T0346519

Goodnews River

ALSO BY SCOTT SADIL

Angling Baja: One Man's Fly Fishing Journey through the Surf
Cast from the Edge
Lost in Wyoming: Stories
Fly Tales: Lessons in Fly Fishing Like the Real Guys

Goodnews River

Wild Fish, Wild Waters, and the Stories We Find There

Scott Sadil

STACKPOLE BOOKS

Guilford, Connecticut
Blue Ridge Summit, Pennsylvania

STACKPOLE BOOKS

An imprint of Globe Pequot, the trade division of
The Rowman & Littlefield Publishing Group, Inc.
4501 Forbes Blvd., Ste. 200
Lanham, MD 20706
www.rowman.com

Distributed by NATIONAL BOOK NETWORK

Copyright © 2019 Scott Sadil
First Stackpole Books paperback edition 2022

All rights reserved. No part of this book may be reproduced in any form or by any electronic or
mechanical means, including information storage and retrieval systems, without written permission
from the publisher, except by a reviewer who may quote passages in a review.

British Library Cataloguing in Publication Information available

Library of Congress Cataloging-in-Publication Data available

Names: Sadil, Scott, author.
Title: Goodnews river : wild fish, wild waters, and the stories we find there / Scott Sadil.
Description: Guilford, Connecticut : Stackpole Books, 2018.
Identifiers: LCCN 2018039716 (print) | LCCN 2018043109 (ebook) | ISBN 9780811768115
  (e-book) | ISBN 9780811738064 (hardcover : alk. paper) | ISBN 9780811771245 (pbk : alk.
  paper)
Classification: LCC PS3569.A2375 (ebook) | LCC PS3569.A2375 A6 2018 (print) | DDC
813/.54—dc23
LC record available at https://lccn.loc.gov/2018039716

(∞)™ The paper used in this publication meets the minimum requirements of American National
Standard for Information Sciences—Permanence of Paper for Printed Library Materials, ANSI/
NISO Z39.48-1992.

"Middle Ground," "Putnam's Bend," "Bottom Line," "Chandler," "Gunny," "Bahía Magdalena," "La
Ventana," and "Beavertail" previously appeared in *Gray's Sporting Journal*.

"Goodnews River," "Swedish Wedge," "Klickitat Fall," "Rattlesnake Canyon," and "The Arroyo"
previously appeared in *The Flyfish Journal*.

"Triple Threat" and "Klickitat Summer" previously appeared in *The Drake*.

These are works of fiction. Names, characters, places, and incidents either are the product of the
author's imagination or are used fictitiously. Any resemblance to actual persons, living or dead,
events, or locales is entirely coincidental.

For Gary Bulla

Passion is not so much an emotion as a destiny.
—JEANETTE WINTERSTON

Contents

ACKNOWLEDGMENTS

My deepest gratitude to Kerry Ruef, David Melody, Nan Noteboom, Leigh Hancock, Keith Ligget, and Susan Hess for help with one or more of these stories.

I would also like to thank James Babb, Steve Walburn, Russ Lumpkin, Steve Duda, and Tom Bie for selecting some of these stories for prior publication elsewhere.

Middle Ground

IT'S OVER BEFORE EITHER OF THEM KNOWS IT. THEY BOTH MAKE EVERY effort, some of them sillier than others, to keep the spark alive. But by the time they reach the peninsula and the first sharp scent of the sea, not even the blue skies and pungent mudflats and pond green forests offer the faintest glimpse of hope.

Four hours of highway and Starbucks coffee leave them each convinced of the sour truth.

"Great weather to be here with someone else," she says, watching the spruce gallop by.

But when they cross the Quinault below the lake, she looks downstream into the broad sweep of milky river, glistening in the midday sun, and nothing in her heart can prevent her from imagining the late-winter natives poised within range of a swinging fly. What have they lost but time? The forest casts them in shadow again and she recalls a fish the previous year on the Hoh, a thick, ice-colored beast that threw itself into the air as though trying to escape boiling water. She never turned it, never did more than lean against it with all she dared while it raced downstream, twice more erupting from the river until the whole effort seemed, even in the midst of it, yet another instance of her inability to control anything beyond her own skittish breathing.

She can do this. As they descend toward the Queets, skirting clearcuts stretched to the edge of the park, she steals glances at Penner Brink, the man she believed in until—what? There's a way he holds his mouth when he refuses to say what's on his mind, unwilling to get baited into a fight. A waste of energy, he says. As though the aim is efficiency—like swimmers trying to conserve oxygen.

He drives right past the turnoff to the Clearwater. They could at least go *look* at the water. But Lockjaw loves a plan; God forbid anyone suggest a detour. She was taken, at first, by a certain quiet attentiveness. A history teacher at the high school, he had just taken over as head coach of the softball team; he was moved by how different it was coaching girls from boys: "Guys go a whole season and you have maybe one come-to-Jesus meeting. Girls need to sit down two or three times a week to talk about a simple change in the lineup."

Somehow this was all reflected in his fishing style. Or she wanted him to be that kind of guy. Was there any difference? He was either patient, methodical, committed to repeating what had worked in the past—or an unimaginative dullard, incapable of a fresh idea if it bit him in the back end. When she finally lost the fish on the Hoh, her heart all but yanked from her chest, he scolded her for her reckless ways.

"You knew if you hooked a fish there, you couldn't possibly land it. Why make the cast in the first place?"

And why say a word if the conversation might head south. *Waste of energy?* Maybe he's just afraid of getting his butt kicked.

When they cross the Queets above South Beach, she can't tell with the sun on the water if the river, milky and green, needs a day or a week before coming into shape.

"Looks high," says Penner.

"It gets higher," she says.

Penner frowns at her. She knows he'd love to tell her that's about the dumbest thing anybody could say. But just imagine what might happen then.

She'll keep trying.

They reach the lodge at Kalaloch beneath a bank of low clouds spilling off the water. She lets him check in alone. At the edge of the parking lot, she watches tiny waves roll up the creek mouth and splat against the tangle of logs left by storms and winter tides. She imagines sea-run cutts threading through the shadows. A bite of wind snaps at her hair, already damp, smelling of salt air. Perfect Queets weather. They'll get their shot.

By the time Penner returns, she can't imagine why she possibly gave up smoking.

He hands her a plastic key.

"The rooms all have two beds," he says, already heading for the car.

———

She insists they start in on the Queets. Penner wants to hold off, give the river another day to come into shape—a point he flogs mercilessly while he fashions his steel-cut oats, stirring in measured doses of raisins, dried cranberries, the walnuts he buys direct from an organic grower in Winters, California. She steadies her coffee mug with the tips of her nails. Why not just chew a little betel nut? Outside, the surf sighs as though the tide has finished rising. She opens the door of the woodstove and immediately snaps it shut.

"What's the rush?"

Penner gestures with a wooden spoon.

"The rate we're going," she answers, "one of us could be *dead* tomorrow."

He lifts the lid and stirs. Already in waders, he looks poised to serve breakfast in a cafeteria.

"Look," she adds, "I've never caught a fish on the Queets. That's reason enough."

"There's lots of rivers around here you haven't caught fish on."

"*Are*. There *are*. There are *lots* . . . There *is* a lot!"

She's outside before she knows it. Her breathing starts her septum vibrating like the reed of a tenor sax. She hates when she pulls this crap. It's *beneath* her, for God's sake.

She stands at a corner of the cabin and tries not to blame anyone but herself. Breaking waves, rising from out of the mist as if flocks of birds, make her feel even smaller. Her father, a Conrad scholar at Amherst, used to keep her awake in salmon camps, deprecating the grammar of other guests, a pet theory that held language as the final arbiter of class. Later, when she discovered it was her mother's money that gave them access to waters shared with these men her father loved to criticize and slander, she suffered her first crisis of faith. Her father full of it, where does a ten-year-old turn next for answers?

Thirty years later and—what? Daddy's bratty little grammar goon, after all? By the time she was a teenager, she was cussing like the Irish hockey hoods from south Boston. All through high school she liked to make her father flinch, pronouncing the *th* in athlete as a pair of *f*'s: *aff-lete*. And then, as though to make matters as bad as she could imagine, she attends school in Oregon, where she falls in love with a doe-eyed steelhead guide with the pedigree of a tumbleweed and not a clue about the subjunctive.

Like that ever had a chance. And Penner? She was sure at first he was the real thing—sharp, educated, attentive, kind, fun in bed—and for awhile she felt certain he enjoyed watching her catch fish just as much as he liked catching his own.

She takes a deep breath, trying to picture the quiet swing of her fly, a magnet aimed at a single steelhead needling its way through a haystack of hidden currents.

Or she could just go buy some cigarettes.

Or Maui Wowie.

"Okay, you win."

For a moment she fails to recognize Penner. Something about his posture, as if a dog come home lame. Then she sees the wooden spoon, held lightly aside his wadered hip—aimed just so, she suspects, should she decide to go for him.

"We'll head to the Queets."

She looks past him, drawn to the shadow of the nearby forest, imagining the clarity of the river improving like the light through the morning mist. The Queets. A victory—but not one she feels very good about.

Penner cocks the spoon toward the cabin door.

"The oats are done," he says.

The water's even better than she hoped—the usual glacial smudge, but once in it she's able to follow the contours of the cobbled bottom deep enough to give her confidence a steelhead can see her fly. All morning she's sure they're going to find a fish. Each time they park and make for a new run, she leaves Penner behind, hurrying along elk trails through dark hollows brightened by birdsong beneath the quiet old-growth firs.

Her mood shifts when she spots a guy with a two-hander at the bottom of the string of pretty lies she recalled from an earlier trip as the trail crossed an old side channel lined with young alders. She tells herself it doesn't matter, there's plenty of river—a thought that does nothing to ease her sudden conviction she's about to see somebody land a fish with her name on it.

She can't watch. She scrambles down the bank, a sharp drop cut by high water. The big fir that fell with the bank rests along the edge of the current, shielding a trough of holding water—an inconspicuous lie, but a tough spot to turn a fish should it head downstream.

Penner arrives and tells her as much.

"When are you going to learn?"

Glancing upstream, she lets him talk her out of anything more than a few half-hearted casts. Why screw around here with all the good water nearby? They get in above him, the guy won't stay.

"He's just some bum," adds Penner.

She's not so sure. She follows his cast, a sharp loop that spears the heart of the tailout. As if aware of their advance, he backs out of the river and returns to a daypack stashed under the trees. He opens a Stanley thermos. As they pass, he gazes their way through a faint veil of steam. He's got all the good gear—Simms, Patagonia—none of it bright and crisp like Penner wears but, instead, a deeper, darker hue, the color of things rarely out of the water long enough to dry.

By the time they reach the top of the run, the guy has disappeared from under the trees. By the time her fly finishes its first swing, he's down at the spot they were just at above the fallen tree.

A short while later, he's into a fish.

Then—what?

Another.

Unlike the first, this one gives the guy trouble. He holds his rod tip low out over the water, trying to coax the fish directly upstream. She reels in and splashes toward the bank. She's got to see this. If he lands it, and it's big, she'll—*strangle* Penner.

Hurrying downstream she remembers the time her father came west to go steelheading. Marty, her steelhead guy, took them to the Salmonberry, a river too precious to fish with clients. March, spring break, her father hooked what must have been one of the big late natives, a fish he failed to stop as it catapulted downstream, headed back to the Nehalem. Furious, her father tried to blame Marty for doing nothing to help, a reaction she was sure was less about the lost fish than the way Marty stood on the bank waving good-bye as the steelhead vaulted out the bottom of the run.

"I thought he was supposed to be a guide, for Christ's sake!"

"Dad, don't be a jerk. He's my boyfriend."

She arrives just as the guy leads the fish, head up, onto a narrow slip of muddy bank. She's never seen one like it—shoulders like a gymnast, not a trace of color, its entire body pale as clouds below the dark, nickel-tinted back running head to tail.

And at least as long as her arm.

"I didn't think it was possible, a fish like that here."

The guy gets hold of the fly and works it free.

He lifts the fish off the water, measuring it by increments she can only imagine. He's that lucky age of men, forty or sixty, nobody knows—and so absorbed in what he's doing, it's as though she isn't there. Then he settles the steelhead back into the river, his hands beneath it even as it starts to disappear.

"What would you have done—if it got down there too far?"

She catches herself making the same nervous gestures she uses when talking about home.

"It's not like there's lotsa options."

"That's what I keep trying to tell her," says Penner.

He comes up beside her, leans his rod against a tree and hops down the bank and introduces himself, offering his hand as if the two of them are coaches before a game.

The guy shakes his hand dry before taking hold of Penner's. "Chuck," he says.

"I was just saying to your sweetheart that a spot like this don't give you lotsa choices."

Penner swings a goofy grin her way.

"But it sounds like you already covered that."

He takes a towel from his daypack and wipes both hands. He's careful and deliberate, like Penner in some ways but there's a difference. Is he bothered they're here? Angry? *Stoned?*

He turns and gives the river a long look.

"The trick is go gentle on 'em—ease 'em upstream so's they don't get excited."

"And if they do?" asks Penner.

Chuck frowns. "You got your jacket on. Get your belt over it, tighten up, and off you go."

He mimes the moves, stepping back into the river and, rod held high, grabbing his nose like a man headed overboard.

"You got five minutes 'fore you start to get wet."

They spend an hour talking about steelhead, flies, the peninsula. She decides Chuck's the real deal, a nomad chasing wild fish from one river to the next. No wife, no family; no mention of a girlfriend. Is that what it takes? All or nothing?

No middle ground?

They fish without luck through the afternoon. Her mood swings this way and that: one moment she feels certain a fish can't help but grab her fly, the next it all seems pointless, prayers raised to an empty sky. Following her through each run, Penner keeps pounding the water, a housefly trying to pass through a closed window—until he asks if she wants to return to Chuck's run.

"I thought you didn't like the spot."

"We saw two fish come out of there."

They're losing light by the time they pass through the old river channel and come out of the alders crowding the abandoned bank. She discovers immediately she can't reach the same water Chuck was fishing, and as the light fades, she creates a list of reasons why this is a dumb idea, she doesn't stand a chance. A guy like Chuck? How can she possibly compete?

Her breathing grows ragged as she tries again and again to hurl her line entirely across the river. Short of breath, she finally gives up—and a quiet loop unfolds from the tip of the long rod. There's some good water in tight to the fallen tree, water she's failed to touch in her eagerness to launch another humongous cast. The fly dangles; she leads it toward the fallen tree with her rod tip. A bump—and for a moment she thinks she's hung up on an errant, underwater branch.

Then her line's alive, the rod throbbing—and her worst fears become immediately real.

"Penner!"

"I'm right here."

Her reel hits a pitch she's never heard before.

"What do I do?"

"You can't stop it?"

"It doesn't even know it's hooked."

She hears the zipper from Penner's jacket, the buckle of his wading belt unsnap. Moments later he's past her, belt up over his jacket, in the river up to his waist.

"Here, give me your rod."

"You sure?"

"What have we got to lose?"

He tightens the drag and, rod overhead, begins to bob with the current.

"Meet me downstream."

Waves tumble up and down the beach in perfect cadence with her breathing. Eyes closed, she relishes the rise and fall of each easy breath moving through her body. Seagulls screech. An osprey squeals. Breeze stirs the window above her head.

God bless this brand-new day.

God bless that *beast* they somehow landed.

"You think Chuck even has a job?"

Penner rustles beneath the covers.

"He's got to have some way to support himself—and pay for all that nice gear."

They turn their heads and look at each other.

"You can bet there's not much else but steelhead going on in his life."

"Maybe that's all he needs," she says, sliding Penner's way.

Putnam's Bend

Putnam senses he may be going too far as he grips the hostess by her ankles, dangling her over the side of the houseboat. The woman's hat, petaled in pink, trembles atop the water; he thrusts her downward, wielding her like a gaff. A fresh gust of wind stirs the surface of the river and sends the hat scurrying into shadows beneath the bulge of the boat's outsized pontoon—and at this awkward angle it's all he can do to hold on tight while he pictures, heroics gone awry, the hostess pitchpoling like a jettisoned raft.

"Got it!" she shouts, her left leg bucking like a landed fish.

"Up we go," says Putnam, hanging on.

He locates a prudent handhold and gives her his best heave-ho. Just like the old days. In a single gesture the hostess rises back into the boat, coming aboard as gracefully as a sea lion scaling a dock—and he keeps her sliding until she winds up sprawled across a table, where her indelicate pose reveals what looks like an open wound torn across the inside of her pale thigh.

"*Oh, my*—"

"It's *okay*," she says, raising a pair of darkened fingers to her mouth. She smiles at him. Then past her lips they go, index and middle finger both, while she squirms free of the flattened berry pie and leftover condiments smeared across the table's Formica glare.

He spends the rest of the evening fending off compliments for his quick thinking and bold resolve. Nobody's ever met a fire-and-rescue guy? He retreats to a view of the river, bigger here than he imagined, an ominous beast lunging between far-flung banks, the opposite tem-per of the dammed and placid waters he lives near five hundred miles downstream. And with trout allegedly the size of steelhead. Yet as he struggles to square the parts, one stretch of river with the other, he finds it impossible to free himself of an image of the hostess upended just so. Each time he crosses glances with her, she waggles the brim of her silly hat, haloed with caddis swarms flooding the boat decks at last light.

"I thought I really blew it there," he says, heading to bed.

He points at her leg, giving them both pause.

"You'll get plenty of chances tomorrow," she finally offers.

Nearby a sharp splash escapes the river's low growl.

She fixes him with a knowing gaze.

"As long as the drakes come off," she adds.

—

A hatch of big mayflies—or another of his typical trout fantasies—seems far-fetched by the time his guide, Curtis, swings the jet sled out into heavy current. The river feels too—what?—*massive* for anything resembling trout water. They skirt the edges of shuddering boils, sudden upwellings that appear to expand and contract as though answering to the dynamics of ocean waves, not the unfettered hydraulics of one of the last free-flowing stretches of the Columbia.

"Hang on!" barks Curtis over the roar of the engine as the big sled rolls up on its chine.

Behind them their wake feathers neatly around a pair of just visible deadheads.

"Frickin' Canadians!" In Carhartt jacket and camo cap, Curtis looks as much like a logger as he does a young fishing guide—until you get to the nylon board shorts and open-toed Tevas. "Government everywhere and they still can't hold onto their goddamn logs!"

Trout water? As they speed upriver, breaching a thin mist he feels in his beard, the pale sky resting atop the serrated crown of the forest, Putnam wonders if he's run out of good ideas. Since retiring from Albion Fire & Rescue, he's fished his way through the West, ticking off river and watershed one after another. But more and more it's all begun to seem the same. Worse, he recognizes his growing boredom, the kind that drove him out of the force, when he could no longer see his job as more than pulling people from messes created by their own dumb mistakes.

But this place? No wonder he's heard little about it. He tries to gauge the distance to shore as Curtis runs the boat into a jumble of currents that leave him reaching for a handhold. Where are the life jackets stored? The river surges and swells, an entire slice of it changing direction as an upwelling rolls into still water, only to recede as though a lull between sets of waves.

He struggles to find his sea legs. Curtis, jockeying the boat into position, pivots this way and that, bouncing atop the balls of his Tevas—until finally he rocks the big engine forward and, still standing, leans heavily into the oars.

"Ten o'clock. Right into that funky shit that looks like nervous water."

Putnam does as he's told, launching an oversized drake that the hostess—Leslie? Lizabeth? Liseth?—hung from the lip of his coffee cup when he arrived for breakfast to meet his guide.

A fish comes up and eats his fly.

Later, glancing over the gunwale, he decides the bright profile circling in and out of view looks more like a skipjack tuna than any steelhead he's ever seen.

—◆—

The morning grows warm, the sun climbing through a windless haze fueled by fires spreading through the eastern third of the state. He tries to ignore a dull stab of guilt; plenty of guys his age are still working. But when a second trout eats his fly, this one heavier than the first, he's quick to convince himself he's really not cut out anymore for anything but what he's doing right now.

As the fish gets close, he hears an approaching boat. He recognizes the guide and an angler from the welcome party the night before. The boat draws near while Curtis lowers the net into the river and then lifts the trout sparkling into the sun.

"Nice one."

Curtis ignores the compliment. He busies himself with the fish, at the same time taking longer than needed to release it so that everyone gets a better look.

"What's up?" he finally asks.

The guide tosses a dry bag Curtis's way.

"Call from the wife. The baby's breaching."

Putnam watches the new guy climb over the gunwales. Even he knows that a wife in labor is an excuse a guide resorts to when too hungover to work—or faced with a client he thinks he might murder if he spends another hour alone with him in a boat.

The second sled drifts downstream.

"You guys can split the cost of Curtis's boat!"

"And the tip, too?" asks the new guy, moving toward the spot Putnam stood while landing his last fish.

The heat climbs. The new guy starts complaining, claiming the weather has put off the drakes—while Curtis keeps running them into tangled confluences where, more times than not, Putnam picks up another good trout.

"Don't fish the upwelling," Curtis reminds them, repeating himself after the guy feathers another long cast into a vein of swollen boils.

"Lefty Kreh watched me cast one year at the Denver show."

The guy stands gazing out in the direction of his fly. There's something about him—and not just the backwards ball cap or his air of contempt for advice. He strips in line as though trying to scare off fish—and then he picks up and launches another tight loop that lands the fly exactly where Curtis told him it shouldn't.

"Said I had the strongest backcast he's ever seen."

"Lefty would know," offers Curtis.

Then Putnam makes the connection. On the lunch-run back to the houseboat, the guy joins him on the center thwart, drawing on an electronic vaporizer as though nibbling a frozen treat. The speed of the boat scatters the mounting heat. Their long wake fans out across the whole of the river, finally fading into a scrim of haze and smoke.

"You know the fish you're catching?"

The guy holds out his vape.

"They don't even count."

Putnam waves away the offering. He recalls the explosion that lifted rafters six inches off the garage walls of the house of the state representative who, for years, had introduced legislation intended to dismantle the public employee retirement system. Working first response, Putnam found what was left of the family terrier, still chained to a two-by-four leg of the water heater platform, beneath which the state rep had stored a back-up bottle of fuel for his outdoor barbecue.

"What are you, a goddamn idiot?" shouted Putnam, still holding the dog's remains when the state rep rushed onto the scene.

For the next month the comment was hauled out and repeated, in one meeting after another, until it grew clear to Putnam that retirement was his best option. And when somebody spelled his name Put*man*, not Putnam, on his twenty-five-year service plaque, it left a taste in his mouth that he still sometimes savors as if running his tongue over a sore tooth.

"You'll see when the drakes start popping," says the Vapester, his tone the same, notes Putnam, as that used by the state representative as the wheels of bureaucratic reprimand squeezed the fight out of him and he finally walked away.

The sun hangs overhead by the time they spot the houseboat. Approaching the dock, they see the hostess just upriver in a kayak, dragging a deadhead toward shore. She beaches her boat on the rocky bank and then carries her line to a single tree standing above high water.

"That's our Lester," says Curtis, reversing the engine as the boat settles against the dock. "A regular Wonder Woman when it comes to protecting her boat."

"Lester?"

"Family name."

Curtis hops out and runs a line around a cleat.

"Bunch of 'em around here," he adds.

Putnam waits at the boat while Curtis, the Vapester on his heels, heads up the dock to check on lunch. Lester's there before them, hopping aboard the houseboat with a spark of sunlight off her wet legs.

He watches her busy herself at the covered table where she ended up smeared in pie the evening before. Heat hovers above the water, the river here a quiet back eddy, a hundred yards long, more like a pond against the bare bank exposed by low water. He feels called to help in some way—but how?

The Vapester returns with a beer and a lewd glint in his eye. He digs through his dry bag and locates a phone.

"Wha' d'you do to the help?"

He comes over and nudges Putnam with his strongest-ever back-casting elbow.

"She keeps asking about you."

Really?

She could have her pick in these parts, he thinks, climbing the trail after lunch to his yurt, one of four lined up in a clearing above railroad tracks and a county road leading to the new Homeland Security fort at the border. On the edge of the bed he pulls the box of flies he tied for this trip from the front pocket of his shirt, outlandish dries with black calf tail wings more jackrabbit ears than the wildest allusion to flight—and every one smaller than the drake Lester gave him to fish that morning.

He swings his feet up onto the bed. And while the heat stirs, washing over him like bathwater, a sudden chill passes through his body as he recalls his last girlfriend, when he realized he had spent his life dating a kind of woman who seeks rescue from herself—her fears, uncertainties, and fragile self-esteem. He closes his eyes, trying to picture each of the morning's fish—the cast, the take, the colors and configurations of the trout themselves—but somehow the trout keep morphing, their sharp outlines melting into splotches of berry pie smeared on Lester's thigh.

He meets Curtis at the dock at three. The heat relents as he passes the houseboat and walks out over the water, the first relief since he lay down attempting to nap. Across the river the forested slopes seem but shadows beneath the hazy sky.

The Vapester appears to have vanished.

"He got started and didn't stop," says Curtis, wagging thumb and pinkie in front of his mouth.

"Can I join you?"

Lester hurries down the dock, one hand pressed to the crown of her goofy hat. She's got on cutoffs and canvas high-tops and a pastel yellow tank top with either a halibut or a ukulele stenciled across the front, he can't tell which without appearing to inspect her pretty breasts.

In her other hand she carries a rod, pitched at an angle that suggests she just may know how to use it.

"You've got an open spot, don't you?"

Curtis looks his way.

"Your call."

He can't think why not.

Wind and engine wail prevent much in the way of small talk. She shows him the fly she's already tied to her tippet—the size of a salmonfly but with wings erupting like the crest of a cockatoo. He watches a cloud of smoke billow as though a thunderhead above a ridge to the east, recalling the excitement he used to feel during fire season—and how one day those feelings seemed part of a life no longer his own.

Curtis takes them back to the stretch of river they started on in the morning. Already sweating, Putnam moves forward and begins covering the water, adjusting his casts as currents shift spasmodically around them. Thermal drafts ambush his loop, bending it this way and that.

"Don't fish the upwellings."

He shoots Lester a look.

"So I've heard."

"Well, all right then."

She tugs her hat tight to her head of wind-blown curls.

"I won't say another word," she adds.

He flings his line about, waiting for Curtis to tell him what else to do. The edge of an upwelling begins to bulge. He follows it as it moves like a shudder across what moments before looked like perfect holding water. His line drags his fly as though a cable from tugboat to barge.

Blanched in sweat, he keeps casting until he realizes he's fishing alone.

"What's up?" he asks, lifting leader and fly to hand.

Lester smiles at him from the edge of the aft deck. She slides a leg over a knee and reties one of her laces.

"Just waiting for you to finish so we can go find some bugs."

———

They swing out of the current around a bank lined with discolored pines, victims of whatever has damaged the local forests. The boat slides into an eddy wider than most rivers he's ever fished. At the bottom of the eddy extends a shelf of sand-colored rocks, their edges worn smooth as if exposed to surf.

On the farthest rocks the Vapester stands casting, a long line riding the overhead swing of a double-handed rod.

"He shouldn't be out there if he's been drinking," says Putnam.

Curtis and Lester look at each other.

"Kind of standard practice in these parts," Curtis says.

Putnam wipes his brow. Recalling his old foe, he needs little to ignore the Vapester's disregard for safety. Curtis tucks them in under a tight funnel of current that creates the sensation of standing beside a waterfall. The boat settles in a slick of still water. Heat stirs in swirls all their own.

"Still gonna wait for bugs?"

Lester looks at him as if trying to decide whether he's being a smart-ass.

"You don't believe it, do you?"

He tucks his rod under his arm and runs his thumb and forefinger along his tippet.

"Believe what?"

"That something special—something new and really special—just might happen."

He raises the rod and sights through the guides.

"Well, what about you? It's not like you're running around the boat expecting to get one."

She doesn't say anything—until he finally looks at her.

"Listen, here's all you gotta know about me." She aims her rod tip at him and gives it a little shake. "I've caught a million of these damn trout.

But when the big drakes come off, and fish are tipping up under them and eating . . ."

It's as if her voice melts in the heat. She nods his way, beads of sweat on her sun-creased lip.

"You stay long enough, you'll see what I'm talking about."

Curtis jostles the oars, pivoting the boat side to side.

"You gonna fish, Les—or just talk about it?"

She rolls her eyes—a gesture that gives Putnam cause to look away.

Downstream the Vapester launches a loop that soars out over the river.

Fish begin showing in the seam between the edge of the eddy and the flume of heavy current. The heat has dissipated, absorbed by the river itself—and drakes or no drakes, they settle into the rhythm of falling light, casting flies over big trout nosing the shadowy film.

He tries to pick out a single fish. The upwelling pushes the seam this way and that. One cast falls short, the next wide. He feels Curtis nudge the boat forward—but the moment he lifts his line he's forced to stop to dodge something glimpsed out the corner of his eye.

"You spooked?" asks Curtis, a big smile lifting his face.

"Some bird or something—nearly hit me."

"That wasn't a bird," says Lester.

She looks over at him, her rod seized in a serious bend.

He watches her fight the fish. When he finally sees it, a chrome bumper skidding through the water, he's sure it's only half the size of other trout breaking the surface, lapping up what look like wads of ash riding the current. Curtis goes past him with the net. As soon as there's room, he steps to the rail and delivers his fly. Fresh sweat stings his eyes. When a trout comes up and eats, he raises his rod tip—and a force like a falling boulder snaps his tippet quick as that.

You have to be kidding. His rod hand, still extended, vibrates like a tuning fork. What was he thinking? Set the hook on a fish like that?

Before he knows it, Curtis has his tippet in hand. He breaks it at the blood knot and then bites off the front third of the leader. He knots on a length of 0X tippet. He ties on a drake the size of a sparrow.

"Just let 'em eat it."

He's set to cast when he sees Lester snug up hard on another fish, her body tensing like a fist. Her hand goes to the crown of her hat; a small sharp sound escapes her lips. She looks up at her rod tip as line rushes toward the river. Her reel sounds like wind tearing through the pines.

She turns his way—but nothing in her eyes says she even sees him.

Ukulele, thinks Putnam. Not a halibut.

He steadies himself against the gunwale and faces the river. The silhouettes of giant mayflies whirl about in the surging currents. The rising trout look like gallivanting otters. The sky, flooded with dusk, spills into the treetops, filling the forest with night.

She's right: he doesn't believe it.

Down on the rocks, the Vapester stands hooked up, too.

But it feels just safe enough to try.

Bottom Line

IT WASN'T HIS OWN IDEA. BUT EVER SINCE BURKIE HEARD IT FROM A KID he had sanding for him one winter, he's made it a practice to hold off closing his books each year until he turns his back on his computer, his check registers, his job files and stacks of receipts and, in the face of it all, goes fishing.

It makes even more sense this year. Can he face another drift boat? Or it's not that so much as it is a question of when he's going to build something new, something different—something *sexier*, for Christ's sake. He remembers his father, dead now ten years, telling him to go where the money is, that it doesn't matter how pretty the boats you build if you don't have a roof over your head, a decent truck, some booze around you're not embarrassed to share.

Or if you can't afford to go fishing.

But at what point, he asks himself, sliding rods on top of waders behind the front seat of his Ford—at what point does the money matter if your life doesn't feel anymore like your own?

What's the money worth if all it's buying is time?

He taps the brakes on the steep drop from The Heights, feeling for black ice. Out over the river a layer of woolly clouds rests atop a pool of quiet air trapped above the water. Against the far hillsides the clouds end in a ribbon of white, a sharp hem of snow and ice etched into the contours of the wooded slopes as precisely as the waterline of a lapstrake tender.

For example, he thinks.

At the bank of duplexes next to the body shop, he waits in the truck fiddling with the defroster until Lalo shows, descending the stairway two steps at a time. Upstairs, Lalo's mother, Milly, appears at the slider; arms folded, she makes an exaggerated show of shivering against the cold. Something up? He follows Lalo in the mirrors, a gloved hand riding the scaly ice gathering in ridges along the rails of the truck. For a kid who won't pick up a piece of sandpaper until he's changed out of his school clothes, he's dressed like he's got somewhere else to go besides fishing.

Then he recognizes his own old fleece, dug out from the bottom of a drawer, that he passed on to Lalo following the first hard frosts of fall.

"Where's the boat?"

Lalo swings his day pack—another hand-me-down—into the truck, riding its momentum into the seat alongside it.

"Not in this cold."

He waits as Lalo unplugs his earphones and stashes his phone in his pack.

"We get wet, we're history."

Lalo makes a face then lifts out a lunch sack already spotted with grease stains.

"I thought you were like some kind of master swim champion." He pulls away from the curb, unsure whether Lalo is teasing him.

"My peanut butter sandwiches aren't good enough for you?"

The windshield fogs up again. The defroster stirs the smell of peppers and fried meat about the cab. He takes the long way to the freeway, passing Walmart and the trailer park, giving Lalo time to show off a handful of taquitos wrapped in aluminum foil before spinning around in the seat and loading them in the cooler.

"My mom. She feels sorry for lonely old men."

"Those aren't going to help you if you go in today."

The wipers leave snowflakes blurred behind lingering smears.

"Five minutes—max."

But this isn't that kind of fishing. No one's going in—not past the tops of their wading boots they're not.

From the freeway the river looks more frozen than still, its surface scuffed with wind from the east just strong enough to score the edges and eddies the color of frost. And keep anyone married to the bottom line at home. Cold like this there's just one real bet anyway: whitefish. They'll be schooled up in the soft water, trying to stay alive until the weather turns. The only good reason today to go fishing is to whack a half-dozen whiteys, fresh fixings for tacos this evening while they see if the Blazers can keep winning.

That, and so he can remind himself there's a point to knocking out boats, one after another, he can build with his eyes closed.

Yet by the time they cross the bridge at Albion and leave the Columbia at the mouth of the Beulah, he's convinced he's finally ready to brave a change. He's got to. To the east the clouds above the river seem to melt into puddles of blue sky. Sunlight sparkles against sheets of corrugated ice draped from the walls of basalt crowding the highway. Is he going to go to his grave wondering if he should jump into new water—even if he can't read the current, how fast or deep it runs?

Deep enough he'll have to let Lalo go.

That's the hard one. But isn't it always the case? His whole life he's been sidetracked by others: two daughters, a wife he never did figure out, a dozen clients a year who want drift boats that look like furniture but only want to pay for ones built like picnic tables.

Climbing the Beulah, the truck swings in and out of shadows cast by the steep hillsides, flaked now with frost and ice-crusted oaks. In a long reach of sunlight he studies a tiny fish Lalo has already managed to carve from an avocado seed pulled, along with his earphones, from his pack—one of a half-dozen miniature animals, each the size of Monopoly pieces, he's mastered these past six months, his fine-boned fingers working a little Japanese paring knife as though he were knitting.

A great kid: a little lippy, yes—but smart, conscientious, a terrific touch with tools.

And there's no way he can keep him on—not if he's building on spec.

Who's going to pay him to turn out a Beals Island lobster boat, for Christ's sake?

———

"Look. One a yours."

Upstream from the Swamp Hole, sure enough, the boat skips gently through the current, twitching with each dip of the oars, extending like wings from the hollows of her exaggerated sheer. He had pushed it about as far as he could with this one; her stems rise from the belly of her deep rocker to the point of affectation. Still, any lingering doubts about her profile are put to rest as she rides through a last steep gasp of boulder-choked whitewater, slipping around the ice-rimmed rocks as though skidding on frozen chines.

"What are you smiling about?"

Before he can answer, the boat bucks suddenly, giving off a resounding clunk that mimics the gunfire of deer hunters throughout the canyon in fall. Low water. Two guys, not a lot older than Lalo, do nothing but look at each other and laugh, their breath visible above a sound like squirrelly dogs barking at wind while the boat swaps ends and waggles awkwardly into the head of the run.

"You teach that trick before you let 'em drive her away?"

"And a swimming lesson—no extra charge."

"So they're safe?"

"Five minutes, Lalo."

"Let me guess: not a second more."

He feels the tap-tap of another whitefish. Distracted, he raises his rod tip too slowly, his hands clumsy, his fingers half numb. Not that it matters. Downstream, Lalo slips another fish from his little egg fly—a fish plenty big enough to kill, the same size, more or less, Lalo's been releasing the last half hour since he hung number five and they both supposedly agreed just one more before they quit this damn cold.

He turns and watches the boat, held steady just above the gut of the run. He loves the look of the oak gunwales and chine battens framing the sapele ply—especially in the soft light, the hint of river mist trapped between the water and colder air. Still, for the life of him he can't remember who he sold this one to. Not these yahoos. The guy on the oars, mad bomber hat and all, pulls hard against the current; his pal, aft and downstream, pitches an indicator alongside the boat and watches it waddle in the current. Twice he rips line and indicator both off the water, launching a shower of spray that sparkles in the sunlight as though ice crystals cast from a nearby pine.

"I thought you said steelhead season is closed."

He looks Lalo's way.

"Your hook's small enough, you can claim you're fishing for whiteys."

Lalo adjusts his split shot, crimping it with pliers before lobbing a short cast back into the inside seam.

"They're not fishing for whitefish," he says.

Who's to say? If they are, they're not doing a very good job of it. Twice more the guy with the rod snaps line from the current—only to shatter the icy quiet with his own wild whoop, a bark of delight that's followed immediately by the frothy flight of a steelhead crashing through the surface. Just as quickly the hook pulls free—which does nothing to diminish the shouts and hollers that rise from the boat, filling the canyon as though echoing beneath a sheet of frozen sky.

What they're drinking from the flask they keep passing back and forth probably isn't water, either.

When they're directly across the river, Lalo calls out and asks how they're doing.

The mad bomber glances at his friend.

"Damn steelhead keep grabbing our flies!"

The two look at each other, mugging shock in response to their rare good fortune.

"How 'bout you guys? Any *whiteys?*"

Har har har.

But when Lalo raises the stringer, showing off their mess of whitefish as though it were a twenty-pound steelhead, neither guy says more—not until they reach the tailout and start whooping it up again, the boat sideways in the current, drifting as if she were on her own.

———

"I don't see why guys like that would even want a boat like one of yours. It's not like they're going to take care of it."

The taquito does as much to warm him as the heater. He can't remember the last time he's had to resort to sitting in the truck with the engine running. It was either that or build a fire by the time he got Lalo to keep one more fish so they could get off the water.

"I'm sure there's a dad involved."

But who? If he needs one more reason to quit schlepping drift boats, this ought to be it. There was a day he could trace the story of every boat he built—just like he kept track of each and every one of his age-group records at the swim club. As though they mattered. Like it added up to something. Like somehow the records and all those boats built one after the other, year after year, meant he was due some sort of reward, like there's an equation that says if you do what you're supposed to do, you end up with something that doesn't just fade into a pool of murky memories.

If there are boats he wants to build, when's he going to build them if not now?

Lalo gets out and checks on the fish, laid out on the sheet of plywood inside the bed of the truck. Neither of them thought to bring a second cooler.

Not that it matters today.

Climbing back into the cab, Lalo makes a show of his breath, gulping in a mouthful of heated air from inside, then expelling a gauzy huff through the open door. His ears glow red against his cap of black hair.

"If we hurry, we can watch them rattle their teeth through Boneyards."

"They're not that stupid. Low water like this, they'll take out at Myrna's."

"Their rig wasn't there earlier."

He looks over at Lalo, surprised again by how much he notices, his attention to details that could just as easily go overlooked.

"Their shuttle just hadn't arrived."

"Whatever you say, sir."

But when they pass the takeout across from Myrna Crompton's old place, tucked up in icy shade beneath a stand of oak he'd give his left nut to own and turn into boats, there's still no rig in sight. Could they have already finished their float? He hurries downriver, lifting his foot off the gas through the shadows, hoping he doesn't spot them—or if he does, before they try something foolish.

Even before he pulls in at the county campground, he sees the truck and trailer parked beyond the last of the empty sites scattered beneath the heavy riparian pines. A hundred yards upstream the river sluices through Boneyards, a pitch of basalt boulders cast from somewhere high along the canyon wall. Downstream the river tilts and plummets once and for all, burrowing through a mile-long cataract to the floor of the gorge below.

Lalo's out of the truck before he sets the brake.

"If I know you, you'll go in when they dump her."

"No one's going to *dump* her." He hops out, checking behind the seat and in back for something that might come in handy. "She rides like a cork."

"Looks like we'll find out soon enough."

They're all wrong even before they start, drifting in the middle of the current through the long gentle sweep of river upstream—a course, should they keep it, that will send them into the second or third rock, depending on which way they try to go once they realize the trouble they're in. Still, they might get lucky; his have always been coastal boats, such that even now, 150 miles from the sea, he takes his lines from the short swift rivers spilling out of the Coast Range and rain-furrowed western face of the Cascades—oarsmen's boats, borne of the need to change direction in a heartbeat, spin on a dime, back up and swivel and swap ends one stroke of an oar at a time.

But in water this low, the best you can do is roll with the punches, try not to hit anything square.

Which is just what they fail to do. The boat rocks once high on her tail, pivoting sharply as mad bomber wrenches on an oar. When she comes down she lands directly on top of that third rock, the impact echoing above the river with the sharp cry of splintering wood. Worse, she stays there a moment, pinned by the current while she rolls slowly sideways until her upstream gunwale suddenly catches and the river pours inside as if a running hose thrust over the lip of a teacup.

"Oh, Jesus," he says, kicking off his Crocs while fumbling with the buttons of his jeans.

The Blazers finally start hitting their three-pointers. They pull within two by the end of the third quarter. Lalo comes in from the kitchen with a plate of tacos reheated in the microwave.

"How 'bout the look on that one guy's face when you finally got him to the bank?"

He watches the steam rise from the crisp edges of the tortillas. He'd still like to know how Milly does it—but he knows if he asks, Lalo will only raise his hands and make quotation marks and say, "Made with love."

"And then he goes, '*It's just a boat, dude.*' We shoulda got *her* first and seen what he had to say then."

"At least his friend could swim."

The Blazers tie it up. He starts in on another taco. He can't tell what's better: the game, the food, the heat from the woodstove—or the shearling-lined moccasins he bought himself for Christmas.

"We going to start in on her tomorrow?"

"If the old man brings by a check."

Lalo carries in the hot water and refills his tea.

"You really didn't remember who you sold it to?"

Not until mad bomber and company made their calls and got a hold of grandpa, a retired judge from Colorado come to the Northwest for steelhead. Old guy nearly cried the day he first saw his new boat.

The check's probably already written.

The Blazers end up winning going away. Only a disaster will keep them out of the playoffs—their first time there in ages. He drives Lalo home, and as soon as he gets back, he goes into his office—the girls' room he still calls it—and sits down and wiggles the mouse, curious what the numbers will show.

He'll see how the playoffs go. After that, he'll make his decision final.

Chandler

CHANDLER PARKS SO THAT THEY CAN SEE THE WATER, THE BROKEN lines of surf spilling toward the beach. He waits a moment for the view to absorb them, the scent of salt air scored into the light. So far, so good. Hardest in all of this is how his father will fail to track the simplest of narratives. Where are we? Whose truck we in? How come *those* guys are here? Sometimes they are not even words anymore that spill from his father's mouth. They both fall silent, both confused. Chandler holds a host of theories about the disintegrating mind—but more and more he's convinced that none of them matter, that his own mind steeped in reasons why invites but the sharpest and bitterest suffering.

He unloads their gear and gets his father headed toward the sand. Their weekly date. Or that's the idea, even as he grows increasingly uncertain whether his father still recognizes weeks at all. Or one day from the next. When he fails to show, wrapped up in the easy derelictions of a realtor's life, he has no evidence that his father misses him, that his father retains a concept of time strong enough to fuel disappointment or anger, loneliness or fear. What is an emotion, anyway, that slips from memory as soon as it has passed? What is time in a dream that swings between day and night, between darkness and light?

Theories. He spears the rod spikes in the sand. His father, barefoot beneath blue board shorts and a wind shell faded gray, steps to the edge of the water and stops, dropping his gaze. A ragged hem of wash slides over his feet. His hairless legs all but glow in the morning light, the pale skin the texture of a coastal moon.

Nobody needed theories about his reaction to Penny's death. Chandler slips the rod butts, one then the other, into the pair of waiting spikes. His younger sister, she went suddenly, a merciful end following two years of treatment for a cancer that did little more than flinch in the face of modern medicine. Tying tippets to the stocky leaders, he recalls the moment outside the home in Carlsbad in which they've placed their father when he and Kendra, his older sister, delivered the terrible news. Confused, their father slowly seized the source of their grief. Then instantly he was back on earth, feet planted in the raw truth, wailing like a wounded child—the purest expression of his father's emotions Chandler has witnessed his entire life.

But does he remember any of that now? Or does *anyone* recall but a shadow of pain? He watches his father turn and pick his steps across the sand. Beyond him a pair of pelicans slide along a fold of gentle surf, their wings as quiet as the fins of resting trout. From a fanny pack hung from his shoulder, he takes a handful of flies stashed in plastic sleeves, a pattern a new client from Seattle raved about while going through a million-dollar dump in Leucadia he thought might make a smart investment for his wad of Microsoft money. *Squid Vicious.* Reports of the strange fish washing up on California beaches spotted the evening news. Fantasizing an unlikely commission, Chandler agreed yes yes yes with everything the guy said. Later he thought *Why not?* At his vise he copied the pattern from a website, resisting the impulse to embellish based on his own loose fly theories that seem more and more to have little or no effect on the number of fish he hooks in the surf.

A half-dozen flies and two gin and tonics into the session, he could picture the appeal of the fly to the odd halibut that still shows up in fall, while reminding himself that with his father in tow, he is never seriously fishing. Still, somewhere into the third drink he suddenly recalled a long-lost photo of himself—Ray-Bans, red sweatshirt, cigarette cocked skyward from the corner of his mouth—fighting a big sheepshead off the rocks in El Rosario, the first time he and his surf buddies thought to bring frozen squid to go along with the mussels and sand crabs they typically used while waiting for waves in Baja during that awkward spell after college when he still didn't know if he wanted to be an outlaw, a sportsman, or the next James Dean.

"Water warm?"

His father gazes at him and then shakes his head—a gesture Chandler understands to mean nothing in context but this: Can you believe what I've become?

Yet when they both wade into the wash, he has already recognized once more the quiet gestures of his father's resilient competence the most devilish and disturbing aspect of his decline. How is it his body retains so much and his mind so little? Not only retains but still processes and evaluates and employs. His first afternoon with a little two-hander and a squeezed down Skagit head, he looked as if he were sixty years old again, lofting chip shots to a practice green with his pitching wedge. In a month his loop looked like you could hang laundry from it; his stroke grew shorter and shorter, smaller and smaller, until now his casts can give Chandler the odd impression of a man stealing a moment to cinch his belt. If you don't pay attention, the cast is already finished, the fly back in the game.

How does he do it? Chandler lofts his own casts without haste or resolve, aiming for nothing more than a fly that lands at the end of a straight leader, a cast that's fishing as soon as it touches down. An eye on his father, he resists the urge to get caught up in the game, a tendency that has cost him, by his own reckoning, two marriages, innumerable girlfriends, and, recently, the company of his teenage daughter, who described his behavior on a beach not five miles to the south as "an asshole chasing its own shit." Better, he tells himself, to think of these outings with his father as a chance to get on the water and tune up his stroke—a tempering note even as he swims the big squid pattern nearly to his feet, inspecting its action through the roiled yet transparent wash.

His father, anyway, appears free anymore of the hungers of sport. Without discussion or example, he's taken to simply lifting his line above the water, holding his rod tip high as waves and wash do little to disturb what is essentially a fly at the end of a heavy head hanging taut in the push and pull of current. As a boy, it infuriated Chandler that his father wouldn't *do more*: walk the beach, change flies, drive someplace new. Later, he understood his father was the better angler because he *didn't* do the things Chandler felt compelled to do in the face of little or no action.

He pitches a long cast out toward the trough beyond the rolling waves, recalling the big halibut his father caught thirty years ago off the beach at Santa Rosalillita before shifting currents filled the inshore channels with weed and muddy sand. The shallows that trip were lined with tiny halibut; his father, perched along a rocky ledge exposed by summer swells from the south, spent two straight tides landing and releasing these undersized juveniles, some no bigger across than sand dollars. The fishing disgusted Chandler; they traveled halfway down the peninsula for *this*? Both afternoons he hiked at low tide out onto the sheer wave-scoured headlands and in the teeth of the onshore wind wrestled calico bass out of the frothy kelp. But the third day his father, still perched on his rocky ledge, found the fish he knew had to be around somewhere—a big bull halibut that measured closer to four feet than three, a fish they were still feasting on when they arrived home, where they discovered that the world record fly-caught California halibut weighed, at the time, all of eight pounds and a few so-what ounces more.

He watches his father deliver another pretty cast, the alarming result of his terse compact stroke. From this distance his hands appear to circle and feint and snap to a sudden stop, as if the gloved fists of a good light heavyweight working an opponent's body. Really, just how the hell does he do it? All his life his father struggled to stay under two hundred pounds. Now he can't possibly go one-sixty, one-sixty-five tops. He remembers running down the beach, rod in hand, when he realized his father was into something big, something entirely different from the little halibut he had been screwing around with for two days straight. Then suddenly his father dropped his rod and pitched forward into the water—the first genuinely awkward move Chandler witnessed his father perform all his life.

"Son of a bitch had a mouth I could put my fist in," his father said afterwards, handing Chandler the bottle of Cazadores. "I kept looking at all those teeth and then the fly came out and—well, you saw the rest."

And then? And then when his mother died, or was driven to her grave—who knows what it was—his father, on his own, retreated from life, growing more and more remote, tethered to the television by the

Padres, the PGA, women's tennis—practically anything on ESPN until—what? Something happened—all at once or over time—until one day he and his sister understood that their father could no longer keep track of even the simplest things—his food, his whereabouts, his medications, a teapot on the stove, blood on his sleeve—could no longer live alone.

Was this the result of withdrawal?

Or the cause?

Theories. He watches his own line settle onto the colorless water. From behind him he hears cars hurrying along the Coast Highway, smells the rank and fecund flats of the tidal estuary spread in lobes of muck weed and invasive grass. Has the wind changed? The lip of a standing wave rises as if surprised by the pivoting wind. The wave spills forward, a gesture of humility, the physics of grace. Would a better son give in to the gravity of his father's care? Would it matter to a mind that lives without context of the past?

His line stiffens. A cruel joke? He leans into something heavy, a sensation he immediately dismisses as he reels against nothing but quiet resistance, reclaiming the better part of his cast.

His father turns and looks his way.

The weight explodes into life.

It isn't a run so much as a ferocious lunge, something a dog would do when startled from behind. He gives the rod tip to it, sick with the certainty of loss until the reel begins to whine, the worst moment past while he still feels how bad it was. Like maybe pay attention now? The fish doesn't go far, a halibut he's sure—exactly what they're fishing for had he sense enough to keep his mind in the game.

Like father like son?

The thought startles him so badly he's relieved to see his father headed his way. He's not completely lost. He still gets it: a good fish hooked, taking line.

Maybe they just need to fish more.

Maybe he ought to first see if he can land this beast.

It's only a halibut. He gives it some wood, persuading it to come his way until he gets it aimed into the wash, when it bolts again. This time he's ready; he relishes the startling power. Who needs half a brain when you're equipped like that? An elegant ambush artist, its entire body a flexing fin that propels it, in one fell swoop, wherever it need go.

Then he sees how big it is. Nothing like the one his father landed long ago, but—*Jesus*. He lets it hang in the wash, waiting for a set wave, something to lift it so he can slide it beyond the surge. A lifetime of this nonsense teaches you—what? Good things get lost when you get impatient.

A wave retreats and he holds the halibut so that it doesn't slide down the sand, back into the shallow trough at the edge of the wash. A risky move—but he's ready to end it. The wave he's been waiting for spills toward the beach. He moves the fish this time and it's over.

But it doesn't move. He levels the rod on its side, leaning hard now, the tip of the deep curve aligned with the halibut's bug-eyed snout, the rod bending into the cork, his hands flexing as though fighting the limb of a tree.

Then the fly pulls free. Everything goes soft. He staggers back a step and at the same moment he sees his father splashing through the wash, nearly on top of him. *Perfect*, he thinks, already changing direction, moving toward the halibut himself, the fish exposed but not quite motionless in the retreating wave, sliding backward across the sand as though dragged by the tail.

He hesitates before aiming at something to grab. All those teeth. Still, what's there to lose—besides a finger or two. He pauses an instant longer before starting for the mottled tail—time enough for his father to swoop down in front of him, reaching to stop the fish just as it lifts from the sand on a fresh lick of wash, free now to pivot, jaws open, and lunge for his father's hand.

—◆—

The ER nurse treats him like some kind of cur. What sort of son brings in his aging father splashed in blood? From the beach, no less.

While they stitch up his father's hand, Chandler wants to ask the nurse—young enough to be *his* son—when's the last time he took *his* father fishing?

But maybe that's not the point.

He waits in a chair outside the curtained operating station, reluctant to expose himself to further scorn. Halibut have teeth, for Chrissake. His father isn't always with it anymore. He recalls as a boy of five or six being bear-hugged by his mother while a dark-skinned doctor put a stitch in the middle of his tongue without the aid of Novocain or whatever they used back then for numbing an open wound. "The shot'll hurt just as much as the stitch," said the doctor. He's long suspected his mother was persuaded as much by the discounted treatment as she was his immediate pain—while at that age all he could think of was his father's inevitable anger, his response whenever he or his sisters suffered injuries or pain.

Finally they wheel out his father, his hand wrapped in a bandage the size of a deflated volleyball.

The doctor keeps leaning in the direction of other patients as he explains how he went about repairing the damage.

"Nasty bite," he concludes, standing up straight, either proud of his work or just long enough to give Chandler a look that questions his sense in taking his aged father fishing. "Didn't seem to bother him too much, though."

"Not a lot does."

Chandler takes hold of the wheelchair.

Out at his truck, he has to help his father buckle his seat belt.

His father holds up his bandaged hand.

"Your mother's not gonna like this."

Chandler loops around the back of the pickup. He can't tell if the blood on the halibut is his father's or from the kick he landed across the eyes on the side of the fish's strange head.

"Mom's dead, Dad. You know that."

He settles into the seat, his hands spaced evenly on the wheel. For a moment he feels like a child again, gazing out the windshield, pretending to drive. At the end of the parking lot stands a row of palm trees fidgeting in the breeze. He's sure if he sits still long enough, they'll even begin to hear surf.

Beside him his father waits, shaking his head.

Gunny

GUNNY KNOWS HE'S GOING TO HAVE TROUBLE AS SOON AS HE SLIPS
under the railway bridge and out into the Columbia, tugging on the tiller
to keep from heading up into the wind. Whitecaps spill toward him as
far as he can see. He gets the dory pointed downwind, feeling everything
go squirrelly under him as the first wave picks up the stern and the current, running hard along the riprap, turns the tiller into a leash on a dog
fighting to run free.

But he's going to have a lot more trouble should his mom or step-
dad find out he crossed the river in the first place. He scooches his
butt up onto the aft thwart then decides immediately he's better off
down low with the loose lines lying in the bottom of the boat. His old
canoe pad settles into a puddle of sloshing water. Where did that come
from? He turns and watches the crest of a wave topple toward the lip
of the transom, while at the same time experiencing the odd sensation
of coming to rest, before the wind, as another wave races off past the
dory's slender bow.

He'll be okay. How many times has Grandpa G told him about getting chased home, in this same boat, by dirty weather? He tries to picture
his mother's father scrunched down between the thwarts, pressed against
the tiller, mainsheet wrapped in a knobby fist—but all he can see is the
old man's vanishing body, frail as bird bones, lying beneath the sad white
sheets in the room he shares with another old man, just like him, the both
of them staring at the ceiling with nothing but oxygen tubes pinched to
their nostrils tethering them to earth.

A wave splashes over the rails. Cold water swirls up into his crotch. A horn blares, startling him—and suddenly he imagines one of the big river barges bearing down on him, a blunt wave rolling before it, driven by a rumbling tug coupled behind.

It takes him a moment to find the train on the far shore. If he gets caught, he thinks, he'll lie—tell them he hooked his second fish and by the time he landed it he was all the way down to the Little White Salmon. His limit, two chinook, lie stretched out along both sides of the daggerboard trunk. Pretty as his girlfriend's thighs, they seem almost alive still with the rise and fall of the boat. Drano Lake, inside the mouth, has been stacked with fish for a month. Why should he have to wait another two years for a driver's license—when it's just as easy to sail or row from home?

Fuck his stepdad. Like he'd have the balls to fish in a wind like this. Gunny glances back down the gorge, picturing the mouth of a dragon spewing flames, not wind, up the river. Wads of cloud cling to the forested walls, layered one in front of the other toward the distant invisible horizon.

The stern lifts again, a steep wave clawing at the transom. The dory picks up speed; a low growl rises from outside the vibrating hull. Settling into the trough, he grabs his bucket and tries to bail, but when he swings the water over the gunwale, it blows back into the boat—and when he tries pitching another scoop over the opposite rail, he's suddenly sideways to the waves, the boom bouncing as though delivering blows, until he finally gets the rudder to bite again, wresting the tiller as if trying to wake from a darkening dream.

—◆—

What's with the kid, anyway?

Gunny's stepdad, Warren Ecke, points the nose of a stand-up paddleboard into the wind, aiming for a patch of smooth water hovering alongside a heel of basalt that protects the beach below his new wife's riverfront property. Or nearly smooth. The closer he gets, wind ringing in his ears, the clearer he can see the tail-end folds of heavy chop fanning around the landmark rock, the even lines a miniature version of surf sweeping around a point, spirited by storm raging far out at sea.

And what the hell's he doing out on a day like this?

But he already has his answer. Before him the river flexes and unfolds, its surface a bedlam of whitecaps between waves furrowed into the current; through his board he feels the changing textures as he glides into the lee of the canted rock. Ever since he began dating Gina Marie, Gunny's mother, he's recognized the boy's terrible lust, the need to do something or prove something to separate himself from the pack—the same need or hunger or simple animal urge that drove him at that age into the surf, holding him there for the next two decades, refusing to relent long after he grew certain there was nothing to prove, nothing he needed to do that he hadn't already done in wild waves around the world.

Gunny. Maybe all boys—of a certain stripe—are the same.

Maybe there's your fever of restlessness that takes such a long, long time to cool.

But Gina doesn't like it. She wants him to help. Now. He steadies himself with his paddle, sculling the water alongside his feet. Their recent fights, new to their marriage, all follow the same disheartening path: Why doesn't he talk to Gunny? Take him windsurfing. Get him interested in something besides fishing from her father's old dory, hauled west years ago, all the way from New Jersey, when the old man found out she was marrying Gunther Gilderhaus, a salmon fisherman from Astoria. Go skateboarding with him, for Christ's sake.

Today's gripe? *He* should have made sure Gunny was back in time to go with her to visit the boy's grandfather.

Or was he too busy shaping boards, now that he had a place on the river without need to make a real living?

Without it, in fact, costing him a dime?

He shoves the heel of his palm against the grip of the paddle. The wind, nearly silent here, seems to press down on him from directly above. He didn't suggest to her that maybe Gunny's not quite a boy anymore— at least not the kind of boy she'd still like him to be.

He didn't mention, either, that a rich wife—like a rich husband—can make you pay every day.

Three hard strokes drive him out into the wind. Of course he didn't say anything, anything at all. What good would it do? Gina's scared: one day Gunther Gilderhaus crossed the bar at the mouth of the Columbia and never returned. Now her father's dying—the two best men in her life, she reminded him once more today.

He pivots the board, paddling hard now, bucking across the chop. This late in the summer, he's surprised how good the sun feels through his wetsuit, the bite of the river resharpened daily by the west wind funneled up the gorge. Pushing the salmon and steelhead upstream, Gunny once said—arguing with his mother why he should be fishing every day, not dicking around the property like some minimum-wage grunt.

He could tell she came close to swatting him for that one.

A lot of good that would have done.

He punches through the lip of a wave, riding up over whitewater and slipping down the back as though paddling through a set, nearly caught inside. Beats Idaho, at least. A train horn sounds and in the wind he can't tell if it comes from upstream or down—or from the tracks a mile away on the other side. This far from shore, he can finally see the circus of kites and sailboarders downwind near the hatchery, a parade of plastic crisscrossing the river, racing back and forth emphatically nowhere. Upwind the river lies empty, a stampede of whitecaps galloping against the current, nothing more on the water as far as he can see—

—but a spot of white off in the distance, a small sail rocking this way and that, a tiny white flag in a battlefield of wind and water and current and waves.

Goddamn Gunny, he thinks, delighted in every way.

—◦—

He'll make it.

He has to.

His grandfather will never forgive him if he loses her now.

He tugs the zipper of his hoodie to his neck, watching the forestay slacken and snap tight, the heel of the mast shifting heavily inside the step. On the steepest waves, the dory roaring, he can barely follow his thoughts; the long pause between waves seems worse, the tiller going soft as he watches the back of a swell slide beneath him and then race ahead of the dipping and rearing bow. He refuses to dwell on the feeling that his grandfather knows nothing anymore. He recalls, instead, the dreamy spell, long ago, after his father vanished and Grandpa G showed him how to scrape and sand the bottom of the overturned dory, a sequence of images recurring repeatedly until one day, just like that, his grandfather told him the boat was his, handing him a pair of brand-new oars that he could barely carry by himself to the water.

Below the highway tunnels he finally glimpses the familiar rock beyond the end of the beach at Ruthton, property that came to his mother following final word of his father's death. In the gut of the river the waves look denser, darker, more tightly packed; sooner or later he's going to have to jibe, try to make it across. He still feels pretty sure of himself—as long as he holds the course he's on now. "The whole point of these boats," his grandfather liked saying, "is to get you to fish."

If only the river were straight.

If only he didn't need to cross.

"And after that, get you home."

With oars, maybe. But before he can question his grandfather's wisdom, he's already blaming Warren, his dumbass stepdad, for rigging the dory this summer with sails, an idea he loved from the start even as he curses it now.

Grandpa G claimed he never liked sailing—an opinion held ever since he ended up capsized his first summer in the gorge, where the wind, he said often, had a mind all its own. "And a terrible one at that," he liked to add. But he rarely let wind—or anything else—keep the two of them off the water. Long before his body failed, his grandfather gave up rowing, leaving it to him, pulling from the forward thwart, to take them up and down the river in search of fish—salmon, steelhead, sturgeon and shad and smallmouth bass. Over the years he learned to watch his grandfather without really looking at him, pretending to study his own hands, the pivot of his wrists, the angle and sweep of the oar blades— while glancing toward the stern of the dory, where Grandpa G sat gazing, even then, at who knew what, his eyes drifting from the river to the steep forested walls of the gorge. He remembers hoping for a sign of approval, some word or gesture that would let him know his grandfather noticed his rowing, how it had improved, how true his course ran even in current and wind. But all he got was his grandfather's drifting gaze, a kind of dreaming it seemed, punctuated by sudden claims that occurred like puffs of wind darkening the water.

"You'd have more chance getting across the Atlantic in this thing than half the boats they build today."

The other side of the river would be fine right now. If only his step-dad had rigged him with a simple lug or spritsail—not this sloop shit he's still afraid to reef in wind like this.

But of course dickhead wanted the boat to point higher, sail faster—because he doesn't understand the idea is to go fishing, not ride around on this fricking wind.

～～

He doesn't see Gunny go over.

One minute the little sail seems to pivot in the wind, swinging on the mast as though buffeted by indecision.

The next it's gone, its feeble image washed from view by spray off the vaulting whitecaps.

Gina doesn't get it. Not a clue. He finds a line between wind and waves, a course to cover distance even if he can't see yet exactly where he's headed. The board slides easily up and over the spilling wash. There's a moment, slipping across the face of each wave, when he picks up speed, briefly surfing. He recalls his own father, dead now as long as Gunny's, sprinting down a beach in Baja, diving in amongst rocks to pluck him out of a hole dug deep by shorebreak currents. The story seems apocryphal, family legend, how he was carried back to his mother, arms outstretched at a cluster of towels to receive him.

"Ecky! You were swimming!"

"Swimming?" Yet he can still see the blood—at five the first time he'd seen it—streaming from scrapes on his father's knees. "I was *drowning*."

Gina thinks they're supposed to protect Gunny. Shield him. Steer him toward safety. When danger is part of the call. He spots the dory, washed on its side, its sail puddled in the water. Gunny hangs from the rail, righting the boat slowly—only to lose his grip, the boat lurching free as the wind flattens the sail again, dumping it back into the river.

She'll figure it out. Or lose him completely. He waits before hollering, hoping Gunny can manage on his own. A good kid. Fierce. Of course he might not be in this mess if he had stayed put for more than a single sailing lesson.

Of course the damn kid couldn't stand being together in the boat any longer than he had to.

Which makes it *his* problem?

If only Gina could see the two of them now.

He digs the paddle into a wave, watching Gunny haul once more on the rail, fighting lines, a loose oar, trying to right and enter the dory at the same time. But it's impossible: the boat rolls up again and he sees immediately how low the gunwales sit, blurry below the ragged surface of the river. There's no way Gunny will be able to bail—even if he could keep the boat standing.

— • —

The boat all but buried, he still thinks he's fine. What did Grandpa G say? "They're your sweetheart, not your mother."

Even after the boat rolls a third time, maybe the fourth, overpowering him again despite his every effort to keep the sail upright, hold the dory steady, figure out what to do next—even then he's sure he can manage, do something that will fend off the worst.

Then he sees the daggerboard. He spots it floating away, naked as a severed limb, its varnished surface casting spasms of light as it rises and falls with the waves, riding upriver against the current—already farther off than he wants to swim even if he did dare leave the dory.

Even if he were sure he could make it back.

For the first time he feels a clutch of fear, the grip of cold river and hard wind suddenly different than it felt before. He swipes at water spilling down his face and then frantically wrestles the boat up on edge just far enough to hang over the gunwale and glimpse inside. Both fish are there, tethered through the gills; his rod and tackle box remain lashed to the thwarts. The weight of the mast and sails draws the boat back over once more. Why didn't his stepdad warn him about the daggerboard floating free? Why didn't he rig it somehow to prevent losing it?

He slides his hands along the rail, struggling with tangled lines, an oar jutting over the gunwale. Now what? The boat won't sink, he knows that, but—what?

"Gunny!"

The hell? Startled, he spins toward the far side of the river. His step-dad, standing, paddles his way, sliding like a skier through the waves.

Even from this far he can see his dumbass grin.

"Gunny!"

He starts to holler back. But nothing comes from his mouth. For a moment he wonders how he thought he was doing something—or about to—that ends up as nothing at all. He spins back around and starts again to try to right the boat. He knows he needs help. He knows he's going to get grounded—probably not get to see his girlfriend for a week. Worse, he was supposed to get back in time today to go with his mother to visit Grandpa G—but suddenly none of it matters, nothing other than the cold welling up inside him, shaking him head to toe.

———

"If you're cold, Gunny, you need to go in."

Warren drops to the board, straddling it as though about to lie down and catch a wave. The paddle, across his lap, acts as a kind of outrigger, steadying him in the heavy chop. In the wind he can hear road noise, either the interstate or the state highway beyond the opposite bank.

A hell of a long way from Malibu.

Abruptly he slips into the river, grabs the board by the tail, and points the nose Gunny's way.

"Take this. I'll lash the paddle to the boat."

Gunny, draped over the rail of the dory, glares at him.

"I can paddle standing up."

"Fine. Take everything. Just get going."

Gunny ignores him. Surprise. He rests both arms across the board while watching Gunny wrestle the boat upright again. The sails rise, spilling water like drenched tarps, until the gunwales, coming to rest, appear to sag beneath the agitated surface of the river.

Sure now Gunny doesn't have a plan, he slips free of the board and goes aft to the windward rail.

"You have to head up a little into the wind."

He floats the paddle between the gunwales and follows it into a tangle of lines. He finds the mainsheet and frees it from one of the oars, the oarlock still secured in its socket. Then he slips back outside the perimeter of the dory and gets ahold of the tiller and eases in on the sheet, his weight settling onto the rail.

The dory, still buried to its gunwales, begins to creep ahead.

"Just try to keep her steady."

Gunny, shivering, turns his way. He follows Gunny's gaze upriver— where the paddleboard rides upstream on the wind.

"Daggerboard's gone, too."

He glances back at Gunny. They make eye contact, exchange a look. Screw it. Gina's probably right: he's got it so good he doesn't even have to sweat new gear.

Of course, he's been making boards so long he stopped worrying about new ones eons before he met any Gina Marie "My Wounded Son" Gilderhaus.

The dory keeps heading in the right direction.

Later, still tight to the sheet, he finally mentions the fish.

"Your grandpa'll be stoked. Where d'you get them?"

Gunny, hanging from the rail, appears half-asleep in the long August shadows cast across the gorge.

He takes his time answering.

Or maybe it's the cold.

"Drano," he says finally.

They look again at each other, the wind filling the silence.

"We better not tell your mom."

Goodnews River

Foster wasn't a cook but his friend Neal said it wouldn't matter. As long as he knew how to buy groceries and fend for himself in a kitchen, he was qualified for the job. The guides were easy as long as he had a half-dozen good ways to fix salmon and he never, ever, ran short of desserts. The guests could get pissy—but screw them, said Neal. A new group arrived every day, so even if you blew a dinner, you could make it up to them at breakfast, set a pretty sandwich buffet for lunch, and they were gone by mid-afternoon on the plane that brought the new bunch to the out-camp from the lodge.

Short-term relationships suited Foster just fine these days. He'd been fending for himself nearly two years now, ever since his college sweetheart dumped him the very week she finished her degree in non-profit management, a specialty she claimed at odds with his budding interest in the sport of fly fishing. Go figure. Raised in Milwaukee by an unmarried father, he had grown up with a type of seasonal salmon fishing that seemed, on most counts, close kin to deer hunting and rooting for the Packers, an excuse for drinking and chest-beating that provoked in Foster an air of juvenile contempt. Had his girlfriend been smarter, she might have seen through his act, pointing out to him what an obnoxious prick he could be, especially since buying a fly rod. Instead, she simply left him, chasing a lead on a six-month internship at a cycling co-op in Minneapolis.

He switched his major the following term for the third time in two years, transferring what credits he could from environmental studies to cartography. Then again, maybe he would really rather move to Maine and become a boatbuilder. Or take up beekeeping. Nobody owned too many good candles. He had no stomach for calculating the extent of his student debt, but as long as he remained enrolled half-time while making credible progress toward a major, he could renew his loans, exempt from the shadow of genuine adulthood.

He met Neal the next year at a meeting of the Badger Fly Fishers. He had never been west of Denver, so when he heard it possible to land a summer job in Alaska with the lodge where Neal guided, he went online and made a case for himself. He could stop in Oregon and catch a steelhead. Or see the ocean. Come finals week he grew too excited to study. He loaded up his Cabela's Visa, outfitting himself with Carhartt overalls, buffalo plaid wool shirts, and a low-crowned, flat-brimmed black Stetson. Plus, a twelve-inch hunting knife, its bright blade hidden inside a tooled sheath that, strapped to his thigh, made his heart soar.

He had never worked so hard as he did constructing camp. Every bit of gear and material was flown out from the lodge, and after piling each load at the edge of the landing pond, he and Devon and Gage, the camp guides, packed it by foot over a rise in the tundra and down to a terraced site overlooking the Goodnews River. Neal and his own guiding partner Lew from Ohio showed up one day to help, a treat for Foster until he understood that his camp was behind schedule, a fault he felt fall squarely on his own tired shoulders. The plane arrived a second time that day, delivering another mess of gear, one that would last them half the night, he calculated, while Neal and Lew made one final pass along the length of the pontoon and climbed into the plane.

"See you in September!" Neal shouted, slamming the tinny door—a note that Foster continued to hear as he watched the plane taxi toward the far shore, its broad wake dissolving in a silvery chop.

"Waiting for somebody?"

Gage, the lead guide, Foster's age yet a six-year veteran on the Goodnews, threw his hands at the pile and hauled up a duffel bag nearly half his size. He spun and left as abruptly as he arrived, passing close enough that Foster could smell him. Pressed to the edge of the clearing, Foster knocked loose a fresh shower from the willows. His gaze fell forward, coming to rest on his own hand, red and wrinkled and all but numb, clutching the handle of his knife.

Maybe it was the rain. It hadn't stopped since he arrived. He'd bought himself a pair of Simms' best waders, but he hated the risk of ruining them before he stepped in the river, even after he could see they were the only thing that were going to keep him dry. Gage and Devon were wadered up 24/7; from what he could tell, they hadn't brought any other clothing—just waders and boots and fleece and fancy Gore-Tex jackets, which they hung on hangers from an aluminum rod that ran down the center of their tent, one end to the other, dividing the space as if carcasses inside a packing plant.

They insisted he take one half of the tent for himself.

He could see right off it was going to be this way. At least at the start. Gage and Devon inhabited their own private world, the two of them growing more and more removed from the domestic operations of the camp once the decks were built, the tents raised, the kitchen and bathhouse plumbed. They wanted to go fishing. *Research*, they called it. Foster made no effort to join them. He claimed a corner of the galley for his guitar, his chessboard, his volumes of poetry. He pored through a half-dozen cookbooks he had picked up used at Powell's in Portland, composing menus and lists of auxiliary spices while sipping *maté* from a stainless steel *bombilla*. The first dry evening he set a chair on the deck outside the galley door, only to find himself unnerved by the empty landscape, a vast tract of green nothingness, rimmed in all directions with distant white mountains that vanished into the low gray sky. He moved the chair back inside. Above the stove his socks hung dripping from a clothesline. He launched into his first batch of cookies, doubling the butter, brown sugar, and chocolate chips, waiting for the sound of a johnboat to stir somewhere along the river.

The night before the first clients were scheduled to arrive, Devon and Gage brought back a sockeye—the first they had killed, they said—and asked he do something special with it. He could tell they'd been drinking. They gave off the air of smug dopiness that his father and two close friends, Rudy and Tyrone, would often share after a day on the lake trolling for salmon, a prelude to the kind of drinking that ended in imagined slights and raging arguments and sometimes even fisticuffs—especially if it were only Saturday when it all began. Hourlies all of them, his father and friends prided themselves on their readiness to face another week of work, whatever the shame or self-hatred that haunted their hangovers. They lived without women, each one of them for his own elaborate and not quite private reasons, a liturgy of sins foisted upon them all by girlfriends, fiancées, and ex-wives alike.

Foster didn't know what to make of these two.

He decided he should try something simple. Most of the recipes from the cookbooks he'd brought claimed he needed to both skin and de-bone the fish; all he'd ever done was fillet salmon and cook it, warning anyone he served to watch out for bones. He tore up the first fillet pretty badly, finally stopping to resharpen his knife and then sprinkling coarse salt over his fingertips to help grab hold of the skin. The pin bones proved easy enough to find; it was like running his fingers up his ex-girlfriend's legs and discovering a spot she had missed shaving. He plucked out the bones with a pair of needle-nose pliers he got Devon to retrieve from one of the tool boxes stored in the johnboats. Both guides dressed for dinner, the first time he had seen either of them in anything but their waders or Capilene underwear. He poached the salmon in a deep bath of California Riesling, excited the recipe called for a pile of peppercorns and pods of star anise he had purchased at Zupan's in Portland, unaware at the time how he might possibly use them.

Neither Devon nor Gage seemed to notice when he overcooked the slivered green beans, ending up with servings that looked like puddles of blanched seaweed next to the steamed rice and rosy salmon. Or they just didn't care. They finished off the first bottle of Malbec and then went through two more. They kept stepping outside, as if to check on the weather, the improbable daylight spilling in around them no matter how many times they swung open the galley door. Were they smoking something, too? Foster felt nothing but goodwill toward both guides, delighted to descend at last into a spell of spontaneous revelry. He got out his guitar and began a rendition of "Quinn the Eskimo," making it through two verses before Gage tumbled from his chair, collapsing to the floor in a shatter of laughter.

"Dude, you're my new hero!"

Gage struggled to catch his breath. He steadied himself on all fours, peering at the floor as if searching for a small trout fly. His hard angular body suggested a homely coffee table set in everybody's way. He shook his head once and pushed abruptly to his feet, rising as if a boxer following a mandatory eight-count.

"Are you for real or what?"

Foster remained silent, his guitar across his lap. He waited for Gage to reveal whether he was teasing him or just another mean-spirited drunk.

A head taller, Devon hooked a hand around his partner's arm and steered him toward the door.

"We better get some rest, man. Show starts soon."

Gage shook himself free.

"No, I mean it." He crossed the floor and stood in front of Foster's chair. No older than Foster, he shared with Foster's father and friends an aspect of bluster or despair, it was hard to tell which, that made him seem from a different, earlier generation.

Or somewhere lost to the world today.

"What's with the getup, anyway? The hat, okay. But that frickin' knife—enough already."

Gage stabbed a hand toward Foster as if to strip the sheath from his leg.

Devon stepped close and again caught Gage by the arm.

"Maybe he's afraid of bears."

Gage allowed himself to be pulled toward the galley door.

"Lot a good that'll do him."

Left alone each morning, Foster finally managed to dismiss his fears and escape the confines of both the kitchen and camp. The pitch of the river reminded him of home; the dark surface slid silently through the empty landscape without the theatrics he had pinned to his fantasies of the West. He grew bold enough to climb into his waders and step into a gentle run that swung beneath a bank of willows before swirling past the mouth of the slough where the guides landed guests and beached their johnboats. He had no clear picture of what he was trying to do other than cast a fly across and down and keep an eye out for anything rustling the bushes. Growing up around his father and his father's friends had taught him that watchfulness, not courage, was the most that he could expect of himself. In the steady current he felt relieved of this tiresome shame, the press of the knife vibrating against his trembling thigh with a life that seemed all its own.

The first time he saw fish in the river he fell prey to fresh spasms of doubt. Whatever gave him the idea he could catch these things? The salmon seemed magnified by the empty landscape, their nervous movement an occlusion within the stillness of the distant horizons etched into the half-lit sky. He retreated toward the bank, imagining himself in some sort of danger. Here and there fish troubled the current, their bright bodies breaking into view before the dark water swallowed them again, leaving him to calculate all that could go wrong should he ever actually hook one.

He usually returned to the galley well before the guides came speeding back to camp, their johnboats wailing with delight. But today, intent on watching the salmon, he remained on the water, making casts that proved he had no business expecting results of any kind whatsoever. Gage marched his clients up the elevated walk, their steps echoing through the pressure-treated planks. Again Foster failed to straighten his leader, watching the fly collapse into a puddle of line already resting on the water.

"Quit breaking your wrist!" Gage hollered.

Caught off-guard, Foster tried immediately to launch a backcast, forgetting to take into account the coils of slack line clinging to the surface of the river. He waved the rod tip as if signaling a plane. When the leader finally slid free of the water, the fly jumped lazily his way, with just enough giddyup to reach him, where it settled with a tangle of line around the brim of his Stetson.

Yet by the time he reached the galley, he had sorted out a fresh way to think about the timeless problem of wrist-breaking—so much so that he had stayed out on the water, making passable casts, until he hurried back to camp to start coffee and, while he was at it, set out the plate of macaroons he had baked first thing after breakfast.

Gage and Devon showed up while he was arranging sandwich fixings on the counter between the kitchen and dining table. They paused outside the doorway, squinting in at the guests as though their eyes were adjusting to the light. Gage leaned toward Devon and said something that set both guides to laughing. Had they already begun celebrating the arrival of the floatplane, the guests' departure—the start of their one day off a week?

Either that or his bungled backcast had been added to his tally of miscues.

He made the guests wait while he carried cookies and mugs of coffee—one with creamer, the other milk—out the door.

"I can't tell you how much that tip helped."

He handed Gage his coffee, pleased neither guide asked anymore if he got it right.

"Made a world of difference, that's for sure."

He raised his free hand and motioned as if ringing a bell, his wrist rigid as rhymed verse.

"Why? You catch something?"

Devon turned away and headed inside without waiting for an answer. Both sides of the table made elaborate gestures offering room for him to join them.

"Did you?"

Gage sipped from his coffee, making no move to join the others. Behind him the wilderness rose as a wall enclosing the camp. The wind or the river sounded like a heavy load dragging in the distance. Alone with someone, anyone, for the first time in weeks, Foster felt the sharp thrill of intimacy—as if waking up and stepping out of his bedroom and running into his father, arriving home in the morning following a night out drinking with his pals.

"You hook something?"

Gage raised the mug again to his lips, his blue eyes curious, free of the sarcasm that Devon seemed to crave.

Foster shook his head no. A lump of disappointment lodged in his breathing, unlike anything he had felt while casting for the stirring salmon. He hated to let anyone down.

"But that's not the point," he said. "Is it?"

———

He got his chance to find out first thing the next morning. Courted during lunch, Devon had decided to fly back with the guests and spend his day off at the lodge. Gage considered his partner's act a sacrilege—worse, a breach of loyalty. Wasn't the whole idea behind guiding in some miserable bush camp so you could throw flies at big wild fish whenever the schedule allowed?

Wasn't the point to stick some pigs?

"You'll see!" hollered Gage, hanging from the tiller while the johnboat raced upstream. Foster felt his breathing stutter as a wall of willows shut like a curtain one last time across his view of camp. He sat with his back to the river, trying to make out everything Gage said. They bucked their way through a narrow bend, the prop raising puffs of mud despite Gage's attempt to keep the boat on edge, rocking it chine to chine.

Wasn't he driving awfully fast?

Was he already drinking?

The river grew smaller, the bends tighter as they weaved upstream. Gage seemed set on trying to impress him, running wide open even when they had to duck their heads beneath willows overhanging a channel alongside a shallow riffle. Foster recalled returning as a grade-schooler from a day of salmon fishing with his father and his father's friends, his dad slurry-speeched drunk yet refusing to slow down in his unwieldy F150 pickup. He remembered how clever he had felt when he realized that there was nothing to worry about in these situations, his father didn't want to die any more than he did—an argument he understood, years later, didn't always hold true.

Yet it was the same argument he tried making to himself now, growing more and more anxious as the johnboat skipped and skidded recklessly upstream. What else could he do? They faced each other without speaking, penetrating the wilderness. Get mad? Throw a fit? He was along for the ride—the same place he'd spent so much of his life.

Later, he could pinpoint the moment he recognized something was going terribly wrong. Above the willows he watched a pair of ducks shoot across the gray sky as if desperate to escape a hidden danger. He ran his gaze over Gage's unshaved face, searching the expression beneath the bill of the cap, behind the sunglasses and wind-tinted cheeks. So what if some guide was trying to intimidate him, put him in his place? Guy has to feel pretty sorry about himself, he remembered thinking, watching Gage's mouth form the shape of a perfect circle the moment everything came completely undone.

———

"You mean to tell me you were just cruising along and—"

"Who said anything about *cruising?*"

Foster drops his bags at the foot of the dock, leaving room for the swirl of guests spilling out of the lodge. His pal Neal laughs benignly, shaking his head as if clearing water from his ears.

"That still doesn't explain how you run into a goddamn bear."

Neal sets down Foster's satchel of cookbooks and spices and fishing gear. His own gear sits at the far end of the dock, two massive duffels stacked alongside the bags and equipment of guests headed out for a night in the bush. Since the accident, the lodge has been scrambling, trying to fashion a new lineup while the top guide at one of its two showcase camps gets put back together at the Providence Medical Center in Anchorage.

Foster leans down and adjusts his pile of bags, aiming for the tidy appearance the guides seem able to create no matter the mess their big duffels hold inside.

"He was driving like a maniac. I never saw a thing."

"A *bear.*" Neal smiles as two guests, approaching the dock, glance sharply his way. He allows the word to hang there without comment, making no attempt to conceal his assessment—age, clothing, carriage—as they pass. "You came flying around a corner and lo and behold—"

"They're around."

"Really?" Neal doesn't try to mask his mock surprise. "In Alaska?"

As the next guests reach the dock, Neal asks about the bear's size in such a way that Foster refuses to respond.

He waits until all the guests have nearly reached the plane.

"You think I'm making it up?"

Neal takes out his tin of Skoal and frees a wad and inserts it behind his lip.

"What happened to your knife?"

"Why? What's that got to do with it?" At the end of the dock the floatplane roars to life.

Neal waves he's on his way.

"Seems weird, is all—the way you've been carrying that sucker around since you got here."

They both glance down at Foster's unprotected thigh.

"He wouldn't let me leave him there unless I left it, too."

Neal turns and spits into the lake. "It's not like he was going to get up and chase after you."

"I figured he needed it more than I did."

"While you hiked back a half-dozen miles through the goddamn bush?"

Foster listens to the sound of the engine, wondering if he can make out a change in pitch as the oil pressure begins to rise. He recalls sitting as a boy in his father's truck, following the uneven rhythm of the idling engine, waiting for his father to drive him to school after stepping back into the house for a cigarette and who knows what else.

"I wasn't about to stay out there all night. Not with him."

From the plane someone shouts for Neal to get his ass in gear.

"So how come you got shit-canned? Why not Gage?"

He rejects the impulse to tell another lie. Everything is settled. He closes his eyes against the bleak forest rising from the far edges of the lake, trying to shut out the terror he felt following the river, making promises to a vague idea of God in exchange for a first glimpse of camp.

"When I finally gave him the knife, he offered me a hit from his flask. Said I was turning out to be a real guy."

Foster opens his eyes.

"All I had to do was say I was driving."

What's a little lie if it saves your old man's ass, his father once said. *Hell, we're fishermen, for Chrissake.*

"And you agreed?"

He hears the pitch of the plane engine change.

Or he's just making it all up, trying to make sense of a bum deal.

"He said I don't have a future in guiding. What's it matter if I lose a lousy cooking job?"

"And you agreed?" Neal asks again.

Foster looks over at the best friend he's got.

"He's right. Isn't he?"

New Lies

It couldn't last.

In the face of abysmal dam counts, emergency river closures, and a general sense of the things going to pot, Jenkins kept getting fish. Not like the old days, no, nothing like that—when over the course of a couple of evenings after work, he might have moved a dozen steelhead to the fly, hooked and landed half of them, and most years rarely gone without fresh fillets in the fridge from hatchery fish all fall. This was different. Retired now, he went at it as hard as he wanted—which of late, on his home river, could feel like pounding sand down a rat hole. Until this sudden hot streak. Or at least warm: a single fish nearly every morning by just poking around, moving upriver and down, dodging crowds, swinging the fly through odd new lies forged by high water from the gnarliest winter anyone had ever seen.

He felt sly as a henhouse fox.

But the deck was stacked. He knew that as well as the next guy. Too much he couldn't control. Too many lies now that *didn't* hold fish.

He knew better than to test the strength of his luck during the busy weekends on the river; such caution, naturally, allowed him chance to stumble. He felt his attention slip, his resolve waver. She wasn't a neighbor so much as she was a friend of friends, a gal, twice divorced, who lived against the backdrop of orchards at the edge of town. She'd been working on an old farmhouse at least as long as he began passing that way after taking over the second language program at the middle school, in charge of helping children of migrant workers learn English.

The house, when he thought back on it, had progressed with the pace of the seasons, passing through phases of reconstruction and remodeling as though the appearance of blossoms and then ripening apples and pears in the orchards, followed over and over by the stillness of winter. He would have never considered the slow but steady progress of the job in such lyrical terms had he not finally seen the extent of the work, bold and sublime, from inside.

And by then it was too late.

———

The days shortened. He didn't have to crawl out of bed so early—or he had longer to himself after he did, time for a fire, a second cup of coffee, a new length of tippet knotted in good light to his leader *before* he reached the water. And a real breakfast—fried eggs on top of buttered toast with a spoonful of steelhead roe, from a recent hatchery hen, spread over each egg, the dainty sacs the color of some exotic jam but with the surprise and delight of salt and the open sea as he squeezed the tiny balls until they popped in his mouth. She insisted food like this would kill him, send his cholesterol through the roof. She couldn't watch him ruin his arteries—another reason, she said, she stopped rising with him, seeing him off before dawn.

He agreed; only a fool failed to pay attention to what went into his mouth. But the matrix grew more flexible before and often after a day of fishing. Which was part of the appeal. Especially steelheading, when a meal needed to hold—when some years the only parameter he understood in the equation to success was how long he stood in the river and cast.

All he really knew, at this point, was he would grow old and die. Everywhere he looked: his father, his sister, the famous athletes and entertainers, the victims of disasters and acts of appalling violence. Or too old, anyway, to fish—unless he was so lucky to be struck down first.

Lucky?

Besides, wasn't he old already?

Maybe she was right: sometimes it seemed like he knew nothing at all.

He climbed into his waders, carried his wet boots from the laundry room, and pulled them on out in the garage.

There. That ought to make her happy.

The bright spark of Venus floated above the ridgeline long after daybreak flooded the eastern sky. He parked at the gate and made his way on foot upriver into the mouth of the canyon. The cold bit hard into his face and fingers; come full light he was surprised, this high up the river, both the alders and cottonwoods remained plush and green, their limbs stretched far off each bank, leaves all but grazing the water. Even the oaks, crowding the canyon walls above the riparian pines, seemed to fret already the onset of fall, their color bleached by the chill of dawn in the wake of weeks of dry, sun-shot days.

He fished through the first run, an old favorite, with decreasing confidence. Halfway down, his casts all but clipping the far branches, he sank into the sense that he was warming up, practicing, not really fishing at all. He hadn't found a fish here the entire season. Had others? Yet the whole idea that he could show up at old lies, do things exactly as before, and expect to catch steelhead grew more and more remote each year. It was a guy thing, he had come to believe, that steelheading, like love, was a linear proposition: you start here and intend to get there. When lately he sensed his steelheading success followed a circular line—in some way, he felt, the same as women experienced love, coming to it and then backing away, sometimes even rejecting the entire trying messiness it brought into one's life until, what do you know, there it was again with all its unexpected glory.

You understood that, you still had a chance.

Higher up the canyon Jenkins stands gazing through a tangle of cottonwoods at a piece of water he's never noticed before. Was it here in the past? Just above him, where he's headed, one side of the river threads its way through a string of boulders before spilling into a deep trough tucked beneath the shade of the trees; last visit he swung a fly on short casts down through the trough, telling himself there had to be a fish there, when, sure enough, his line tightened and bucked and a steelhead exploded into the air, twisting and bending all but in half with the sort of breakneck acrobatics he rarely sees with sea-run fish this far from the ocean.

But this? Through the shadows and heavy trunks he watches how the current below the trough settles into calm water at the same spot the river from the far side tumbles over a broad tongue of freestone rocks, some of it spilling through the quiet pool. He climbs down the bank, skids in up to his knees. His first short casts lie inert; the little Muddler hangs beneath the surface as though a drowning grasshopper. He lengthens his line a pull off the reel at a time, finally reaching the shallow riffle alongside the pool, where the fly comes under tension and opens a wake that slides silently through the shade.

The fish breaks the surface and is on the reel and into the current in the same frightful moment. Downstream he sees no way to chase it; he staggers toward the lip of the riffle, looking for a place to carry the fight. Worse, he thinks, when you haven't been catching fish—cinched up hard now, leaning heavily into the rod, feeling the line come his way.

Still, much as he tries, he can never quite keep track of it all. And the next three visits, when he fishes the pool and side channel and finds nothing, the single steelhead fades toward an abstraction, an idea in his mind that grows farther and farther away from the heat of the running line, the weight through the rod, the growl of the reel, the broad wrist of the tail cold in his hand as he wrenched the Muddler from the hard mouth and pointed her head, slim and unscathed, into the breath of the gurgling current.

A fluke?

Will he ever get one right there again?

He found her note on the table. Rather than try calling, he gathered ingredients and started a pot of chili, enough for several meals so he wouldn't have to bother with cooking the rest of the week if he didn't bring home fish. While the meat stewed he stoked the woodstove and sat near the window in one of the two ragged armchairs she allowed in the great room, as she called it, where she still had wood flooring to install, the trim to stain and varnish, granite or marble, she couldn't decide which, under the woodstove where two layers of WonderBoard now lay directly on top of the plywood subfloor. It made him tired just looking at all of the unfinished work, even though for her, he imagined, it was sort of like fishing, just something she did all of the time, not like she'd ever reach a point and say, *There, I'm done.*

His eyes were closed when he smelled the meat about to burn. He got up and turned off the heat under the skillet and dumped it into the pot of simmering beans. When he woke next time the room was dark, the fire a bright fist of coals hovering behind the glass. He wasn't sure where he was—not until he saw the two paint cans on the floor beside him, a sheet of notepad paper lying on top, arrows pointing toward each lid with a big question mark scrawled in between. The dot in the mark was enlarged into a little heart—with two eyes, one shut, winking, it seemed, as he heard her moving around in the bedroom upstairs.

Triple Threat

It feels like an insult. Or a mean trick of fate. No sooner has Scribner escaped the rain, steering his daughter into the boozy welcome gazebo, than he finds himself shaking hands with Cody Knapp, one of the toughest little shits he ever expelled during his seventeen years as principal of Beulah River Valley High School.

Sergeant Cody Knapp, 1st Marine Special Ops. Any other former student, at least one as old as Knapp, he might have failed to recognize. He signals for a drink and then lets his gaze linger on the soggy dock and pair of de Havilland Beavers, a postcard view flirting with trembling water and dark forests and the promise of pale Alaskan nights. Seventeen years. At what point had all the kids started to look like so many smallmouth bass?

Thank God he got out when he did. Yet Cody Knapp, he recalls, accepting his Scotch from one of the bubbly lodge girls, was different from the start—and not just because of the angry scar running from the bridge of his nose to the corner of his unforgiving mouth. A ragged wound, it had creased his face into a permanent grimace or sneer, impossible to tell which—an expression he appeared to still wear with pride, lifting his own drink to his lips while peering out at both Scribner and his daughter with the bright predaceous eyes teachers had hated and coaches all loved.

"You fish here often?"

Cody aims the question at Madison. Scribner watches the tip of Cody's tongue slip into view and settle into the deep crease folded into his upper lip. Madison shimmies her glass in restless circles, swirling her red wine as though unsure of her answer.

"No, never." She looks over at him before turning back to Cody. "He usually leaves me behind."

"Alone?"

Cody offers them both his damaged smile. Scribner recalls the moment he decided to expel the boy, forcing the baseball team to enter the playoffs without its star pitcher and number three hitter in the lineup, by all counts ending the Bulldogs' chances for a third straight state title. Cody's word against Tony Wharton, the state representative's son. The girl, whose father needed someone besides her to blame, appeared another victim of circumstances that extended far beyond the walls of any public high school. Not even Coach Kavanaugh, in his last year before retirement, had questioned the final decision.

"What about you, Cody? You get up this way much?"

He follows Cody's tongue as it again seeks out the divot in his lip. What was it about him—more than all of the other troubled and damaged and often simply obnoxious students he had dealt with during his career—what was it about Cody Knapp that he had found so disturbing?

What did he find so troubling about him now?

"You kidding?"

Cody makes a show of inspecting the other guests. Clustered, drinks in hand, they give off an air of excitement that Scribner suddenly no longer shares. Guides and the pair of pilots and the two grinning lodge girls hover along the fringe of the gazebo, their expressions pitched in sharp relief against curtains of rain draped from the eaves. Cody smirks and rolls his eyes. He's dressed in a canvas jacket and coarse wool pants and rubber rain boots, a perfect foil for the latest Simms and Patagonia wear adorning the guests and help alike, as though all of them belong to a single team from which he's excluded.

"Closest I ever got was stories my dad told." Cody eyes Scribner from beneath the tilt of his smooth brow, his pale crew cut appearing to glow in the low wet light. "'Course that was before they ended up pulling him and his truck out of the river."

Scribner follows Cody's glance as it probes his daughter's reaction.

"I'm sorry. I never—"

Cody shakes his head dismissively.

"Nothing to be sorry about." He glances all around him, taking in the guests and help once more. "Saved me and my mom a lot of hurt having him and his drinking out of our lives."

Madison reaches out and lifts Scribner's empty glass from his hand. "Will they let the rookies fish together?" she asks.

———

The stab of fear was so sharp that now, as he lies waiting for sleep in the stubborn midnight light, Scribner recalls the voice of Brad Wharton, years ago, growing more and more menacing as he made it clear what could happen to Scribner—and his job—if Wharton's son Tony missed even a day of school or a single inning of play just because some Hispanic girl claimed she'd been raped by one guy, maybe two, she didn't even know which, following a weekend party on a notorious sandy beach along the Beulah River.

He follows the rhythm of Madison's breathing, trying to decide if she's asleep yet across the room. He has no way of knowing if anything Cody Knapp says is true. The head guide Jerrod—or Gerald—made it all but impossible to oppose the pairings when he offered the odd-man slot to Scribner, assuring him the chance to fish his big two-hander during tomorrow's search for Togiak kings. Of course he could have just said he wanted to fish with his daughter. Yet he relishes the opportunity, the rare gift of room on a johnboat with no one but his guide, the chance to swing the salmon rod unobstructed from the bow, launching a heavy head and big fly from here to kingdom come.

Cody's father—and truck—fished out of the river? Maybe. Who could keep track? A high school principal was privy to more bad news than anyone should be asked to absorb—the reason, he suspected, he had grown to cherish these far-flung escapes so that now, even in retirement, he clung to an itinerary of roving destinations, a piecemeal schedule with little more logic to it than a calendar showing the school musical, winter prom, and yet another homecoming week.

Rain rattles against the single window to the south. He's left the shade up because—why? He never tires of the logic of midnight sun. Even when they're socked in. He watches as his daughter stirs, tugging restlessly on her covers. Has he risked too much coming this early in the season? Just for a shot at big kings fresh from the sea? No doubt she would have had more fun—and probably success—fishing silvers in September. But she's game, God bless her, for anything. Anything to please him.

Which is the real reason, he decides, he finds her reaction to Knapp's mention of his father's death so vexing. Had her eyes actually glistened? More and more his daughter has become what teachers had called, with little or no irony, a *pleaser*—the kind of girl who seemed always on the verge of new drama if not outright disaster. Daisy Castro, for example, the girl either Knapp or Wharton—or both of them—had assaulted in one fashion or another.

"Honey? You awake?"

He uses his best father's voice, different from the principal's tone he still calls up for solicitors, his insurance broker, the occasional haughty guide. Madison is twenty-two, about to begin her teacher certification program—but like many single fathers, Scribner has a hard time seeing his first and only daughter as a genuine woman.

"No." She pulls a blanket over her head. "I'm deep in sleep dreaming about salmon."

Scribner rolls up on an elbow so he can see his daughter more clearly.

"I'm just going to say this one time about Cody Knapp. Whatever he says, whatever he claims he's going to do, he can't be trusted."

"Trusted how?"

Madison folds down the blanket and raises her head.

"Just that," says Scribner. He tries to sound both light-hearted and serious at the same time. "I hate to say this, but—"

"Then don't." Madison rolls away from him and faces the wall. She pulls the blanket over her shoulders. "Lots of kids are problems in high school but turn out fine. I've heard you say that a thousand times."

⌒⌣

The fish are bigger than he expected. Lying in a row on the muddy bank, they look like sacks of feed ready to be pitched onto the two johnboats already nosed up on shore beyond the floatplane. Eric, Scribner's guide, eases their boat through the eddy, casting glances his way even though they both agreed, all day, that the fly was a long shot, especially this low in the river, especially this early in the year, when there was virtually nowhere to wade along decent holding water.

No matter how well he could cast.

At a makeshift table another guide manhandles one of the big kings, lifting away a slab of candy-colored flesh that looks broad enough to paddle into the river. A second guide portions out fillets and flops them into a five-gallon bucket. Beyond the guides Madison and Cody raise what look to be bottles of beer, greeting him through the mist and drizzle, the two of them just far enough apart from the pair of Minnesota developers that Scribner feels his bowels contract and a sudden damp chill seep into his bones.

"Those are fifty-pound salmon," says Eric, helping Scribner with his gear as he climbs stiffly out of the boat. "I told you they're here."

He hasn't doubted him. Still, the dead fish on the bank call up a category of animal completely different from anything he's ever hooked on a two-hander, offering consolation, however small, for brandishing the heavy rod he's nearly worn himself out casting all morning.

Madison hurries his way, her wading boots squirrelly in the mud. Coming down the bank she lets loose a measure of rising squeals that remind Scribner of footsteps tracking rain down the high school hallways. She throws out an arm, which Cody Knapp is there to receive with the reflex disdain he once reserved for his warm-up jacket, carried out to him after another hit between his pitching duties.

"Dad, we killed 'em!" His daughter takes his arm and leads him toward the lineup of dead salmon. "Two of them were mine."

"They still are, honey." Scribner finds himself standing between Madison and Cody. "Looks like enough there to last until your first teaching paycheck."

Eric hands him his rod, passing it to him as if it were a shovel or tall broom. Another guide comes over and collects two more of the salmon, hoisting them through the gills and dragging them to the table. Madison walks to the johnboat and looks inside.

"What about yours?"

Scribner shakes his head.

"Still in the river."

His daughter turns to him, her lower lip extended in an exaggerated pout.

"Maybe it's your equipment." Cody smiles or smirks, running his fingertips up and down the length of his scar. "We got 'em on plugs."

"And WD-40." Madison returns and pulls up the zipper of Scribner's jacket. She reaches out and tugs on the brim of his hood, shielding his face from the rain. "You ever sprayed any on a fly?"

He doesn't answer. Instead he wanders off, looking for somewhere to relieve himself. The big salmon stir his imagination, even though he never felt, all morning, that he was really in the game. He climbs the bank toward a break in the tall grass, shedding his jacket and top layer of fleece and unhooking his wading belt.

He'll get his share.

The trail leads into the willows. He glances back at the river—the plane, the boats, the guides still busy with the fish. The current passes in a slow even glide, all but featureless beneath the low gray sky. They're in there somewhere. Madison and Cody approach the Minnesota developers, who hold out fresh beers to welcome their return.

The crime was that he didn't know. But he had acted as if he did. Cody Knapp or Tony Wharton. Or both of them. Or—what? His job?

The politics of power had chased him off into fly fishing, where he now hid out playing like a kid on rivers and streams and seas, trying to prove himself. To whom? He had wanted to educate, open minds, inspire. He'd been a fool to believe the job was about anything else but imprinting the earmarks of class.

He turns back toward the bushes. Stepping beyond sight of the others, he starts to roll down his waders, only to find his way through the flattened grass blocked. In the middle of the trail lies a pile of bear shit, enough to fill a small wheelbarrow. For a moment Scribner stands and studies the dark mound, fresh as the dead salmon on the bank, contemplating again how little he knows.

— —

He feels the line tighten. Again. Reduced to a state of dreamy grace, he leaves the rod hanging at his side, giving the fish the fly, letting it turn with it while he stands there motionless until the line pulls stiff and the reel squawks and he swings the tip firmly in a wide arc toward the bank, pivoting his hips until the bend of the rod sinks through his hand and far out in the current the line slices magically, at a sharp angle, upstream.

Another chum? Zack, one of the two guides at the out camp, raises his fist from the bottom of the run and starts his way. Scribner waves him back; he doesn't need to interrupt anyone else's fishing. This late in the day, long after dinner, Zack's been off the clock for hours, long enough for either of them to wear the point off of any sort of salmon horn.

He edges his way back toward the bank, a steep incline now that the tide has risen, flooding the vast pool below the cluster of tents that make up the camp. The fish doesn't feel like another king. Like two of them make him an expert? He watches the line cut sharply through a wind-blown chop moving opposite the current, picturing the two salmon that came completely out of the water, not big fish like those landed on the Togiak by the others earlier in the day—not much bigger, really, than the chum. But bright, bright and bold, both kings hurling themselves into the pale evening light, a faint blue blush still lingering in what must now be practically the middle of the night.

Midnight salmon fresh from the sea—who knows how many of them riding this very tide, a great wave swollen by the solstice, a first surge of summer just now starting to sweep upriver across the land. He can't help himself. His thoughts stir some profound welter of his imagination, leaving him helpless to quit. One more. And another. Until the darkness seems real at last, a sudden gloomy shadow draped across the empty landscape. He staggers up to camp and makes for bed—only to discover his daughter gone, a fresh jolt to his imagination, her absence an imprint on the coarse wool covers as clear as the scar etched into Cody Knapp's cheek.

Cody and the guides mill about smoking on the deck outside the door of the kitchen tent when he and Madison finally arrive for breakfast. The sky has lifted, suspending the sun behind a veil of frothy grays, the smudge of pale light the first chance Scribner's had to confirm his bearings. As they come up the slatted walkway, he's sure he can smell the sea, a faint scent of salt and low tide and mudflats riding the onshore breeze.

They sit in silence on opposite sides of the table while Derrin, the cook, pours coffee into heavy ceramic cups. He hasn't said a word to Madison about last night. He can't devise an innocent question. Is there such a thing? he wonders, stirring granola into a bowl of yogurt. Or did he lose the ability to question out of curiosity, not design, when he left the classroom and moved into the front office all those years ago?

Cody, anyway, has sense enough to steer clear until they get back on the water.

They split up between the two guides, Zack and Gardner, spreading out on a pretty run just above the big tidal pool and confluence of two low-gradient streams meandering off into the tundra as if promising mangrove creeks. Zack has convinced him that they could leave the two-handers in camp; this will prove a completely different kind of sport. They're looking for kings, Zack explains, that arrived on the last tide, fresh fish that will hold in these lowest tributary pools, resting or waiting for dark on their first day back in freshwater.

"Fish this hot in water this small." Zack's voice trails off. He shakes his head, leading Scribner toward the top of the run. They stay back from the water, edging up into the grass above a muddy bank as if approaching a sweet spot on a Montana spring creek.

"You ever see really big ones in here?"

Scribner searches the pool as they slip upstream through the grass.

"We taped one last year nearly forty-four pounds."

"In water like this?"

Before Zack answers he halts and aims the lip of the landing net at the ground.

In the wet soil the bear print looks big enough to cover a Griswold skillet.

Zack stands up straight and glances around.

"Goddammit. Now I gotta go back and get the protection." He looks down again at the paw print. "You might as well get started. Just run the fly along the far bank."

"I'm okay here?"

Zack looks downstream in the direction of the two johnboats. Madison and Cody stand knee deep, a cast apart, in the current.

"You oughta be. We haven't had to spank one yet this year."

Scribner's thinking as much about bears as fishing when he's startled by something take hold of the fly and move it and then let go. Shit. Is that what he's after? He pays attention to no effect until he's passed through the best water. Downstream he sees Cody tight to a fish, his rod straining against the empty gray sky.

Without waiting for his guide he returns to the top of the run and drops the fly near the shadow along the far bank and lets it slide in a sinking swing into the soft water inside the current. That's just about where he was last time. Even with a ten-weight, he feels more like he's trout fishing than trying to scare up a Pacific salmon of any sort fresh from the sea. Could have been a whitefish last time for all he knows.

But he's sure it's something else entirely when he sets up on a heavy fish that's immediately on the reel and taking line.

A lot of line.

———

"Forty-four by thirty-two," says Zack, slipping a coin-sized measuring tape into the front of his waders. He pats Scribner on the back "That's a fifty-pound fish, professor."

Scribner cradles the fish a moment longer before it twists free and steers itself out into the current.

"A fifty-pound king," says Zack, shaking his head.

Scribner rises and looks all around him. Downstream he pictures waves rolling in against the push of the river, the one current cleaving the other. He's not sure where he finally beached the fish, not after they crossed the stream three times, maybe four, and passed through at least as many bends. A damn lucky fish to land but he did it.

He really did it.

Zack leads them back upstream. He's still carrying the landing net and rusty sawed-off he had in hand when Scribner came splashing downstream, trying to keep up with the big salmon threatening to spool him. On a rise above a tight bend of the stream, they both get a good look at the long pool where Scribner hooked the fish, empty now save for the two johnboats, their square bows resting on the bank.

"Where're the others?"

"Damned if I know," says Zack, hurrying ahead.

They plow through two different tailouts, plunging upstream until they see them, Madison and Cody at the top of the run, Gardner downstream—while in between a bear as big as a half cord of wood muddies the water, pawing about the shallows in an attitude of confusion that suggests to Scribner a runner caught in a pickle.

Zack slows down and then stops, waiting for him a couple of long casts below Gardner.

"I hope they have enough sense to hold still."

Scribner barely hears him over the waves of his own labored breathing. Somehow this is Cody Knapp's fault. He's sure of it. He starts forward but Zack grabs him by the arm and stops him short.

"The best thing right now is do nothing."

The bear rises to its hind legs, pivoting its head this way and that. Can it hear them? He looks past the bear and catches a glimpse of Cody eyeing his daughter, recalling the glare of outrage and hatred the boy had fixed on him when he understood that the decision was final, that he alone was being blamed for whatever had happened—whatever really happened—that night on the river with Daisy Castro.

And a rich kid named Tony Wharton—who was getting off scot-free.

Do nothing my ass.

He pulls loose from Zack's grasp and races upstream. Zack shouts once and Gardner and Cody and Madison look his way. The bear takes a step forward and then drops to all fours and lumbers up the bank, only to stop where the grass stands in a long bright brow above the steep lip of mud.

Scribner yells, waving his arms overhead.

The bear turns and starts his way.

He pulls up short. Wads of muscle and rolling fir-colored hair, the bear comes directly at him, pressing forward as though relieved to finally find itself with something at which to aim its confusion or fear. It's bigger than Scribner has ever imagined a bear would be. He stands there watching it, unable to move, studying the bear's small dark eyes, pitched at an angle of near-sightedness that makes them all the more frightening.

Behind him he hears Zack shouting over the slap of his wading boots running across the mud.

Gardner hollers something else he can't understand.

Then beyond the bear he spots Cody, his throwing arm raised, charging forward in the manner of an unschooled outfielder daring a runner to advance. From ninety feet back he lets loose a softball-sized river rock that follows a graceful arc and lands directly at the back of the bear's broad head.

The bear stops, tips up its face, turns toward Cody, who has already pitched himself down the bank, free of the line of fire—all of this giving Zack the perfect broadside target to unload a shell of steel shot from a roar that rolls like thunder across the empty green tundra.

—⁓—

"Quite the toss by soldier boy."

"Thank God. I'd be afraid to spank one of those sonsabitches in the face."

"You hurt 'em bad enough they'll come grab the gun off you and shove it up your ass."

"You'd be praying that's all it did to you."

Both guides nod Scribner's way. They each take another pull from the plastic flask he's produced while they listen for the plane. He usually waits to pass out treats until they're about to board.

Now seemed the appropriate time.

He studies the wildflowers clinging to the rise between camp and the shallow landing lake. Their gear sits neatly at the edge of the narrow mud beach where the plane will eventually taxi to shore. A breeze off the sea has pulled the ceiling down low. As they await the sound of the engine, there's the added excitement of whether the plane will even arrive.

From here they can also see Madison and Cody, strolling along the wind-scuffed water lapping at the shore, the two of them side by side.

Zack pulls at the single malt again.

"'Course a guy who can land a fifty-pound king on a tiny tundra stream can probably kick some serious ass, too."

"No doubt." Gardner reaches for the flask. "Soldier boy doesn't bean the cub, our professor appeared ready to bend it over his knee."

Gardner drinks and then holds out the flask.

"You've known him awhile, haven't you."

Scribner watches his daughter moving along the shore.

"Not really. He was just another kid at the high school."

Gardner shimmies the flask, waiting for him to take it.

"Seems like a good guy," one of them says.

John Day

Nothing seems stranger in an ardent fishing career than those curious spells of indecision when we can't seem to find our way to the water. Real guys, we imagine, never suffer such failures of purpose, returning again and again to river and stream—day after day, season after season, year after year after year—with the billowy enthusiasm of gusty bird dogs. Most of us, on the other hand, fall prey to periods of resistance, an insurgency of will that drags us into psychic tugs-of-was more commonly associated with postponed chores, temperance, or schemes of self-improvement.

How can anyone not want to go fishing? we ask ourselves, later, when the fugue or depression finally passes. How did I deny myself all of that time? Yet find ourselves in the midst of these maudlin spells of uncertainty and we savor the unlikely but bittersweet possibility that maybe we were wrong all along, there *are* better ways to spend our lives than trying to fool mindless creatures with brains on the order of dried mung beans. Maybe the ennobling virtues of a life of service make meaningless a well-crafted Comparadun. Maybe love, not a tight loop, makes life worth living.

I mention love with reluctance. Haven't we all, at one time or another, found ourselves a little carried away? These days I'm a sober man, recognized throughout the community for my modest bearing, yet for months I've found it virtually impossible to indulge in angling pleasures, so great have my affections grown for Maritza the X, whose spirited company deserves a metaphor lifted directly from these sporting pages.

"Chuck," she said recently, responding to my wishes. "It's bad enough you write and talk so much about fishing. Do you have to lie there with that expression of a fish on your face, too?"

Maritza. The X is short for Ex, the perils of love having dealt her a peculiar rash of petulant blows. But she liked the way it looked on a marquee, she explained when we first met—and the anonymity made it less likely she'd be tracked down by former husbands or old boyfriends now that she had moved upriver and started dancing professionally again to restore her independence and emotional ballast.

"You have a real name?"

Made bold by music and dim lighting, I raised the question while following a trail of sweat to the corner of her chin—only to have it plunge into shadows tucked between a pair of crimson lapels.

"Chuck," she said. "It *is* Chuck, isn't it?"

I nodded—and here, I recall, she studied my hands, looking first, I'm sure, for sign of a ring, only to be taken in by their disturbing lines, a gaze of sympathetic interest slipping into her eyes while she gathered up the front of her robe in a small, tidy fist.

"I doubt either of us has time anymore to relive the past."

She likes the sharp difference in our ages. But what's a couple of decades when two minds meet across the dark recesses of the vast existential night? Of course I harbor no illusions; our species, I suspect, is compelled to collide—wherever we find ourselves—by a force as sure as gravity itself. Yet was it luck or fate, you ask yourself, after your eyes have locked the very first time—in our case directly above a pile of neatly stacked twenty-dollar bills, a quaint but effective invitation for company after stopping at the bank with payment from one of a half-dozen magazines that continue to cushion the steady fall of the worth of my monthly disability check.

Still, I allow her every opportunity to embrace the postures of youth. Professionally, she needs to project an image of health, vigor, carnal exuberance—while as a writer about fly fishing, I'm supposed to sound wise and experienced, if not old at least grizzled, whiskered, ironic, deep.

Which is pretty much how I've played it. Maritza, of course, knows otherwise. What is love if not access into the deepest recesses of one's true character? Naturally, there are risks involved. Why wouldn't there be? The rewards, need I say, are boundless.

Even if you can't keep up with your fishing.

—⁓—

I explained everything to Maritza after she moved in. By then I was sure I could smooth over the rough spots marring the edges: the real income of even a widely published fishing writer; the sorry particulars of a disability settlement once lawyers finish bargaining and the stock market collapses as if made of hay; the caretaking arrangement with the orchard owner in exchange for the double-wide overlooking the river; the point of a backyard dope crop rather than bowing to a system of submission and capitulation for my stash of medicinal marijuana. Unlike regular visitors to these pages, Maritza had to take this all in at once. For those same readers, I'll try to keep redundancies short.

Fortunately, these belated details did almost nothing to disturb our descent into the cadence of domestic harmony. All Maritza asked for in return were a few personal odds and ends she had done without since her last divorce. Flannel sheets. Silk nightwear. Waterpik and electric toothbrush. Coffeemaker, espresso machine, conical burr coffee grinder. Laptop. A low-mileage Subaru Outback.

This last was a reach. We had to sit down and talk about it—or at least Maritza sat, perched on a stool at the counter sipping her pre-shift latte while I pivoted about the kitchen making dinner for two. Nothing fancy—we'd been working our way through my latest batch of *machaca*, a style of spicy pulled pork I learned years back from Mayra Gálvez, the wife of the orchard foreman who ended up owning the Barrett property next door. To tortillas I added guacamole, *queso seco*, diced tomatoes and lettuce, and my homemade salsa: a mean burrito. I can cook like this for Maritza. Between dancing and an exercise routine that would challenge a gymnast, she has the appetite—and energy—of a surfer.

And the waistline to match.

"Chuck," she said, aiming her smile at me. Above the lip of her cup she exposed the gap between her front teeth, accent to all that attracted me from the start. "What about when you go fishing?"

"I haven't gone since we met," I reminded her. I set down my food and glanced out the window, taking in the riparian hardwoods just beginning to turn in the fold of the canyon. *There are steelhead in that river*, I recall thinking, *and every day that passes, these are fish I'll never have a shot at again.*

"You'll go," said Maritza, turning to follow my gaze. "You know that."

When her eyes returned, moist as prunes, it seemed they were brimming with all that ails us when love—or trust—goes awry.

"It's only a matter of time."

How did she know? Granted, I'm not as complex as I might care to imagine—hardly the Renaissance type.

But am I *that* transparent?

For the truth is, I did have plans to fish. A week away in my date book was a trip to the John Day, a chance to swing flies for wild desert steelhead on a stretch of the lower river running through private land. A buddy of mine, a fly shop owner, had met the son of a ranching family that had been on the property for over a hundred years; the son had an idea to create a seasonal fish and eco camp between two of the best runs, reported my friend, that you could hope to ever find. I'd been called in as a so-called expert to assess the fishing possibilities—with the idea that I might also write a piece to spark interest in the project.

There was mention, as well, of the son's tastes in marijuana, which my friend felt pretty sure I could gratify with a bud or two from my recently harvested homegrown stash—thus ensuring us future sport even if the business prospects went up, so to speak, in smoke.

What's more, I had invited my sister, Riki Swanson, she of the long-running sitcom *Gaia*, where she's made a name for herself over the years as the oft-jilted but always alacritous New Age airhead, Marjorie Doe.

So why hadn't I told Maritza about these plans? I admit I was wary of her response—which suggests I didn't yet feel entirely secure in our relationship. Yet I'd argue, today, that my caution sprang from an intuitive need to protect the both of us and even something beyond—that my failure to wet a line, in fact, during six weeks of fall, the magic months of Northwest steelheading, belonged to the kind of heart-centered genius available to all of us who embrace love as a guiding principle—and perhaps, more so, to those of us who have been damaged—literally—in the course of our uneasy, confusing lives.

For I sensed, even then, that Maritza had it in her to go absolutely ape-shit—should she not get her way.

Maybe it's the pot makes you think like this.

"Chuck," she said, tilting back her head to get at the last of her latte. She lowered the mug and licked a blister of foam from the edge of her lip, her tongue appearing as if through the slot in her teeth—while at the same time, as she shifted atop the stool, the insides of her thighs made the sound of a breath of wind passing through the nearby trees. "Just a regular old Subie. Something simple. Plain. White. I don't care."

She set the mug on the counter and lowered her eyes—until I could feel them on my hands, a reminder of my ragged past.

"You know I don't need much."

In a sense, I suppose, love is all about finding a place in this world, somewhere one belongs. I don't imagine it's easier from one person to the next. We all feel like strangers so much of the time, separated from those around us by our disobedient tastes and desires—and then, when we happen upon someone with whom everything feels as familiar as home, we revert, I believe, to a kind of childhood trust that feels both timeless and beyond reason. How can this be happening to *me*? we should be wondering—while in our hearts we believe, deep down, we've been blessed, finally, with what we deserve.

My sister Riki, however, held little stock, at this point in her life, in the promise of love. Nor in the possibility of grace in any of our unreliable lives. Her lack of faith seemed posited in perverse contrast to the nimbus sophistries she ventured onscreen, generally in the wake of yet another heart stomping that, nevertheless, left Marjorie Doe slipping hopefully, show after show, into the deepest currents of romance once more.

Riki's own marriage had imploded during a protracted bout with breast cancer, and her only child, my nephew Blaze, seemed intent on patterning his life after a character concocted in the sordid imaginings of a television scriptwriter one step removed from the melodrama of afternoon *novelas*.

Blaze made life tough on Riki, no doubt about it. On arriving in Wasco, a scramble of dark geometry bypassed by a numbing reach of state highway, Riki had just finished visiting Blaze at an Outward Bound–style rehab in the high desert east of Bend, flying up from LA to assess the return on her latest investment to curb her son's serial addictions. At first light we left her rental, as instructed by Stan, the ranch son, in the lot of the feed store; I could tell right off Riki was a bad mood waiting to happen. I hadn't seen her since both the cancer and her divorce, but she sounded just like the sister I had always known when I asked about Blaze's new treatment.

"Lot of fucking good it's going to do him."

She glared at the windshield as if angry it wouldn't break.

"Just a bunch of rich kids still sucking the gold tit."

In the back seat Jeff, my buddy the fly shop owner, fired up a bowl that glowed, momentarily, as though pageantry in the dawn's early light.

It seemed to help. Riki fell silent as we glided across the rolling landscape, studded with tracts of wind turbines quiet in the frosty fields. Buoyed by the pot and Riki's retreat, I launched into a rambling soliloquy on the good fortune of my relationship with Maritza—failing to notice, as I spoke, that what I took for my sister's sudden sedation was in fact a classic case of her growing more and more agitated by the mile.

We dropped into the flattened canyon of the lower John Day and followed a rough two-track etched into the scrubby rise just above the meandering floodplain. The plan was to meet Stan on the river near the family homestead, long abandoned for more accessible land beyond the canyon rim. Excited by glimpses of the river, riffled and blue in bends outlined by faded willows, I made the mistake of not only enumerating to Riki the blessings of my love life with Maritza, but also listing, in detail, the gifts I had bought her in celebration of our passionate coupling.

Including the Subaru.

"You bought her *what?*"

A moment passed before Riki could even look at me. On the deck in front of a funky plywood cabin Stan had built as the first phase of his grand design, my sister assumed the tortured body language of Marjorie Doe, victim of yet another assault on her every notion of common decency. She looked shocked, hurt, dismayed. The morning light cast her gestures of despair in elegant relief, and it occurred to me she recognized she stood, more or less, on stage, while a cold wind blowing upriver did what a thousand directors have tried to do, by any means imaginable, to the heroine's disheveled hair.

I offered that my gifts to Maritza were simply a matter of love.

"*O Jesus fucking Christ, Chuck.*"

My sister's well-known expressions of pain sharpened into a frightening, ecstatic scowl—a cross between a look of gratification received and her own self-inflicted release.

"She's *using* you, Chuck. Women like that are hardwired for this kind of shit."

At a loss how to respond, I brought over the bag of waders and wading boots from the van. We were still waiting for Stan to show up. Jeff remained huddled on the backseat, out of the wind and range of my sister's angry glare.

"They got the tits and ass to dance around half naked on stage," she continued, pulling waders up over her fleece, "You can bet they expect a lot more from you than love."

Riki tugged at straps and adjusted the fit of the wading belt. She sat down on the steps and jammed her foot down the throat of a boot.

"She sure as hell isn't after your body. Look at you."

I stood waiting with the second boot at the bottom of a pair of two-by-six steps resting directly on the dusty river loam, practically eye to eye with my sister, trying not to have the one thought that does a man no good in this kind of discussion.

Riki's gaze dropped to my hands.

Women, I thought—failing to take my own advice.

But in the wake of that dangerous epithet, I looked not at myself but at my sister, she of the fame, fortune, a following of men her entire life, some of them worthwhile, a couple of them trustworthy, maybe even honorable. Where were they now? And what was *she* doing up here in Noplace, Oregon, her California tan and tool-straight nose and candelabra of bleached hair as though a corsage of orchids displayed against the weather-blasted terrain, going fishing with her half-handed brother and his stoner friends while a hundred miles south her son was probably taking sagebrush soaked in coyote piss straight up the nose?

I confess my own dope can still get to me, too.

Yet there was more to my restless view of things than the urgings of my smoky mind. The morning sun remained hidden by hillsides upriver, the shadowy sweep of overgrazed grasses highlighted by a skein of basalt exposed through worn-away soil—and already you could feel the breeze of the cold dawn settling, the sun asserting itself in clues brushing the river nearby so that suddenly I grew anxious imagining the steelhead themselves beginning to stir in that curious way that seems, on some rivers, their own inclination to rest at dawn or simply wait until the day feels fully fledged.

But even the thought of my first fish all fall failed to free me from the odd sense that this day might be bigger than that—that maybe my sister, bitchy as ever in so many ways, was trying as best she could to tell me something I needed to hear.

As if this were her way of offering love.

All of which now seems etched in relief against the backdrop of perfect hindsight. For this was the same moment I finally noticed that my dear sibling, the famous Riki Swanson, the famously *compliant* Marjorie Doe, was now—in the wake of it all—as flat-chested as a teenage boy.

It seemed absurd I wouldn't have known this. My own sister. Or that I hadn't noticed. Or somehow put two and two together and—

They must have her wear fake boobs now, I thought, *when she's in front of the camera.*

Riki stood up, booted and wadered, ready for a rod.

"How do I look?" she asked.

"Terrific." I raised a fist to my chin, spinning the other round and round alongside my head—the old charades gesture for movies—while wondering, for the life of me, what else must lie contained in our separate, unspoken lives.

"I couldn't agree more."

Climbing steps to the river, our host, it turns out, Stan Albright, rose into view, his gaze swinging this way and that, the practiced detachment of landowners approaching anglers—or anyone else—on their riverfront property. In one hand he carried a spinning rod—with a bright waggle of metal hooked to the reel.

"I've been parked downstream since you arrived. I like to see what's around before guests arrive."

Stan's gaze had settled on Riki—while his voice seemed aimed directly at me.

"Find anything?" I asked.

"Big bright buck." Stan offered Riki a toothy, good-ol'-boy grin, one that suggested, right here at the start, that the words *big* and *bright* and *buck* might apply just as much to him as to anything that swam in the river. "Native. Probably still there just waiting for your fly."

You never know about first impressions. That's all it took for me to fall for Maritza—but in this case I experienced the kind of ugly distaste I don't really care to feel toward anyone anymore—unless I'm sure they deserve it.

Can't you see she just had her tits lopped off, for Chrissake!

Stan set down his rod and swung himself up onto the deck, a move that confirmed the impression of health, agility, and a readiness for play. He ran a hand over a stiff brush of gray hair and maneuvered his eyebrows through a brief sequence of schnauzer-like tricks. Riki, I could see, was taken by this act; her expression, so stern and judgmental just moments before, grew as soft and compliant as Marjorie Doe's in the throes of yet another fateful swoon. Stan unlocked a pair of plywood doors, forcing them loose with a loud blow from the toe of his irrigation boots, and then crossed to the far end of the garage-like cabin, where he opened a blackened woodstove and began filling it with newspaper and chunks of two-by-four.

When the fire began popping, Stan bounced back out onto the deck and did a few more dog tricks with his eyebrows. This time he looked at me while he spoke.

"Now what about this bud of yours I heard about?"

Riki had already taken Stan's hand and allowed herself to be pulled to her feet. Just like that. At the same moment, I recalled the first time Maritza and I watched an episode of *Gaia* together, one in which Marjorie Doe conceals from her new lover, Cy Flack, a rodeo enthusiast, the most recent mishap of her teenage biological son. Hobson has totaled Marjorie's Karmann Ghia in yet another night of drunken street racing; Marjorie decides to replace the car, at exorbitant cost, with an identical replica, so that Cy doesn't think he's courting a spineless single mom. At the crucial moment following a night of call dancing, Cy, who doesn't own a car himself, pulls Marjorie out of her bucket seat and halfway into his own, running a hand up a fishnet-stockinged thigh until the camera follows his gaze down to the Hamm's beer logo stenciled onto the gearshift knob—a blatant affront to the Pabst Blue Ribbon emblem we've seen Cy both privately admire and tenderly touch earlier in the show. Suspicious all evening of Marjorie's anxious behavior and roundabout explanations and barely concealed lies, Cy halts his advances and begins another volley of pointed questions—only to find himself smothered by a kind of pragmatic venery that few cowboys anywhere have the capacity to resist.

Fade to black. At which point Maritza, rising from the Half Moon Pose that she had held, remarkably, throughout the last five minutes of the episode, adjusted her exercise thong and then turned to me and said, "She's not acting."

I felt this a harsh assessment of my sister's stage skills, regardless her limited range. Maritza, eyeing me, dabbed the sweat from her face, using the hem of a pale Lycra top that did virtually nothing to conceal what stood out underneath.

"She's *supposed* to be a lousy actor while trying to fool Cy," I said.

"No, I mean she wasn't pretending." Maritza took the tall glass of ice water I held in my lap and emptied it completely, revealing the whorls of her distended trachea. "She wasn't making it up. That really happened to her. I'm sure all of it's true."

For a brief moment Maritza looked at me, in that way she does, as if she still wasn't quite sure what to make of me. Or us. Then she set down the glass and leaned over and kissed me on the forehead.

"How do you know?" I asked, raising my face toward hers.

"Chuck," she said. She took my hands, both of them, and guided them, as if they were cold, up inside the Lycra.

"Chuck," repeated Maritza, her voice low, measured—a register that suggested I was a fool to ask how she knew what she knew.

And for a second it seemed my hands *were* cold, so radiant was her flesh.

"And she's in love, really in love, with that guy Cy. Cy *Clone*. Whatever his name."

While Stan led Riki off to the confines of his kindling plywood hovel, a fat blunt of mine between them as if they were two dogs blessed with a steak bone, I recalled how struck I had been on discovering Maritza's observations correct. Denton Erickson, Blaze's real father, tracked me down in Albion, hoping to fish and, need I say, score some exemplary Northwest pot. This was the same guy who abandoned Riki during her bout with cancer—but since I hadn't known, at the time, the extent of Riki's illness, I felt as Blaze's uncle that I should at least offer a cordial welcome to his father. Also, according to Denton, the real problem, marriage-wise, began long before the MRIs and chemo, when Riki fell for a *Deadwood* extra who later played the character Cy Flack in *Gaia*.

Of course I'd had no way to verify any of this—not until Denton recounted the tale of a one-eyed rooster caterwauling atop a three-legged jackrabbit, causing Blaze to lose control of his mother's baby-blue Hummer, which she later replaced, surreptitiously, etc, etc—the exact details of which I had just read about that week in an essay Blaze wrote for a college application and sent to me for editing and comments.

Readers here have already seen this same story, which I later shaded just enough to make it sound like something that had happened to me. I see no point in repeating myself.

Yet I confess I suddenly felt confounded—if not disturbed—by these Chinese boxes of narrative points of view nesting one inside the other. Alone above the river beneath the rising morning sun, it occurred to me that maybe all of our lives were fashioned after make-believe characters we had decided, for whatever reasons, we should emulate. Were any of our lives really real? Maritza, it seemed to me, in all her naked directness, offered the best example of an authentic self. And yet according to Riki, Maritza's was an act, too—a way for her to get what she wanted from me.

But isn't that always the case, I asked myself, heading for the river, if what we want is what we treasure that someone else already has?

⌁

The fishing that day, as we can generally predict, meant more to me—the one engaged in the act—than to anyone reading about it. This seems a heartless admission. But there you have it.

We can probably all use a little more truth in our lives.

Still, there were steelhead caught—wild desert fish slipping upriver through skinny water that seemed, in places, hardly deep enough to hold, much less hide, these extraordinary creatures. Writers often wax eloquently about steelhead. But these John Day fish—unadulterated by hatchery efforts and probably as pure as any run left in the lower forty-eight states—shared the kind of startling configurations and aboriginal integrity that have nothing whatsoever to do, at last, with all the drama and exclamations in any language or in any of our lives.

Borne off by his own private cloud of sedation, Jeff seemed to have disappeared completely. I was left alone to sort out a long, nearly straight run with nothing to indicate its suitability as holding water beyond the deepening of hues in a wavy ribbon of current along the far, willowless bank. And that Stan had reported landing a fish here. One pass through offered nothing new in the way of clues—but when I returned to the top of the run and started in again, I decided I had missed most of the good water, allowing the fly to swing too quickly rather than slowing its pace on a long line angled far downstream.

The beauty of a two-handed rod is that you can make that cast—even if you're only moderately able. In my case I probably wouldn't have been fishing at all could I not have held the rod and cast it using both hands. Or what's left of them.

I've written enough about my profound debt to the Spey or double-handed rod. Ours is a bittersweet relationship based largely on its capacity to keep me in the game when it appeared that fate, chance, or my own stupidity had swept me off the field. Neither one of my hands is good enough, on its own, to hold and manipulate a fly rod. Together they manage—in most cases—to get the job done.

The first fish came from the very top of the run, up inside a quadrant of soft water I was able to present the fly through only by wading out into the middle of the upstream riffle and making a cast virtually straight downstream. The fly landed, hung, began to move—and the fish ate it. My first steelhead of the season, it offered repeated chances to leave me completely unnerved, cartwheeling downstream and then turning and running directly at me, only to jump again, while I frantically worked to retrieve line.

Were it not for Maritza, and I had enjoyed, instead, the usual number of steelhead by this point in the year, I might have felt it was good enough just to have hooked such a fish, so spirited was its fight.

No, that isn't true. Had I lost it, I wouldn't have felt that way at all.

What is true, however, is that when I finally landed the tired, unmarked steelhead and cradled it for release in my ugly, nearly fingerless hands, I experienced one of those goofy but nevertheless real moments of grace that offers a schema of order to keep us from feeling like so much cosmic dust buffeted about by blind winds emanating from the void—even if that happens to be the case.

Faith, perhaps, is nothing more than trying to hold onto these moments of alleged understanding. For I saw right then a kind of exquisite symmetry, a balanced duality, between the fundamental components of my life—a union between desire and what we need in order to feel fulfilled. Clearly my hands were part of this equation: what one can't do anymore, with the other it does just fine. But there was more to it. I saw, of course, the obvious connection between me and the steelhead I had just landed—but then I quickly glimpsed the elegant coupling Maritza and I had conspired to create, the delicate pairing of me and Riki, of Riki and her son Blaze, of Riki and Stan, Jeff and me and on and on: everyone seemed, for the moment, perfectly connected to the thing or person it or any of us needs most.

Maybe I was just stoned.

Yet it seemed more than that—emphatically so when, later, four fish into my sudden escape from the throes of a season-long slump, Riki and Stan joined me on the water to inform me they wanted to go see Maritza dance.

Exquisite symmetry? I thought. *Or . . . what?*

I was suspicious of their motives. Especially Riki's. In the time it took me to fool and land four wild steelhead—fish that brought to mind fragments of lightning sparking across the surface of the desert stream—no telling what had gone on inside the nearby plywood hut. And I'd be the first to admit the reckless shenanigans one can devise or agree to in the wake of acts of intimacy. Would there be a scene? At the same time I hoped this might prove some sort of conciliatory gesture on Riki's part—or at the very least a way for her to show respect for the woman to whom my heart now belonged.

About Stan I wasn't sure what to think. Clearly his intentions were canine at best—and yet when had Riki ever desired otherwise? No, she was the one I worried most about. There was a wide streak of nastiness that my talk about Maritza had exposed, and I felt my sister capable of any sort of devilment when it came time for Maritza to bare herself and romp upon the stage.

Was I wrong?

Let me be brief. Slumps end. Spells pass. Steelhead, like rivers and rust, never sleep.

And deadlines loom.

Maritza, God bless her, will also be home soon, hungry from another night dancing for grateful eyes cast upon the In Gorged Inn's half-lit stage.

Much like the night, I suspect, that Riki, Stan, Jeff, and I found her, the magic of her sculpted body revealed in greater clarity with each spin and turn and triumph through the margins of swirling light.

The crowd had grown threefold in both size and enthusiasm since the first time I saw Maritza dance. Is there any question why? We had her to thank for a rare brand of physical beauty, not unlike the elegantly contoured bodies of the wild steelhead I had hooked and landed and released that morning, as exquisite in detail as the fingers and nails on a newborn's hands. I looked at my own hands and felt, for a moment, the profound disgust we nearly always feel on looking, at first, on the damaged, the maimed, the ugly, and it took all of my presence of mind to keep from burying my ragged paws in my armpits. It seemed perverse, yet miraculous, that these same hands had come to know Maritza's body so completely, and at the same time I sensed there might always remain something missing in our lovemaking since my hands themselves felt so incomplete.

Then Riki was on the stage—just like that, moving to the music in precise imitation of Maritza's practiced routine. Or was this Marjorie Doe, easing herself free, already, from the stirrups of her fallen fleece? The audience hooted and hollered, surprised to get two dancers on stage at once, the promise of something new, perhaps extraordinary. The stage itself seemed suddenly smaller, the bodies around it larger, pressed more tightly together than before. I found it difficult to breathe. What was Riki trying to prove now? And yet despite a good twenty years on Maritza, she gave away little in terms of looks, legs, a lithe and lively waistline, the timeless gestures of longing, invitation, appetite, resolve.

And maybe nothing by way of expressing, truthfully or otherwise, a libido slipping from its moorings, her reptile brain about to run off lickety-split.

Poor Stan, I thought. This is not a woman you can expect to croon to for long above the gentle banks of the merry John Day. Maritza, I'd come to believe—despite my sister's claims—maintained a clear distinction between her role onstage and the woman who returned home each night to embrace me. Still, was it this very separation of roles or characters—or *selves*—that left her dancing in dives on the lower Columbia, shacked up with her fingerless fishing fool, while Riki Swanson achieved worldly success doing what looked not so much like acting but, instead, playing out the reckless impulses of her genuinely wacky self?

She began plucking at the snaps of an oversized cowboy shirt. Stan's? Eventually, I was relieved to see she had on some sort of slinky camisole thing underneath, draped over her featureless torso in the same sad attitude of a lover's lingerie left behind on a hanger in a closet. The crowd fell quiet, confronted, it seemed to me, by the unlikely prospect of a stripper without breasts. Yet Riki herself showed no signs of relenting, popping the last snap and flinging away the studded shirt with the flourish of a magician revealing rabbits turned to doves.

Had she stripped before? Dumb question, I told myself. My sister, I felt certain, had done *everything* before.

Everything except . . . *this*. For suddenly there she was, dancing as if coupled to Maritza, with nothing on but her ribbon-thin thong and, above it, waist to head, nothing at all, her figure as slender and refined as my beloved's but for the bold, puckered scars that had replaced her own once-shapely and suitably proportioned breasts.

The crowd, God bless them, erupted in cheers and vigorous applause. *Men*, you might think. Yet I'd contend there was a generosity of spirit at work in that crowded strobing tavern, a magnanimity fueled by beer and shots, no doubt, but a high-minded kindness nonetheless—one to remember, perhaps, when so much before us appears ready to unravel.

And Maritza? How do I reach the high notes of praise that I haven't yet aimed for here? She, too, seemed genuinely moved, despite this sudden and profound intrusion upon her stage. Perhaps that's the difference, I recall thinking, between those of us who identify ourselves with the characters we portray on page or stage, and those who maintain a clear distinction between who we are in real life and who we are when we perform for accolades and pay. Maritza didn't appear troubled, put out, or surprised in the least. To the contrary: she swung her body into the full force of Riki's sexual verve, without so much as a questioning glance, and certainly nothing to reveal a hint of alarm for the scalding display of Riki's damaged flesh. Her hands rose, instead, in a gesture of submission, one I'd never seen before in any of her dances, nor in any of our countless tumbles through ecstatic delights. *Lady*, said Maritza's hands, *you got balls to be up here on this stage with me*—and Riki took the cue and concluded the dance with a series of head-to-toe spasms that left little if anything for the crowd's imagination.

I looked over at Stan. He appeared cross-eyed with desire. Only later did I discover that Riki's gyrations were only partially to blame. Stan *is* cross-eyed, Maritza pointed out to me, and the dog-like acrobatics he performs with his eyebrows—which bothered me so much when we first met—are his way of trying to focus on what he really can't see.

Maritza. I'm awfully lucky. It takes a woman like her to notice that kind of thing. I can't wait to get her whatever she asks for next.

In the meantime, I just need to fit more fishing back into my life.

Swedish Wedge

Lofton wakes when he hears Nils zip shut the tent and shuffle out of camp. He wonders if it's morning, nearly dawn, until he gets his bearings and through the screened windows finds stars and darkness in all directions, the desert sky dense with night. He sinks into his bag, the delicious warmth of down. The secret at this point in life, he reminds himself, nestling his hips and shoulders just so, is no less than three good sleeping pads—a genuine cushion between their worn bodies and the hard, unforgiving ground.

And no beer after sundown.

At first light he's surprised to find Nils's bag still empty, wadded up in a pile as if laundry dumped there waiting for someone to fold. He pulls on fleece against the bite of the morning chill. Nils probably did return, and now he's just up early, off looking for those good fish that will set up in the tailouts, feeding on drifting midge larvae, sight fishing as tough as it gets. Despite a case of something he refuses to talk about, Nils hasn't quit, fishing as hard today as they did when they were fifty years old, as though he can still track a size 22 midge at the end of his 7X tippet—when they both know damn well he just swings it downstream and now and then something grabs.

Outside the tent the cold air feels metallic, it's so dry. Daylight has burnished the stars from above the sharp rim of the canyon, the pale globe of dawn scouring away the dark. He lights the stove and starts the coffee. On the clothesline stretched between the shade tarp and tent, he sees that, sure enough, Nils's waders are gone, along with the little two-hander he's been casting this year on the Wolf—further evidence he's fishing downstream on a tight line. Not that it makes any difference—as long as he doesn't go on about another wedge-shaped loop that put the fly over a big fish he could have never covered with a one-hand cast.

The coffeepot lid starts rattling just as he gets the fire going, a pretty piece of work thanks to the split oak and cedar kindling he brought from Albion. In *his* truck. Again. Not that who drives makes any difference, either—an argument he's been making to himself ever since Nils announced, in March, that he'd started meds that made it impossible for him to take his turn for the first time in—what? Twelve? Thirteen years?

He turns down the stove. At least he hasn't had to make the seven-hour drive alone. He finds his cup in the dish rack and pours just enough coffee to check the color and warm the mug. Daylight has flooded the canyon, washing away all trace of night but the cold, and as he waits for the coffee to finish brewing, he works hard to convince himself that just because Nils can't drive doesn't mean he can't get up at O-dark-thirty and try to prick a couple pigs in the shallows. More power to him—him and his double-handed wedge-shaped loops creasing the width of the Wolf.

He falls still, cup in hand, trying to capture the quiet of the morning. He imagines, instead, the air in the canyon already beginning to stir, set in motion by the fire, the rising light, the constant rub of the river, the insistent whisk of Nils's rod. Mornings come and mornings go—whether anyone's ready or not. He fills his cup and a Stanley thermos and returns to the warmth of the fire. He could probably find Nils—or climb into his waders and go fishing himself. But as he settles into the sling of a camp chair and the fire's embrace, he finds it impossible to turn his attention away from the smell of the coffee, the snap of sparks leaping from the good dry wood, the first chatter of chukar scrabbling in the rubble at the base of the canyon wall directly across the water. He doesn't want to give up any of this—no matter what Nils might be up to. He's never really sure, anyway—not since his own ex-wife married Nils Sorenson way back when everything they did seemed to matter.

He hears Nils long after he's let the fire die down, a steady blue and orange flame nesting between a pair of oak chunks positioned just so—what they both call a Swedish wedge. A thousand desert campfires together have done nothing to diminish the effort they each put into finessing a store of firewood—a practiced study to keep a flame alive long after other fires would have lapsed back to smoke.

Nils says the fishing was unreal.

Of course.

Then nothing except the sound of him pulling off his boots and waders, stirring about getting dressed inside the tent. Have they *ever* had much to say to one another? What's different this morning? Their contract, as Lofton's always thought of these monthly trips to the Wolf, rests on the agreement that it's better to fish with someone than go alone—a line of reasoning that's made more and more sense with each passing year. Even before they grew old, their options in a town as small as Albion were practically nil, reduced by a history that left both of them treated throughout the valley as musty rogue males nobody knew quite what to make of.

Neither of them would say more about Carla Lindquist, the woman they had both married, than was absolutely necessary should a story pivot on her dangerous looks or withering moods. Once, only, somewhere in the middle of the past twenty years, when they could both still drink with abandon, they worked their way one night on the Wolf through a fifth of Glenfiddich and allowed themselves an exchange of candid memories, an evening of intimacy as deep as they had ever shared. *She drank like an Indian*, he told Nils. *But she had a liver like the Irish*, Nils countered. The next morning, under the weight of their hangovers, they both felt they had said too much—and if there was anything either of them still felt the other might not know about Carla Lindquist, they never shared it, no more than they would have offered up the details—unless absolutely necessary—of the condition of their bowels or the decay of their sexual vigor.

"You already eat?" asks Nils.

He comes out in khakis, a frayed sweater, and his new fleece cap, one he's been wearing for close to ten years now. Puffy-eyed, stooped, unshaved, he appears all but destitute without the attitude of his high-end gear, an appearance Lofton feels certain they share in the morning light.

"I would've started something," he says, "had I known when you'd be back."

He rises from the fire, pushing himself upright in a series of small careful movements, bothered by arthritis in both hips and the irritation in his own voice. Across the river, sunlight spreads about the twisted rock walls as though a tide beginning to move.

"There're muffins," he adds. "Fruit and yogurt. Coffee in the thermos."

He watches Nils dig through the food bin and pull out the trail mix—always the first thing to go. Neither of them feels much like cooking anymore. Nuts, cheese, hummus, good bread—they're a couple of old goats, thinks Lofton, lighting the stove for a fresh pot of coffee.

Nils drifts off like a tired dog into the sunlight—and then tells him to come check out a fly.

It's a big deer-hair concoction, spun and clipped, as close in size and shape to a tarantula as it is to the mouse it's supposed to approximate. Dangling from the reel, the fly looks like something Nils found dead and brought back to show—a bat or bird or weird, regurgitated lizard.

Lofton immediately recognizes what Nils was up to last night, this morning—whenever he was on the water.

"You know as well as I do it's illegal to fish at night."

Nils rests the long two-hander along the loops of bungee cord holding the eave of the tent to the aluminum frame. From a front pocket he takes Velcro straps and secures the rod to the pole at the eave. He grabs the pole and shakes it to make sure the rod will stay put should the wind blow.

Lofton follows him back to his coffee cup.

"That's breaking the law," he adds.

Nils swirls the last of his coffee inside his cup and then casts it into the fire.

"Yeah. And so what?"

Lofton steps past Nils. He stoops down and with his bare hands adjusts the halves of his wedge, the legs angled just so. Quickly the flame brightens and spreads.

"Laws are laws," he says.

Nils goes to the tent and unzips the door.

"You're right, Lofton." Nils kicks off his moccasins. He closes his eyes, and for a moment he stands there as if relishing the morning sun. "But I'm doing it because, one, seeing if these big browns get excited about a mouse swinging across the river was something I'd been thinking I'd like to try, something I just wanted to find out about. Two, it doesn't really matter, does it? Whether I break the law or not, I'm just about done here."

Lofton eases himself up again and waits until Nils opens his eyes.

"We're all going to die," he says.

Nils nods and gives up a tired grin. "But it so happens right now I finally know it. Before March it was kind of an abstract thing."

Nils turns and spits into the stony soil along the bottom edge of the tent. Sunlight holds the features of his face in sharp relief. For a moment he seems younger, his outline a reminder of the past—until he pivots and enters the tent, moving like an old man climbing into a car.

"You're still wrong, Nils." Lofton follows as far as the door of the tent. He peers through the screen as Nils straightens out his pad and bag. "Just because there's an end in sight doesn't mean it's okay to start—what? Driving on the wrong side of the road? Ruining public property? Stealing your neighbor's wife?"

He watches Nils lower himself to his knees and then stretch out on top of his bag.

"We were always gonna die," he adds. "There's still right and there's still wrong."

On his back Nils drapes an arm over his eyes.

"I didn't steal anybody's wife," he says.

━━◆━━

Lofton fishes alone most of the day. He waits, drinking coffee, while the sun warms the canyon to a point that finally prompts him to remove his outside layer of fleece, a reading on his body's own thermometer he knows from long experience will translate soon into bugs on the water.

Shortly before noon the PMDs begin to pop. He takes a pair of classic Wolf River browns, eighteen- to twenty-inch fish, each one found feeding so close to the weedy margins that it seems his little yellow fly, riding gently downstream, can't possibly avoid getting snagged—when suddenly the nose he's targeted pokes through the surface and eats the fly in a gesture of perfect faith. The fish are heavy, belligerent, dangerously clever around boulders scattered throughout the river, while in the net they seem as beautiful as tropical birds, spotted in some cases as though with the juice of Albion's famous cherries, in others the flanks almost silver like those of sea-run fish.

He passes through camp on his way upstream to fish a favorite riffle come the start of the afternoon caddis hatch. He leans his face against a screened window of the tent and finds Nils sleeping—still on his back, an arm thrown across his face. He wonders if he should wake him but decides if Nils can sleep he must need to. Plus, he remains troubled by their morning exchange, his sense that something has shifted, a change that surely started in March after all the years they took turns driving, Nils one trip, he the next—back and forth without question or discussion, a rhythm as simple as moons.

It's nearly a mile to the upstream caddis riffle. By the time he reaches the bend in the road above the best water, the heat has slowed his pace to the point that he thinks twice about climbing down the loose riprap, wading the tailout, and poking through the willows that he then has to circle behind in order to start in where he can find a good drift in the stiff current. He pulls his water bottle from his vest and drinks. He's going to need to eat, rest, get out of the sun—get ready for the evening action. Check on Nils, too. But then he sees fish moving—pale flashes slashing in the slots between the broken water, the big browns feeding on rising pupae—and as he starts down from the road, he begins to spot fish tilting through the surface, quick, lunging takes completely different than the measured rises to mayflies in the slow water downstream.

—◦—

The gunshots begin while he makes his way toward camp, following a game trail at the foot of the canyon wall on the far side of the river. He quickens his pace, stepping carefully across the uneven footing, concerned that Nils has a problem and is trying to signal him. But as the shots continue, he pictures Nils with his .357 and snake loads smacking down a row of targets—tin cans, beer bottles, anything he could find—as though there's nothing better to do on a hot afternoon along a desert trout stream in June.

Beats hell out of taking your sexual frustrations out on yourself, Nils used to say.

Typical. He turns down to the water just as he meets the sharp smell of ammonia from the rattlesnake den in the jumble of rocks, stained black, above the long run where they like to swing soft-hackled caddis patterns at dusk, coaxing rises that seem just short of eruptions in the fading light—the same spot where Nils must have fished his mouse pattern during the night. Fording the tailout above the run, he decides what's bothering him is simply that he's allowed Nils to get on his nerves. Years back, after Carla died and, eventually, they began fishing together, he was often put off by Nils's behavior, his tedious banter with cashiers and waitresses, his need to make fun of the Les Schwab mechanic or inexperienced clerk at a fly shop—anybody he felt wasn't as smart as he is. All he could think of then was Nils having had his way with Carla Lindquist—the woman he had loved right up to the day the grief she caused him was suddenly no longer worth the companionship and pleasure. Nils moved right in on that vacated turf. He'd taken over like a guy sliding in behind the wheel of a great-looking used car.

A lot of good that did her.

In camp he finds Nils seated in the shade, cleaning his gun at the fold-out table in a blue light cast by the tarp overhead.

"You see any of our friends over there?"

Lofton hangs his vest from the corner of the tent and lays his rod next to Nils's two-hander.

"Not in this heat." He rolls down his waders to his waist. "You can sure smell them."

Nils gets up and goes to the cooler. He chips ice with his pocketknife into his cup and splashes it from their bottle of Beefeaters. He fills the cup with tonic, slices a wedge from a lime, and squeezes it into his drink.

"We ought to go see if we can find a couple. Clean up this neighborhood."

"Why now?"

Nils sets his drink on the table. He spins the revolver's cylinder and then presses it shut.

"So I don't have to worry about them tonight."

Lofton pulls a beer from the cooler.

"I thought your point is now it shouldn't matter."

As soon as he says it, he wishes he hadn't. It's low, mean-spirited, a cheap shot. He doesn't even know what's ailing Nils. What's he going to be like when someone gives him the bad news?

Would he rather see Nils go out like Carla?

"That's your plan then? More night fishing?"

Nils gestures for the beer. He pops the lid with the opener on his knife.

"One night more, at least. See if what happened was for real. Or just a fluke." He hands back the bottle. "Then I'll know."

"Why's that matter?"

Nils doesn't answer. He sits still and looks off in the direction of the river, his unshaved cheeks a watery blue in the shade of the tarp—the same blue, thinks Lofton, as Carla's eyes before they turned gray with drink.

And for the millionth time in the past twenty years, he wonders how he and Nils Sorenson ever became fishing pals.

"What if we never make it back?" asks Nils, still looking away.

"We will," says Lofton. "Next month. Even if I have to drive again."

"You'll have to," says Nils. "But I'm not sure I'll be with you."

Nils makes quotation marks in the air.

"'Treatments,'" he says.

Lofton drinks deeply from his beer. He goes out into the sun and gets the second chair from next to the fire. The halves of his Swedish wedge have settled against one another. He resists the urge to tip them apart, see if it's warm between them.

"I'm still going to argue it matters what we do now." He sets the chair in the shade, rocking it side to side until all four legs settle into the stony soil. "Whether either of us returns isn't the point."

"Fine," says Nils. He swirls the ice in his drink. "Then why don't you just tell me what the point is."

Lofton drops into the chair, the first time he's been off his feet since morning. He should pull off his waders, escape their steamy scent—but for the moment the effort seems more trouble than it's worth.

"Isn't honor its own reward?" he asks. He reaches across the table and picks up Nils's revolver. "Knowing we're going to die doesn't change anything. That's just giving up, saying nothing matters, it never did. None of it. Not even this." He gestures with the gun at the river, the canyon, the blue sky. "It's like Carla drinking herself to death."

"I don't think she tried to do that," says Nils. "I think she was doing the best she could."

Lofton looks down at the gun in his hand. He sets it back on the table.

"I don't buy that. She could've stopped."

"She tried," says Nils. "Plenty of times. You know that as well as I do." He gets to his feet and moves to the edge of the shade. "She needed help. But all she had her whole life were judges—honorable judges." He turns and looks at Lofton. "The sad thing is, neither man she married was able to give her what she needed."

"What was that? What did she need?"

Nils steps to the table and picks up the gun. He turns and aims at the remains of the morning fire.

"You were married to her. You tell me."

—◦—

The shot wakes him, a single blast that rings in his ears while the canyon fills with silence, an absence of sound so deep he feels himself straining to hear something more, another sound, as if underwater needing air, his heart racing.

He lies in his bag listening until he can't stand waiting any longer for a second shot, a shout—something. Outside the tent he calls Nils's name. The quiet deepens, and for a moment he imagines not only the sounds of night life retreating from his voice, but the river and the wind and the stars falling silent, too.

He finds Nils's rod standing against the willows, awash in the acrid scent of the rattlesnake den. The light from his headlamp reveals the mouse pattern hooked to the reel. He touches it, finds it dry. He recalls the fish he hooked, hours earlier, at dusk, the shadowy swirl that suddenly animated the precise point where the little wet caddis initiated the wedge of its wide wake.

"Just like that," Nils had said, watching from the bank. "Only the fly—and *fish*—are bigger."

He's in the river with Nils's rod before he thinks more about it. How else say—good-bye? To a—friend? He shuts off his headlamp. The little two-hander throws a long line. But he has no trouble finding the big mouse skating through the dark.

Bahía Magdalena

SERVED ON A SEPARATE PLATTER, THE EGG SACS OF THE SHORTFIN COR-vina, *Cynoscion parvippinis*, look like pudgy fingers or oversized pea-nuts—or an aspect of the male anatomy that produces from the four women around the table a flurry of murmurs and subtle glances—plus a few crude comments that Marilyn Crowley, helping herself, imagines getting entirely out of hand.

But it seems tonight, at least, her twin sisters, Anna and Elizabeth, fifteen years her junior, are too deep into the margaritas again to offer their typical flavor of jest.

Set next to a pair of corvina fillets on her own plate, the neat wad of eggs, fried to the color of dust, appear distinctly more vegetal than a product of flesh—a fruit or root or rhizome. Slicing through the trans-parent sac, she recalls her inability to come to any final understanding, her entire life, of the difference between seeds and eggs. There's science, she had argued, again and again, with their father—and there's vocabu-lary. He'd dismissed her reasoning, laughing warmly from that place of pure air he found each evening above his tall glass of Scotch—and sud-denly she longs insensibly for one more conversation with him on this, the anniversary of his self-inflicted death.

Vocabulary.

The eggs taste vaguely of flour. Or lima beans. It's the texture, she suspects, moving the chalky paste about her tongue as she watches her sisters and Margaret Hardwood, her best friend for thirty years, come to terms with the unusual matter. Bathed in the lantern light beneath the blue tarp shielding them from sand and the evening dew, they seem, as one, a composition painted from a single palette—as much the same, perhaps, as the countless tiny corvina eggs stirring in their mouths, the shortfin themselves spawning in the nearby esteros.

Eggs or—*seeds?*

"Shit's like baking cocoa," says Anna, her pretty nose scrunched up as if filled with dust.

"More *salsa!*" pleads Elizabeth.

He pooh-poohed all of it as so much semantics. She squeezes lime juice over the length of the fillets, separates a single segment with the tip of her fork, and lifts it to her mouth. Beside her, Margaret gives up a quiet, guttural *yum*—a sound laced with the layers of innuendo and irony and generous goodwill that have made it so easy for men to play games with her—and her silly last name—all these many years. Turning to her, nudging her with her thigh, Margaret bulges her eyes—an expression of mock ecstasy that suggests to Marilyn, against her will, some deeper truth to their father's opinion that the words themselves, in the end, don't matter.

Their father, Marilyn reminds herself, *is* dead. This is not a debate she will win. Manny, their cook and camp hand, serves red wine from a platter of juice glasses. Too big to pass from the kitchen tent down either side of the crowded table, he leans in next to her, the great girth of his belly forcing her to one side. She smells the sweat from his damp flesh and sleeveless T-shirt—and for a moment she imagines the heat and animal pulse he shares with his boyfriend in La Paz.

Men.

The words, she concedes, make none of it more or less true. At some profound level, thinks Marilyn, everything is timeless, infinite, the same. Form changes; things come and go. Yet in the end? What is, was; what was—is?

~~~

The moon has risen, spilling a wide splash of light across the water, by the time they wander, slow with food, past the tents and kayaks to the edge of the bay.

The plan is simple enough. Tomorrow, beneath the first full moon since the solstice, they'll scatter his ashes in the bay—a place he came to love, in no small way, in light of the corvina that lace the currents and move so readily to the fly.

She and the twins, Margaret, and even Manny were privy to that love—a lifelong affection for the inshore *Cynoscions*, reaching back to the weakfish he caught on silver spoons near Montauk, where his own father, a retired naval officer, refurbished a surf dory and took up with the last of the baymen, testing his wife's patience and the strength of his pension against his profound inexperience and dwindling stocks of striped bass and bluefish, scallops and seed oysters and clams. Later, stationed in San Antonio for his early medical training, he began visiting the inshore waters near Corpus Christi, where he learned to fly-fish for speckled or spotted sea trout, a species that seemed perfectly married to flies and fly rods and the fertile, grass-covered bays and estuaries inside the barrier islands that stretched in both directions along the Gulf.

Then on leave during his residency at the naval hospital in San Diego, he drove a Ford pickup down the length of Baja on the newly paved highway, and along the way he caught corvina in the surf, from rocks and gentle beaches, along open stretches of coastline where, he said, he felt certain nobody had ever cast flies for shortfin before.

They became, she thinks, the fish he lived for—the fish he talked about most often when he could no longer go fishing, when the incessant bile that threatened to kill him had already made it impossible for him to travel the long harsh roads of Baja, the miles of dust and jarring insult in promise of a coarse unruly campsite at the edge of the surf and some godforsaken sweep of wind-blistered blue sea.

She closes her eyes, lowering her head against the bite of the wind, a wet onshore breeze crossing the island from the surf to the west. Atop a dune pitched steeply down to the inshore channel, she tries to imagine him at his best, standing in this very spot, where they camped, many a chilly June, to fish the swing of the big solstice tides. He loved this kind of sport—the simplicity and lack of glamour, the need for self-sufficiency, the inshore fish that money couldn't buy—until there wasn't enough of him to love any sport or even life at all.

Enough is enough, he told her, just before the end—an argument bigger than any of the words. There was more to it, she's sure—but he didn't stay around long enough to explain, leaving her with the secret of his sudden departure and little if anything else.

———

"Rin? *Rin?* You there, Rin?"

She opens her eyes as Elizabeth, the oldest by personality or chance, makes a knocking gesture, backlit by the moon-bright sky.

"You okay?"

Beyond Elizabeth she sees the sudden flare of cigarettes being lit, an exquisite dereliction that stirs her deepest affections for both Anna and Margaret, the two of them hopeless pranksters, so very much like her father. The smell of tobacco fills the night, wet with dew and the salt air—laced moments later with the scent of marijuana drifting past as if carried by the tide.

"Full moon," she answers.

The shame of it is she can't tell anyone—not Margaret, not her own sisters. Thirty years of counseling—couples, families, women—have grounded her in the practice of confidentiality, a commitment to restraint that often seems the same as secrecy, costing her, she believes, any chance she might have had for the sort of intimate relationship she's tried so often to encourage or shore up or repair.

It's just not fair he's dead, she thinks—a thought that immediately seems so absurd she wonders if the mere smell of pot has triggered some sort of psychedelic reaction.

"Tide should be just about high now," she adds, closing the hems of her sleeves in her fists.

"Well, we sure as hell are!"

Anna, approaching along the rim of the dune, appears to struggle with the shadow tangled about her feet.

"Sister Maggie down yonder's got some *good* shit."

Anna turns and waves in the direction of Margaret, drifting off down the shore.

"You want some of this?"

A sudden flame illuminates Anna's face—then tips into an ember near her lips.

"Cool it, Nana."

Elizabeth reaches for the half-smoked joint.

"Can't you see she's thinking about Daddy?"

What do they know? She's certain nothing about the actual suicide—yet in the past year her sisters have grown increasingly close, engaged in a kind of conspiracy of knowing that leaves her feeling stripped and vulnerable in their company.

Worse, this sudden tendency toward their own private vocabulary—*Nana? Sister Maggie down yonder?*—words and names and locutions that spring forth spontaneously or out of some secret language that holds them both beyond her understanding.

"He's up there somewhere," says Anna, mocking—who? Her? Them? The point of the trip itself? "Up there where the sun don't shine."

"With a secret address," adds Elizabeth, "*Mama* can't find!"

Anna hoots, delighted by her twin sister's response, then pivots and swings Elizabeth a high-five as if launching a hook shot from the three-point line.

"That's just cruel, you two."

They know nothing—other than they both think of her as an honest-to-god old maid, disillusioned by the stream of unhappy clients who pass through her office doors, a dour odd duck in need of their attention and cheering up.

Still, she turns her back on them when Anna, waving her hands as if dancing, begins to roll her hips side to side while Elizabeth pretends she's unable to grab hold of her by the waist.

She's certainly not about to start talking to the twins—or anyone else—about her most important client of all.

Herself.

And she has her hands full, anyway, arguing with their father.

It's past midnight when she gives up tossing and turning, plagued by moonlight flooding her tent.

Moonlight *and* a mounting sense of panic that tomorrow—*today*—she'll suddenly be alone.

A feeling of weightlessness washes over her each time she closes her eyes. Her father's departure, she fears, leaves her without anything holding her to the earth. She has nothing, no one. She and her life no longer matter.

She knows these thoughts are irrational. Yet nothing she tells herself relieves her from the sensation, swirling about the tent, that her life's emotional gravity has relinquished its grip.

Overcome, unable to lie still, she dresses and crawls outside—only to turn and plunge through the doorway for her father's ashes, stashed inside an aluminum water bottle, just in case, for the flight to La Paz.

She drags her kayak to water's edge.

Dropping backward into the seat, she slips free of shore. The night has grown still. She can hear, faintly, the rise and fall of Manny's snoring. She waits, paddle across her lap, picturing the tide calendar, its sinuous line punctuated by the phases of the moon. She tries to recall the numbers: Moonrise. Sunset. High tide. Low. The bay gives off the smell of sweat. Awash in light, the steep dunes slip past her, moving south.

North, she thinks. *She's* headed north.

The tide's falling.

And rising—*where?*

Seeds or eggs? she asks, tucking the ashes tightly between her thighs.

Margaret's voice, distant and small, carries across the water.

"Marilyn? *Marilyn?*"

She stabs the current, pivoting the kayak, and begins to paddle with the tide.

The moon has passed overhead by the time she reaches the lights of López Mateos. Current presses her toward the abandoned buildings along the riprap waterfront, and she struggles to keep herself safely beyond the reach of the wooden pier near the south end of town, where three days ago they loaded their gear into their outfitter's *panga*.

North of town opens a *boca* to the ocean.

She slips beneath the remains of the sardine factory, its panels of corrugated siding lifting at the edges as if old stamps curling from a page. She recalls the image of the bay's currents black with sardines that Manny described as the *panga* bucked through the wind on their way to camp. She looks at the stir of phosphorescence each time the blade of her paddle penetrates the water, the shimmer of moonlight across the surface of the bay, the tint of color raised by these vast patternings so much the same, she thinks, as those current-darkening sardines, the whales or turtles freckling the tides, the schooling corvina or weakfish or spotted sea trout dispensing their coddled eggs like semen, she thinks, cast into esteros, come what may.

His ashes, she decides, belong *outside* of the bay.

Swept north by the tide, she imagines herself leaving everything behind, giving in, like her father, to powers beyond gravity, beyond emotions, beyond words. She recalls as a girl of eleven or twelve, sometime before the twins were born, wandering in summer heat about her father's front yard wildflower garden, a tangle of weedy mounds that drew angry remarks from both the neighbors and her mother alike. Her father held some high notion about allowing only "natives" in the garden; he used the word as though it were an absolute term, a scientific truth like the boiling point of water. Mostly the yard was filled with California poppies, which had already gone to seed by school's end. He showed her how the capsules, when dry, burst open and discharged their seeds—and for days she delighted passing in the heat of the afternoon through the garden, running her fingers up the curved slender shafts and feeling them pop open, one by one, the seeds vanishing, leaving behind the brittle husks spread into forked, wishbone-like Vs.

She recalls her first real boyfriend, Andrew Moorehead, and how, when the time finally came, she realized her father had already shown her what she needed to know.

To the west she hears the first murmurs of surf. The sound carries with it a new smell, a denser, vaster, sharper scent than the confines of the bay. She wonders if she's making it all up—sounds, smells, the flight of the moon through the stars—or if this begins the start of something new.

Beneath the kayak she feels the pull of the tide strengthen.

She lifts the paddle into her lap, allowing herself to turn sideways in the current and simply drift.

What did he want from her? She loved the outdoors as much as he did, loved the wildflowers in the foothills beneath Palomar Mountain in the northern reach of the county, the birds that gathered in the riparian willows and sycamores along the tentative arroyos and riverbeds trickling toward the sea, the fish he and she found with flies in the chill, vigorous surf. But in high school, after the twins were born and their mother began to levitate toward the dark clouds into which she eventually disappeared, she discovered herself unable to take interest in the sciences he claimed held the answers to the questions she asked. She counted sepals, petals, stamens, pistils—but rather than lumping together things because of how they looked or acted the same, she craved the individual story, the unique narrative, the aspects of one life that made it different from all the rest.

She went into the sciences of the mind—an oxymoron, her father said.

Drifting in the current, pushed sideways toward surf showing as ribbons of white in the moonlight beyond the *boca*, she wonders if he ever forgave her.

—~—

The current compresses, gaining speed and strength between the dunes framing the *boca*.

She feels suddenly as though she's going downhill, as if the ocean is somehow lower than the bay—and she imagines she hears a sucking sound, the fall of water pulling against the vast pool of the bay now piled up behind the *boca*, trying to depart all at once.

Still broadside in the current, she tries with the paddle to straighten herself—only to enter a slow, deliberate spin that nothing she does with the paddle seems able to control. She pulls at the water, aiming the bow of the kayak in the direction of the moon. The next moment her shadow swings across her lap as the kayak pivots in the current, sweeping this way and that as if the needle of a cheap compass.

She twists about, trying to locate herself in the swirling current. She finds the moon again; beneath it, the surf shimmers in layers of uneven light that seem, at one moment, far off toward the horizon, at the next, toppling forward as if to assault her.

She knows better than to keep fighting. At the very worst she can spin here in what she decides is a temporary eddy, biding her time until the tide ceases to drop. At low tide, before the water begins to push back into the bay, she can scramble through the surf.

And head out—*where?*

⁓

Daylight shows faintly over the desert when she finally turns and makes for the surf. Released from the eddy, she aims the kayak at the flat disc of the moon hovering above the horizon. An offshore breeze stirs, carrying with it the musty low-tide smell of the mangrove. Glimpsing dark water and the swells of broken waves reforming over the trough of the resting current, she suffers the sense of barely moving, the wind at her back lost in the wake of her approach toward the surf line rumbling in the distance.

She tugs the ashes tight between her thighs and leans into her stroke.

The kayak rises and falls as she works her way through the scuttling inshore wash. Digging into the trough, she feels her breath shrinking. Her arms grow heavy. The shaft of the paddle feels swollen in her hands. She tells herself to back off, soften the pace—only to find herself in the path of a set of swells, each one bigger than the other, lined up as far ahead as she can see.

The biggest wave rises, steeper and steeper, the offshore wind scouring its face. Spray from the crest showers the moon. She has nowhere to go, nothing she can do—until the wave collapses in a tumbling mass that rolls and wrenches her sideways and seems to press the open kayak as if to flatten it or fold it lengthwise.

She hangs on.

The whitewater carries her to the *boca*, where she comes to rest in the placid pool between the dunes.

The ashes are gone.

⁓

For dinner Manny serves the corvina whole.

That afternoon he asked for nothing but small fish, ones too young yet to spawn.

He serves them wrapped in tinfoil. He's baked them "Mexican style," he calls it, in an oven fashioned out of an old toolbox or some kind of gas can, Marilyn still can't tell which, from the beach where, with the help of their outfitter's *panga* captain, he and Margaret and the twins found her sleeping beside her kayak above the high-tide line on the beach south of the *boca*.

She opens the tinfoil and draws in the scent of the fish and the bay, the last traces of the warm afternoon, Manny's own smells and salsa. She feels as though the night of paddling has left her body porous to touch. The blue tarp snaps once then falls still. The light shifts about them like calm water. Beside her, Margaret hums with pleasure. The twins make smacking sounds with their lips. She lets her eyes fall closed—and the loneliness starts up again, the sensation that gravity could release her, at any moment, from its hold.

She's told no one anything other than that she was overcome by a sudden, irrational need for adventure.

Margaret said she understood.

The twins were delighted.

"Well, hallelujah," said Elizabeth.

"I would have never thought you had it in you," added Anna.

She studies the dish before her. Even this size the shortfin share the orange mouth and fang-like incisors of the genuine orangemouth corvina, *Cynoscion xanthulus*, a species she and her father fished for once in the Salton Sea, a place they both found too demoralizing to ever return to. She peels back the silvery skin and forks a bite of the young corvina flesh into her mouth. At the age of six, she recalls, she had an extra set of her own front teeth—supernumeraries—that the dentist removed along with her front pair of baby teeth. For four years she lived as if suspended in a moment of childhood, waiting for the new front teeth to appear. Finally, another surgery—and ever since her teeth there have wobbled as if a pair of palm trees in the thinnest of suburban soils.

"You okay?" asks Margaret.

She looks at her friend and nods.

"I'm not going to ask you what was really going on."

"Good. Because I'm not going to tell you."

She watches Margaret smile, the single expression she knows as well as her father's amused gaze. She holds her head still as Margaret reaches up and brushes a strand of hair off the side of her face.

"Not yet at least."

Later, when they head at twilight to the water to watch the moon rise, they hear the twins laughing and splashing out of sight beyond the last dune.

Her sisters come bouncing over the crest, drenched and shivering like wet dogs, their still-young bodies outlined softly by their wet clothes.

Anna holds up the water bottle—with their father's ashes.

"Hey! Look what we found!" she says.

La Ventana

First light finds Parker Ferrington looking for money. Undressed, he slips about through the heat, at rest this early as though a mood not yet disturbed by his deliberate search. For the second time since showering he opens, in measured succession, his wallet, a zippered coin purse, the snapped pockets of his old-fashioned passport scabbard—all of them fine tooled leather, all of them void of bills.

He stands at the foot of the bed imagining the worst. But nothing goes wrong in La Ventana. Even the bed, littered with gear on the half of it abandoned, now nearly three weeks ago, by his girlfriend, suggests no worse than another angling idyll gone slightly awry, an example once more of the fallout of faith pitted against reason.

She decided his attempts at a world record roosterfish were a complete waste of time.

And money.

More to the point, he believes, pulling his sun shirt, stiff with salt, from the clutter atop the bed, was the growing discomfort Penny expressed over shacking up in her and her ex-husband's Baja beach house, a stone-walled casita she lost in the divorce in exchange for a monthly stipend that makes Parker's contracting fees look like a teacher's salary.

Last time he *got* a fee, that is, to do anything more than run crews of day laborers through foreclosures from Lake Elsinore to Escondido.

He didn't get far with the argument that her ex should be happy they're checking on the place while it's up for sale in this upside-down market.

"It's not him I care about, Parker."

Penny possesses the thinnest lips he has ever kissed, and when she presses them together, as she did then, they suggest to Parker an old CD case snapping shut.

"This is something he and *I* tried to build. We *did* build. It keeps reminding me we failed."

She stepped through the arched doorway leading onto the patio, a great sweep of the Sea of Cortez outlining her fine-boned body, worked into sharp relief by a lifetime of diet, sport, exercise, and vigilant self-denial. On a long June day a heartbeat above the tropics, Penny Gadwell—twice divorced, mother of three, grandmother to boys as beautiful as her own son—stood alone in twilight beneath the breathing canopy of the patio's *palapa*-style roof, fighting back tears Parker was sure she didn't want to see any more than he did.

Still, he longed to go to her, comfort her some way—but through the rustling of palm fronds caressed by the evening breeze, it was all he could do to keep from hearing the sound of roosterfish, just offshore, crashing bait in the wake of the surf.

Then Penny, dear Penny, also pointed out that she was finding it easier and easier of late to think of him as a freeloading schmuck—especially while he set off each day on his half-cocked scheme to break the who-even-cares record for roosterfish caught on a fly.

Parker noted nothing he could pin down as irony in his lover's somber appraisal.

"It'll pay for the trip, our whole time down here," he countered.

He crossed the patio and stood at Penny's side. The breeze off the surf carried with it the faint scent of dust and dry leaves. He didn't know *how* he would turn a record rooster into money, but ever since stumbling upon a record calico caught on 8-pound tippet while kayak fishing in Oceanside Harbor, he felt as though his life had suddenly begun to change—as though the *universe*, as Penny often said, were guiding him toward his dreams. Working his way through the IGFA record book, he had targeted a list of open tippet-class categories for obscure or under-exploited species, setting three world records for mullet snapper in Golfito, Costa Rica, his first week trying. He set eleven records inside of a year. Since this run of luck coincided with the collapse of the housing market, he had more and more time to concentrate on record hunting, as well as convincing Penny that now was the perfect moment for her to take her ex up on his standing offer to share the keys to their old, up-for-sale Baja pad.

He felt poised for a fish that would change both of their lives forever.

He moved close to her, running a hand from her hairline to the taut muscles rooted to her slender neck.

"This isn't some line-class record for Chinese squawfish you only find in the backwater sloughs of the Indian Ocean," he said. "I'm talking about *rooster*fish. *Roo*ster. *Fish.* Roosterfish—the West Coast's version of every big-game trophy fly-rod fish that ever—"

Penny slipped free of his hand and headed inside.

"I'm close!" he said. "I'm really close!"

He listed out loud, in quick succession, the exact weights of the five fish over fifty pounds he had landed since they arrived in La Ventana.

The record was sixty-two.

"It'll be good for *me!*" he called out, aiming his voice toward the shadow on the threshold where the casita spilled out light.

She was gone the next day when he returned from fishing.

Her note said leave the key with Elena, the divorced sister of Valente, his *panga* captain, whom they'd hired through Penny's ex to cook and clean.

———

It's the sound of Elena, stirring in the kitchen, that pulls Parker back into the morning.

He's told her not to come, that he doesn't have money anymore to pay her. She frowns, lowering her eyes, a trace of stubbornness through her mouth, each time he tries to explain, mangling verbs and syntax in his broken, construction-site Spanish. He believes she understands, that she's ignoring his case, a response he's increasingly grateful for as he fails, day after day, to find a record fish.

When he's dressed he unzips the pocket of his shirt and finds two twenties—leftover bait money and something to go toward a tip—along with flies, the plastic sleeves he keeps them in new, and a pair of Revlon nail clippers. Encouraged, he digs through his fanny pack, the scent of sweat and saltwater rising out of a rat's nest of tippet spools, crusty gloves, sunscreen and ChapStick and pliers and more flies, finally pulling out a crumpled Ziploc baggie with three more twenties, a wad of pesos, another pair of clippers, three more flies.

He's okay. He's already paid Valente for the week. And they can always kill something to eat. What's important, he decides, reaching for his dry bag, is that he doesn't get uptight, concerned about petty shit— which is exactly the state of mind, as Penny would say, that creates the negative energy that inhibits the flow of success, especially abundance, in one's life.

Or maybe she was talking about love.

Hands inside his dry bag, Parker suddenly has the sense of working his way through a series of Chinese boxes: the deeper he looks, the more he finds. The billfold he pulls from the bottom of the rubbery blue bag is also leather, soft, chocolate brown, as flat as an envelope. He can't recall where he got it or when. Or from whom. His ex-wife? A sister? J.Crew? It seems, subtlety he thinks, remarkable that it has taken him this long to find it. *SAN JUAN COWHIDE*, he reads inside. As opposed to—what? Calf? Bull? SAN *JOSE*?

The bills are inside one sleeve. Three of them. Two hundreds. A fifty.

In the opposite side rests confirmation of his flight from La Paz to LAX—now two weeks past.

He'll be fine.

Another week and he's not so sure.

Mostly it's his mood, he tells himself, hauling his gear at first light to the casita gate. He feels diminished by the need to pay such close attention to money. He's not sleeping worth shit. He's landed three more roosters right at fifty pounds, forcing him to consider that they simply don't grow any bigger—at least not in these parts. He misses Penny. The heat keeps making his feet swell. He needs a haircut. He has no idea how the Dodgers are doing.

Then Elena offers him money.

It takes him a long time to figure out what she's saying. She still comes by each morning, fixing him coffee, a lunch for him and Valente. He thinks at first she's talking about the money he owes *her*. They're in the kitchen. She's at the sink, raising and lowering the side of her face toward him while he hangs out listening, over her voice, over the hum of the fan, and, beyond the gate, the chickens and dogs, for the sound of his ride, Roger, a new guy he just met who's joined the other sports at the Hotel El Viento. There's always a chance a new guy might not even show. *How do you know?* he thinks—when Elena turns and faces him, her dark shoulders framed by the window above the sink, the decorative bars outside the glass, and the first hints of morning light.

From the front pocket of her shorts, she tugs free a thick stack of folded bills. Pesos. Lots and lots of pesos.

He understands the word *ayuda*. She wants to help *him*.

She stands looking at him. She raises her empty hand and, with her forearm, wipes her forehead, moving a length of black hair toward the band of yellow fabric holding back the rest of her loose braid. She doesn't smile. Her eyes hold his.

He tries not to get angry. Immediately he feels sweat run down his sides. What's she take him for?

In the clearest Spanish he can muster, he says *Thank you*. He says she's very kind. But he doesn't need her money, he says. He's fine. Everything's okay.

He hears the eager beep of a car horn outside the casita gate.

"Elena," he tries again, still in Spanish. "I cannot have your money."

No puedo tener el dinero de usted.

She turns back to the sink before he finishes.

Outside, the car horn sounds again, this time impatiently.

Parker takes his cooler from off the dining table. He glances once at Elena and receives the flat of her slender back and sleeveless T-shirt as he hurries toward the door.

To the east, the sky through the tops of the palms holds more light than he's used to this time of day. Faint breeze off the water does little but stir the morning heat.

"Sorry for the holdup."

He shakes Roger's hand. Roger, Roger *Hitchcock*, he recalls—earbuds around his neck, a cigarette, lit, at arm's length downwind alongside a little cranberry-colored rental that already looks as though it should have never been allowed on the East Cape roads.

"Kind of bizarre in there this morning," adds Parker, gesturing with his head toward the casita.

He gathers up his gear and stashes it through the hatchback of the little rental.

"They get that way you fish too much," says Roger.

He chuckles conspiringly as Parker folds himself into the passenger seat.

"Hope she's worth it."

Suddenly Parker feels—what? Anger? Sadness? Embarrassment? Remorse? As they navigate the untended side street, already testing the little rental's suspension, he tries to remember what he told Roger Hitchcock the day before when they met at Punta Arenas, the *panga* beach, where Parker was listening, discouraged but happy for the camaraderie, to Valente describe to the other Lucero captains another big rooster they'd caught that morning—another fish that failed to break the record. *Casi nada*, Valente liked to say. Almost nothing. All of the captains love the idea of his world record, thinks Parker, a thought that immediately strikes him as a need to justify himself, his sport, the time and effort and money he's sunk into the past month. But the captains understand. A world record makes perfect sense to them—why any fisherman wants to catch the biggest fish, regardless of the species, the method, the line-class, whatever. They get it, thinks Parker.

Or they're just happy taking money from another rich gringo who complains about going broke but somehow keeps showing up for more.

"Stop the car," says Parker.

Roger, both hands on the wheel, turns and looks at him.

"I said, *stop the car.*"

Roger pulls off onto the shoulder.

Already outside, dust swirling about him, Parker leans in through the open door and says he has to make a quick phone call.

"I hate to do this kind of shit. I'm really sorry. Especially on the way to fishing. But I just remembered something. Business. Money. It'll just be a second."

He doesn't wait for a reply.

Instead he moves quickly out of earshot, tapping his phone with the tip of his thumb. He tries Penny's cell, her home number, her work, the open phone against his ear as he listens, studying the trash littering the edge of the desert, broken glass and plastic bags and bottles and someone's shorts, probably a rag, tangled in the spiny, dust-covered vegetation.

She doesn't answer.

He decides to send her a text—"*Love you. Bills paid? Home soon!*"—and then in quick succession, as if sitting in freeway traffic, he navigates the automated customer service menus for both Bank of America and Cabela's, confirming that, yes, his two Visas remain maxed out, no different than they were before he left home.

Home?

He wonders what that means anymore.

At least he's got . . . Roger?

The sun blisters its way out of the sea, swelling with the morning heat. Parker snaps open the door of the rental.

"Sorry," he says, lifting his sunglasses into place.

"The little woman?"

Roger, grinning between his earbuds, lifts his chin in the direction of La Ventana.

"Let's go fishing," says Parker, staring straight ahead.

They ride in silence, Roger weaving through potholes in the asphalt so that, when he hits them, it's as if he were aiming, trying to beat the little rental into submission. He turns without stopping onto the new pavement headed south. Climbing through the gears, he forces the car into a fresh range of cadences—and by the time he's finished shifting, stomping on the accelerator as if trying to cover a leak, Roger has Parker wondering what he's got himself into now.

What's he know about Roger, Roger Hitchcock, anyway?

All that really matters, he quickly concludes, is that Roger Hitchcock has already hired Valente for four days of fishing. The deal? Roger, some kind of wannabe fly-fishing photographer, feels certain he can sell a photo essay to *Gray's Sporting Journal* if Parker continues to hook roosters that threaten to eclipse Phil "Pancho Villa" Arkin's sixty-two-pound fly-rod record.

Roger's arrival yesterday afternoon at the beach, and the deal that followed with Valente, seemed nothing short of a miracle—even after Parker discovered that Roger had already captured, surreptitiously, his long-faced powwow with Valente and the other Lucero captains before he and Roger actually met.

But he can't find any purchase there. Roger showed up, somehow, out of the blue, the promise Parker needed in the wake of yet another big rooster that left his spirits, like his wallet, all but flat. Maybe there is some justice, thinks Parker—some effect of hope and belief.

Maybe pay attention and keep your eyes out for vacas, he thinks, scanning the roadside cholla and cardón cactus.

Roger slows down after they hit the first of several speed bumps in the town of Los Planes. He holds in the clutch and wiggles the shift lever through a random sequence of gears, his gaze passing sharply side to side as if he expects to see someone he knows on the nearly empty, early morning street.

"You always this quiet?" he asks, removing his earbuds after a long pause tracking something out the driver side window. "I'm not interrupting something here, am I?"

Parker doesn't feel he's expected to answer.

"Oh, I get it. This is some kind of morning meditation."

Roger snaps his head forward and stares wide-eyed straight ahead.

"*Pre-game visualization,*" he says, his voice suddenly different, firm and precise, as if he were opening the broadcast of an obscure sporting event.

"I like that," Roger says, his voice his own again. He turns half around in his seat and begins grabbing at gear piled up in back. "See if you can get one of my cameras out of this bag here."

Parker turns and scrunches up onto his knees. He lifts the entire bag and spins back around and opens it on his lap.

"I'm just dealing with some shit," he offers.

"*Some. Shit*," says Roger, returning to his announcer's voice. He points at the camera he wants. "Let me guess. *Money. Women.* Am I getting warm?"

He takes the camera from Parker and holds it with one hand on top of the steering wheel.

"I hope it's not going to get in the way of your fishing."

Parker offers nothing more until they're well past Agua Amarga, where he finally stops worrying again about cows on the road. Probably see them fine now, he thinks, casting his eyes across the desert, troubled by how late it seems, the sun already up, the sky turning blue. Roger takes his picture a few times, until Parker flips him off, casually and not unkindly, when they turn off the pavement again and start bouncing toward the beach.

But that's all he's going to give Roger, Roger Hitchcock, for now. For the truth is, thinks Parker, something *is* in the way of his fishing this morning, something in his mood, his state of mind. What the fuck's Elena doing offering him money, anyway?

Where's Penny when he needs her?

They cross the salt marsh, the little rental bounding past evaporation pools and tidy, waist-high mounds of salt suggesting staggering stockpiles of some malicious drug. He tries desperately to improve his mood. He's going fishing. The fish are big. He's hammered practically all of the kinks out of his casting. He enjoys excellent health and, when called on, sexual vigor. Anticipating the deep swale beyond the edge of the marsh, Parker presses the soles of his Crocs against the firewall beneath the dash, raising his butt off the seat. To the east, a slender scab of weather remains scraped across the horizon, a ragged tear in the otherwise taut fabric of a seamless blue sky. If it blows today, it'll start late. Swell from distant weather makes the big roosters move, says Valente.

He's pretty sure they get air coming off the lip at the far end of the swale. Roger hoots with delight.

But he can't find it, the excitement that belongs to the beginning of a new day of fishing, the stoke he feels he should feel if today's meant to be a world record day. He wonders if Penny is right—it's all a joke, a pipe dream, a waste of time *and* money. For nearly a month now he's felt a world record rooster was his—a fish he knew with certainty, as though love beginning to stir, was about to happen. He *imagined* it. He *believed* in it. He could *see* the events unfold.

And every day he's come up short.

Casi nada, says Valente.

Nada y pues nada, the old Hemingway waiter says.

The sonofabitch.

—◦—

Later that day, much later, Parker tries again to find relief from his wretched mood.

Thank you, God, for beans and rice—body and blood of Our Savior the Lord Jesus Christ.

It doesn't quite work. But it's the best he can do, at the moment, mopping his plate clean with a stale corn tortilla, listening to the desert come alive in the dark.

Beans and rice. A metaphor, he thinks—what he's lived on, in the past, when he's had nothing else.

It could be worse.

He could have thrown Roger, Roger Hitchcock, overboard.

He leaves the plate on the table on the patio and walks to the back edge of the casita property, a tangle of barbed-wire lashed to the top of an untended palo de arco fence. He holds perfectly still, imagining the barranca in the shadows beyond the light a kind of natural ampli-fier, broadcasting the sounds of quail and rodents, coyotes and snakes, nighthawks, flickers, mourning doves, the snap of a plastic bag in the breeze. He's probably making most of it up, he thinks, a good sign, he hopes, like imagining the grace of beans and rice because it's some-thing, food—and at the end, what else is there? What's the rest of it going to mean?

Beans and rice. Just the sound of it makes him feel better—stronger, more honorable, free of all the bullshit. Not like when he's drinking, really drinking, he thinks, turning to see if he can see, from this distance, how much remains in the liter of Cazadores standing on the table on the patio next to his glass and empty plate. His eyes are still good, he thinks.

He saw that big rooster long before Roger, Roger Hitchcock, knew they were even fishing.

It doesn't matter, he thinks. Beans and rice. We are all absolved, at the end, of our sins.

He takes out his phone.

He opens it.

He closes it and puts it away.

She could call him, he thinks.

He returns to the table and fills his glass. When he switches off the light inside the casita, it's as if the desert were suddenly illuminated by a remote glow slowly growing stronger. It was his fish, he thinks. It was his cast.

———

They parked and unloaded at the edge of the soft sand above the *pangas*, lined up like hopes scattered along the lapping sea. The heat and smell of birds and dead fish seemed sharpened by the harsh sun already climbing the sky—yet he was sure they were only an hour or so later than he normally arrived. Still, this bothered him, too. Valente, as slender and dark as his sister, dressed as usual in a white T-shirt and Levis rolled up to his calves, met them halfway across the sand and immediately helped Roger with his big camera bag, aware from the start, apparently, who was paying for his services.

They put up their rods and launched in flat water, getting help with the heavy *panga* from little Chuy and Fidelito, Elena's sons, whom Valente hired as captains only on the busiest days. Out in the channel they began to pick up swell, long, even lines that rolled white high up the steep beach just beyond the lighthouse. But nothing in the way of wind marred the surface of the ground swell, and by the time they reached the island and found their bait, tucked in tight to shore, his mood, recalls Parker, had lifted.

Especially as they swung north and began nosing up the east side of the island, where for weeks now the big roosters kept popping up in the dark water, riddled with boulders, at the foot of the barren headlands falling directly into the sea.

This one showed itself twice, feeding explosively on Valente's far-flung herring, well beyond casting range by the time the fish, its comb a black-tined pitchfork stirring the light, attacked the bait in the *panga*'s drifting wake.

"*Espera*," said Valente, a hand up, as though he were a traffic cop, while he searched the water in all directions around the *panga*.

Wait.

Parker, on the bow, nudged the coils of loose line alongside his bare feet. Waiting wasn't hard for him anymore. He wiped the sweat from his face with the sleeve of his shirt. He knew what he could and couldn't do with the fly. Roosters don't eat hope.

While he waited, rising up and down with the swell, he listened to Roger take pictures from the back of the *panga*.

When they saw the fish the next time, its shoulders pushing a wave that distended, opposite the light, a bulge the color of a bruise, Valente, from the center of the *panga*, glanced once his way, a look that Parker understood perfectly.

Big.

Stay ready.

Watch me.

Wait.

And maybe that's all there is to ask for, thinks Parker, sipping his tequila at the edge of the desert, *these moments when two of us—any two of us—see perfectly eye to eye.*

He tries to hold that thought, failing when gripped, once again, by the surprise and anger he felt when Roger, Roger Hitchcock, launched a cast in the direction of the horizon.

He pours himself more Cazadores.

"The hell you think you're doing!" he shouted, looking frantically about the *panga* for the roosterfish he was sure was already gone.

Roger, stripping in line, said he was fishing.

"What does it look like?"

Valente turned and tossed a herring in the direction of Roger's fly.

"What if that was my *record*!" shouted Parker.

He couldn't help himself.

"What if *you* hooked it instead of me!"

"What if I did?" asked Roger.

Of course it was nobody's fault, thinks Parker, that they didn't see another decent roosterfish the rest of the day; nobody's fault that, later, after he landed and released a heavy jack, they saw the worn-out fish snatched and devoured by a bear-sized *lobo*, or sea lion; nobody's fault they found a young sea turtle, dead, held head down by a weighted line and an angry bait hook affixed to its serrated beak; nobody's fault that at the shark buoys, looking for dorado, all they found was in fact a shark, a six-foot-long leopard shark, dragging an anchored buoy in circles while tugging against a lug-wrench-like hook and taut, tethered line.

Nobody's fault, thinks Parker. *Unless maybe my own for being such a miserable prick.* He tries to block from his mind the look on Valente's face when Roger, at the end of the day, told him to leave his own goddamn tip. He unbuttons his shirt and shakes it off his back and arms and uses it to wipe the sweat from his face. He might have a better chance figuring out some way to frame this day if he weren't drinking, he thinks.

He pours himself another glass and tries to call Penny again.

What's fault got to do with it, anyway?

"Parker? Is that you? Is there something wrong?"

Encouraged by a note of concern in Penny's voice, he tries to explain his mood, what happened today, how he was fishing with this new guy Roger, Roger Hitchcock, and the whole thing went to shit, they didn't catch anything worth even talking about.

"And?"

"And nothing." Parker stands up from the table and walks to the edge of the patio, cooler there, he notices, looking up at the stars. "I just wanted to call, tell you what's up."

"I'm up, Parker. I'm up listening to you. And I'm wondering just what it is you're trying to tell me—now that you woke me in the middle of the night."

Parker glances at his wrist before remembering he hasn't worn a watch since arriving in La Ventana. He looks at his phone but can't get the time to focus.

He returns the phone to his ear.

"I could use some money, for one."

There's a long pause before Penny speaks.

"You'll figure it out, Parker. You're a big boy."

"I could use some help, Penny. I really could. If you could just lend me a thousand dollars. Maybe two—"

Eventually Parker realizes there's no one there. He looks at the phone, wondering how long he was talking to himself.

When he wakes the next morning, Parker can't remember going to bed. *So what?* he figures, pulling the sheet up under his chin. *This deal's done.* But he can tell immediately he's not going back to sleep.

Beans and rice, he remembers. *He needs to remember something about that.*

Maybe he dozes off. He's not sure. But outside he hears a car horn, somebody honking impatiently.

He scurries about getting into his pants, a shirt, his Crocs. He hates to be late. For what? He hurries out to the casita gate—and there's Roger, smoking, leaning in through the window of the little rental to press on the horn again.

"You look like shit," says Roger.

"I didn't expect you back."

Parker spins around in a circle, trying to remember where he left his gear.

"I seem to recall we made a deal," says Roger. "I still need some shots."

Parker holds up a finger—*Just a minute!*—and then turns and hurries back to the casita. To the east, Venus looks like a man-made signal sent up into the half-lighted sky. Where's that been? he wonders. Inside, he finds Elena, who holds up his blue and white cooler, lunch packed, God bless her, for the three of them—Roger, Valente, himself. He dismisses, emphatically, the impulse to kiss her on the cheek. He'll make it up to her somehow before he leaves. He takes the ice chest from her upraised hand but fails to draw a smile from her with his own, and before he can configure anything clever to say in Spanish, she turns and retreats to the kitchen, her unbound hair doing nothing to hide the stern cant of her shoulders.

Parker pauses, suffering the harsh sensation of disappointing one person after another in his life. Outside, he stashes his rods and dry bag and the cooler into the back of the rental, and then he slides into the cool of the air-conditioning, folding himself in alongside Roger.

"I gotta say, I'm surprised you're even here."

Roger looks briefly at him before pointing a finger at one of his earbuds. He touches the volume of his iPod in the cup holder and then mashes the gearshift into reverse.

On the ride out to the island, Parker explains to Roger what he needs to do to get a good rooster.

"Don't cast until you feel like you can hit him right between the eyes," he says, his voice raised over the roar of the outboard. He rocks forward in his seat and squirts a bead of sunblock on both of his ankles and lathers the tops of his feet.

"They change directions like a fucking pinball," says Roger from the seat along the opposite gunwale, a hand on his head to keep his hat from blowing off.

"That's okay. If you *think* you can hit 'em, you got half a chance."

Parker tears a length of athletic tape from a roll in his dry bag and wraps a cut from handling his fly line inside the first joint of his middle finger.

"The thing is, don't just start casting when you see one. Let the fish come to you. And whatever else you do, keep your eye on Valente. He'll let you know what's happening."

"My Spanish sucks," says Roger.

"So does mine," says Parker.

Through the course of the morning, they get shots at several good roosters. Not records, nothing close—but fish anybody would want to hook and land. Parker doesn't cast for any of them.

Standing on the bow, Roger keeps up a steady litany of half-hearted protests.

"If you don't cast, how'm I going to get my photos?"

"Nobody comes out here just to take fucking pictures," says Parker.

Roger's fish comes to a pretty cast that seems to hover in the air, the fly waiting for the bait to hit the water. When the rooster eats, simultaneously disappearing with a spike of fly line behind it, Roger releases a string of obscenities that draws a concerned look from Valente until he sees line pouring directly from the reel.

"Don't get excited!" shouts Parker. "You might lose it."

Long before there's any chance they'll see the fish again, Roger climbs carefully down from the bow and asks Parker to pull a camera, the little Canon, from his bag.

"Did you tell me these things were this strong?" he adds, losing another long reach of line.

"I didn't tell you anything." Parker finds the camera and points it at Roger. "Don't you remember?"

When Valente finally lifts the fish into the *panga*, Roger claims he can't believe it's so small.

"I bet you it's not even thirty pounds."

"Twenty," says Parker. "That's a twenty-pound roosterfish."

Roger looks at him as if he thinks Parker's kidding.

"You want to weigh it?" asks Parker, pulling his scale partway out of his dry bag.

"Just take my picture," says Roger.

They've drifted offshore and north of the headland where Roger hooked the fish by the time Valente revives it and sets it free, allowing the tail to slip from his hand as if releasing an awakened child's ankle. In the lee of the excitement, Roger sits down and digs through his bag and exchanges cameras. Valente, tending the bait, scoops water over the gunwale with a five-gallon plastic bucket, now and then tossing dead herring over the side. Parker, still feeling he has something to make up to his host, opens his cooler to serve lunch.

Inside, he finds a thick roll of pesos—bound in the yellow fabric that held Elena's hair the morning before.

"*Rooster!*" says Valente, up front near the bait. "*Big rooster!*"

Parker hears the edge in Valente's voice and closes the cooler and grabs his rod. He doesn't see the fish so much as he does the violent swirl of water, a great gaping boil that seems as though it should give off a sound, a thump that reverberates off the barren face of the island. He drops the fly in the water and rips lengths of line off his reel, watching the coils puddle at his feet. He waits. Then Valente does something with his eyes that Parker recognizes as though his own body had spoken in need—and he tightens the line and loads the rod and aims at a target he never even sees.

—

It takes a long time for Parker to realize he did it—that if his scale's still good, if his tippet's right, if Roger's photos tell the truth, he's got himself a world record rooster. If not? *Fuck it,* he thinks. *It was a hell of a fish.*

On the long run back to Punta Arenas, Roger drinks two of three Pacificos Elena packed in their lunch.

"God, what fishing," he says, scrolling through photos in the big Nikon on his lap. "I need to find a place down here. Build something, maybe."

Parker reaches for the third beer, sizing up Roger. What's he know about him, anyway? A room at the El Viento. Good rods, good reels. Two high-end cameras. A pretty good caster. The usual assortment of Simms and Patagonia clothing. A goatee, it looks like, he started the day he arrived.

"You need a builder?" asks Parker.

Roger offers that he might.

"Come by the hotel this evening," he says. "We'll talk about it."

Parker leans the beer bottle against the gunwale and smacks the top of it with the heel of his hand, popping loose the cap.

"Can I bring a date?"

"Why not?" says Roger.

"*Casi todo,*" says Valente.

White Salmon

Halfway through the back doors of the high school, staggering briefly as he frees himself and a pair of steelhead wrapped in a plastic
garbage bag, Martin Silverton spots his new roommate, Jack Cochran,
touch his lips to the mouth of Lydia Salazar, an ELL instructor both men
have talked about in detail since she appeared from God knows where at
the year's first district-wide staff meeting.

The heat of indignation rises like a blister forming on Martin's hairless scalp. *Goddamn him,* he thinks, tucking the fish under his arm as if
a receiver, having broken a tackle, suddenly loose in the open field. For a
moment he's able to skirt Jack's self-satisfied gaze, averted in the direction of Ms. Salazar's receding, pear-shaped bottom. But then it seems to
Martin that Jack exhibits again his increasing knack for noticing Martin
whether he likes it or not, spinning on the heels of his Georgia Giant
Romeos and immediately bearing down on him with the candid gait of
one's most intimate friend or foe.

Jack points a finger at him as if a kid playing guns—as if *he*, not Jack,
just got caught in the act.

"What d'you got there, Marty?"

Marty. It pisses him off Jack rarely calls him his real name anymore.
Instead, *Marty, Martino, Martinito, Marty Pants,* and, lately, *Silverado.*

As if he couldn't do something with the name Jack *Cochran.*

"Give us a look, *ese.*"

Ese? Martin stabs the two wrapped fish under his other arm, shielding them with his body. He tries to picture himself straight-arming Jack

if it came to that. He gestures down the hall with the top of his still-warm head.

"Working on your Spanish, Jack?"

Yet his tone surprises him. What does he care if Jack wants to play kissy-face in the heat of steelhead season? Martin stares straight ahead, the hallway empty again as well it should be at this hour, the same time they both arrive nearly every day—although never at quite the same time, despite having lived together since the new school year began.

Meanwhile Jack has parked himself at Martin's side, allowing his own gaze to retrace his steps. He shrugs, rolling his shoulders as if trying on a new coat, raising his hands enough that his fingertips catch inside the front pockets of his Levis, the backs of his hands cock forward, his thumbs pointed toward his crotch.

"No say," he finally answers.

Eyes still distant, Jack sighs and then presses his lips together, setting into motion a series of expressions that Martin, watching out the corner of his eye, has recently started to name: The Kiss. Blowing Up Balloons. High C on Trumpet. Sucking the Lemon. Triggerfish. Pouting Child. Jack Nicholson Sells Viagra. After years at the same school and now nearly three months more living under the same roof, Martin still can't tell if Jack performs these faces unconsciously, or if this is Jack Cochran trying to act like a guy in deep, detached, thoughtful thought.

What Martin's grown all but sure of, instead, is that nobody should trust Jack with anything more than the promise of a good time.

"*No sé.*"

Jack does his Stinky Diaper look.

"Get it?"

Or maybe he's just a clown, a monkey, an unrestrained or uncultured or uncivilized kid—like so many of the sophomores: six-year-olds in adult bodies. *And* a smart-ass. Martin shifts the weight of the two fish from his arm to his hip, aiming for the spiritual high ground he feels he deserves for having already ventured to the water and hung himself a week's worth of meat. Yet try as he might, he finds it increasingly difficult to dismiss Jack, whose contradictions seem purposefully transparent, as if to undermine all attempts at genuine intimacy—despite the complicities of cohabitation.

"Truth is," says Jack, his face suddenly still, "we better all get bilingual soon."

A tremor of fury runs through Martin's shoulders, his chest, his heart—a sensation that startles him, carrying with it impressions of the desperate fight of each morning fish in response to the sting of the hook. *Bilingual my ass*, he thinks, recalling Jack's face tilted toward Ms. Salazar's. Yet it's this other face of Jack Cochran—now wistful, vulnerable, guileless—that compels Martin to stand there engaged with his roommate—even when, at this early hour, he wants nothing more than to deposit his catch in the staff refrigerator and get on with his teaching day.

"More like you better be careful—around here at least."

Martin turns toward Jack as a tangle of students breaches the quiet through doors at the far end of the hall.

"It can get messy. Especially when things go bad."

"What makes you think it has to go bad?" asks Jack.

Martin takes the fish into both hands, cradling the bundle as though an infant in his arms. He lets the question answer itself. Aren't they both living proof? Or at least prime examples, a strain of the gender, without the capacity to make love stick?

How many failures does it take to prove you'll never get it right?

Martin looks at Jack and wonders: *Is he just dense?* As kids straggle down the hall, Jack adopts his Vacant Look—or, better, *Cara del Perro*—another expression Martin has named and renamed without confirmation that there's any connection whatsoever between it and something, if anything, going on in Jack Cochran's mind. The thought of Jack's loony looks gaining him access to Lydia Salazar's lips—and who knows what else—reignites Martin's anger, and he questions suddenly his own judgment in taking on a roommate whose age, no less, remains a mystery. Gray as a snarl of driftwood, Jack sports the curious male cast of someone who could easily prove far younger than he looks. Or far older.

Irritated as much with himself as with Jack's unlikely romantic success, Martin rocks his twin steelhead side to side, a motion he notices—and immediately stops—on overhearing two boys say something, beneath conspiratorial laughter, that sounds like *Mr. S and Mr. C are having a baby.*

Martin turns and glares as the boys pass.

"So what about that fish?" asks Jack.

"*Two* fish," says Martin. Why is it, he wonders, Jack never seems to hear the shit kids say? "I got *two* this morning."

Jack nods in approval.

"Then that's perfect."

"For what?"

"One for you. One for me."

Jack makes a face as if preparing to bite into an oversized hamburger. "Me and Ms. Salazar."

For a moment Martin considers the possibility that Jack is fooling with him—that this is Jack Cochran's clumsy, juvenile way of showing affection, of letting him, Martin, know that they're good friends, pals, survivors in the trenches of life and love and learning, that he and Jack are close that way, a couple of good old boys, tough guys, real men who have remained on their own because of smarts, wisdom, integrity, a sense of self that defies the shallow belief that one need be coupled to live a full, fulfilling life.

Then Martin comes to his senses.

"Go catch your own goddamn fish," he snarls.

Jack's eyes snap wide; the corners of his mouth fall. Bozo Betrayed. He starts to say something, stops—then he raises his hands, palms up, in a universal gesture of *what the fuck?*

"Look," says Martin. "You and I both have to go teach right now." He notices two girls listening from in front of an open locker. He leans in close to Jack—as close as he dares. "We'll talk about it when we get home."

—◦—

Home?

Throughout the morning the thought torments Martin. What, exactly, did he mean by *that?* Certainly the notion of home has nothing to do with Jack Cochran, who, since tumbling out of a twelve-year marriage, has lived like a gypsy, bouncing from place to place, sometimes on his own, sometimes connected to his latest flame, always on the verge of falling into isolation, obscurity, oblivion—a prospect that leaves Martin dizzy with fear when he imagines his own fragile hold on the matters of life, on order and routine, on what seems to him more and more an existence resembling a house of cards that might at any moment collapse, releasing him from gravity's hold, adrift and alone in the cosmos. Now Jack says it's time he grow up, take responsibility for his life. At meals he pesters Martin with passages from the work of the Jungian analyst James Hollis, brandishing ideas about the "soul's agenda" as if an assortment of newly discovered casts. His plan, he claims, is to forget trying to strike up again with some gal in hopes of lighting a magical relationship coddled by the ardor of heart and home. Instead, says Jack, he lives cheap for a year, he saves ten thousand dollars for a down payment on a house—and he begins, at last, to create the life his "soul longs to live."

"You'll be lucky if ten grand gets you into anything in *these* parts."

Seated at his computer, Martin recalls his own off-handed remarks after Jack approached him one evening in August, near the start of steel-head season, on the final run of the White Salmon—the same spot he hooked and landed his two fish this morning. Had he known about this soul shit, would he have ever consented to Jack's proposal and let him move in? He turns and scans his classroom, his students busy with a lengthy grammar exercise he assigned immediately after taking roll, still livid over Jack's request to feed Ms. Salazar part of his morning limit. Fucking Jack. He should have known what he'd be getting into during that first conversation on the water, the two of them trading shots from his flask in the cool air hanging just above the river, while everyplace but the depths of the canyon lay wrapped in ninety-degree heat. Jack said something about the first-time home buyer credit; Martin pointed out to Jack that divorce didn't mean you started over again. Jack countered; he told Martin he was sure he was wrong.

"I should qualify as a first-time buyer." Jack tipped the flask and emptied it into his mouth. "It's just like if you don't have sex for a year. You get revirginated."

And how would you know, Mr. Jack effing Cochran? You were about to revert to prepubescence—when suddenly you found yourself sucking tongue with Lydia La Vibora Salazar?

Martin knows he's taking all of this much too hard. *He's* the one with reason to celebrate, both fish this morning having come to the waking fly, all but a miracle this late in the season, a tactic he felt inspired to try on the strength of nothing more than a hunch triggered by a deep calm hanging over the river as he descended in darkness through the still black trees, his headlamp launching shadows into fitful flight, the trail a route he has followed so many times now that he's sure he could manage it with his eyes closed, half asleep, abandoned once more to the reckless hope of a steelhead willing to rise.

Yet try as he might, Martin finds himself unable to embrace his success and dismiss Jack's juvenile antics. Nor can he muster the disdain he usually feels for the petty concerns of both students and faculty alike after he's already risen in the black of night and spent two hours caressing the surface of the current with long graceful casts unfolding from the sweep of his Spey rod. During his second period he has a brief altercation with a pair of boys still sizing him up after arriving from the orchards two months into the term. More often than not he relishes these challenges to his authority; few things impress him more about his work than the state of efficiency he has achieved whereby he does as little as possible and still continues to enchant his students, their parents, and the administration with the breadth and profundity of his pedagogy.

Two pickers trying to act like urban gangsters in hopes of gaining the admiration and affection of a classroom of innocent boys and girls are generally the *stuff* of Martin's most inspired moments teaching. He either trashes them outright—to the delight of the other students—with the basest forms of rhetorical abuse; or he exercises the full weight of his institutional authority, sending them off to the disciplinary netherworld lorded over by administrators—ex-teachers who have either turncoated or surrendered, against all logic, to the unlikely notion that in escaping the classroom, they deserve the reward of higher pay.

Today, however, Martin can think of nothing better to say, in Spanish, than to tell the boys they are both ugly as possums—and that from their mouths passes a form of the language that resembles the shit of dogs.

Come lunch he feels the onset of flu-like symptoms creeping over his body. His scalp tingles. His muscles throb. His attention begins to wander. He rejects the idea he's fallen ill, only to find himself shaking as he works his way through the peanut butter and banana sandwich he slapped together before heading to the river. He drains his water bottle. He pulls on his fleece jacket, his watchman's cap. He plunges into the hallways, making for fresh air outside.

The track lies empty. Of course. Nobody uses it during lunch, the kids not allowed anywhere without supervision, other teachers, because— why? A light mist falls from a low gray sky, the same muted weather that inspired him, that morning, to swing the surface fly. *What a brilliant fucking piece of fishing*, he thinks, crossing lanes without stepping on the lines—*while Jack did what with Lydia Salazar who knows where.*

Two laps and Martin, walking as if late—or chased—catches himself replaying the phone conversation he had the evening before with his father. Has he been trying to forget? He recalls his irritation as the vibrating growl of the phone against the surface of his tying bench intruded on the Van Morrison wail playing through his computer. Halfway into his third tumbler of Scotch, fashioning a fresh lineup of waking Muddlers to replenish stocks depleted by the demands of fall fishing, he rejected his inclination to ignore the call only after seeing his father's number and suffering a stab of shame. He rarely calls his father. Since his mother's death, their conversations slide here and there within a plane described by three subjects and little more: the weather, the Padres, and Martin's failure to find a wife.

He's lost all capacity, anyway, to tell if his father is serious—or sinking deeper and deeper into solitude's shadows and doubts.

"So when you getting married?"

Restless with drink, recalls Martin, and the quiet of tying, he announced that he had shopped that weekend at Sears—but failed to find a wife who fit.

During the long silence that followed, he slid headlong toward his deepest guilt, his inability to please his father. *Sears?* It seemed the pettiest claim possible; he hadn't been inside a Sears for years. But apparently he was not above even this cheap shot—a reference to the one store his father would still recall.

When his father finally spoke again, Martin felt chastened to remember that at this stage, any conversation they had could be their last.

"I never once regretted the price of your mother's love."

Yet free of whisky, students, and the immediate shock of Jack's morning audacities, Martin suddenly finds it unlikely that any of this matters one bit. He caught two steelhead this morning! Who else in the school, in Albion, in White Salmon, or you just name it can make this claim?

The bell rings, ending lunch, and as he heads back inside, his body aching but somehow relaxed, he considers the very real possibility that his father sought nothing more than to encourage guilt because of a failure, in his own life, to answer a heroic calling. *This is where Jack's got it right*, thinks Martin, peeling off his cap. He slaps it against his thigh, expelling a scrim of icy droplets. *Eventually there's the mirror and nothing else.* He pulls open a door and plunges into the chaos of students making for class, the fetid currents of heated air filtered through the bodies of the hornéd young. *"I've enjoyed three years of marital bliss!"* his father used to love to declare, decades into a marriage that seemed fueled by a commitment to hang on to the end and little else. *What bullshit*, thinks Martin—just as two boys, Keith Nachman and Chuy Granados, both from his next period class, greet him with borderline vulgarities that make him feel, despite his mood, like the stern but lovable uncle neither of them probably ever had.

"Mr. C says you got a fish!" says Chuy. He looks at his friend and jerks his hand back and forth, suggesting a fishing rod—and much more. "You and Mr. C gonna celebrate?"

"*Two* fish," says Martin. "I caught *two*."

———

It's a long afternoon.

Sipping water from a ceramic coffee cup, he's able to saturate his discomfort into a dull indefinite ache, while maintaining a semblance of order by allowing students to work in pairs on a grammar assignment that ends up taking twice as long to finish as anyone should need. The boredom initiates its own wave of symptoms, which leave Martin uncertain whether he's sick, hungover—or falling into a state of lethargy that seems to afflict veteran teachers, more often than not, throughout the building.

Yet during the second half of the period, he finds himself momentarily uplifted by an old Roethke poem, "My Papa's Waltz," that he's decided to use this year to introduce students to their annual recitation contest, Poetry Out Loud. *"The whiskey on your breath,"* he reads, *"Could make a small boy dizzy; But I hung on like death: Such waltzing was not easy."* Touched by something fresh or unseen, he feels moved by the hint of danger, the threat of violence, even abuse, lurking beneath the rhyme and simple meter. The poem seems a perfect balance between two opposite forces in the world—and suddenly brings to mind for Martin the fundamental tension between the elegant acts of fly fishing and the spirit of frenzy and fear that such acts aim, from the fish, to ignite. *Explain that to Lydia Loose Lips Salazar,* he thinks, imagining himself talking to Jack over the rim of his evening's first glass of Scotch. And his students? He's sure they're able to grasp, in part, the poem's unsettling irony, the dark tone lying just beneath the surface of childlike language, meter, and rhyme—but when he goes to his computer to project an image of the poem on the screen in front of the class, he discovers that the title has been pulled from the Poetry Out Loud list, that it's no longer a choice in the competition.

The bell rings while he's still trying to figure out why. Who the fuck would pull this shit? He googles every state and national arts agency and commission he can think of, sends half a dozen outraged emails—and by the end of the passing period, he sits cussing at an "access denied" message that, apparently, will now exist on a log at the district office.

Fuck them, too.

His body feels as though it's changing colors. He can feel his pulse inside his ears. He hurries out of his classroom and rushes through the empty halls toward the teachers' lounge, trying to imagine who he'd turn to for help right now if he didn't have his prep. He wonders if there was something wrong with the peanut butter in his sandwich, if the banana was somehow bad. What about all those tarantulas they get shipped with? What if Jack did something to him?

Before arriving anywhere Martin pivots suddenly and heads back to his room. He walks carefully, stepping clear of the dark tiles inlaid as boxy letters into the linoleum floor. He tells himself to settle down. This is ridiculous, he thinks. Why should he care about a dumped poem? What's it matter to him?

What's he so upset about, anyway?

Through the narrow window in his classroom, he stares out over the cars squeezed into the parking lot, the sullen leaves of the orchard beyond, the great solitary hump of Mount Arcadia from which, across the Columbia, the White Salmon descends, severed in its lowest reaches by Naughton Dam, its obsolete generators engraved into the blade of the concrete guillotine that stopped the climb of running steelhead and salmon from a time no one remembers now. The fish, the poems, the— language? thinks Martin. He closes his eyes, unable to tell if he's warm or cold, if his body aches or if it simply feels heavy, his muscles freighted with fatigue.

He returns to his computer, the Poetry Out Loud website. He checks again to confirm that the Roethke poem has been pulled. He still can't believe it. Who's responsible? Poring over the site, he discovers, on a hunch, that the old antiwar set piece, "Dulce et Decorum Est," has also disappeared from the list. He quickly finds his copy of the Poetry Out Loud Anthology, published years before, and locates the poem. But on this year's website choices?

Gone.

A fresh sense of betrayal reinvigorates Martin's outrage. He has better things to do, more important things—but he's unable to resist the desire to find out who's to blame for these sordid transgressions, what other crimes of omission have been foisted upon the nation and its unsuspecting youth. He plunges into the list, searching for other exclusions to fuel his anger, his disgust. Danse Russe? To His Coy Mistress? A Song in the Front Yard? The Powwow at the End of the World? The River Now? Leda and the—

He can't believe it's there. It doesn't make sense. He leans his head back, closes his eyes, sighs. Who could possibly be making these decisions, eliminating poems like Roethke's and Wilfred Owen's while allowing Yeats's graphically sexual "Leda and the Swan" to stay? You worry about a kid dancing with his drunken father, a nearly century-old antiwar poem, but you don't mind a god raping a woman—a god in the guise of a swan?

"A sudden blow . . . the staggering girl . . . her nape caught . . . fingers push . . . her loosening thighs . . . a shudder in the loins."

The logic seems irrational. Not those but this? A spasm of pessimism that he likens to the final writhing lunges of a steelhead ready to land leaves him all but limp in his chair. He wonders again who or what's behind this thinking. He aims the cursor at Google and types in the name of the poem, bringing up a list of sites that includes a row of images of the myth, thumbnails of famous paintings showing Leda, naked, in various responses to the swan's irrepressible desire. *This is okay?* he asks himself. And a father's rough hand on a dancing boy's head is not?

He clicks on his two favorite paintings of the myth, both of them alleged copies from originals destroyed when exposed, goes the story, to the dripping fangs of the jackals of sanctimony. The Michelangelo copy has always seemed to him to beg such attention; the attitude of Leda's thighs, embracing the spread-winged swan, offers an erotic tenor to the coupling, mirrored in the emphatic gaze passing between the two lovers' eyes. Swan Fatale. But the da Vinci copy, he notes once more, suggests a much different Leda, a restrained, even demure lover, her eyes cast modestly away from the swan's eager attention, her body somehow chaste despite the full frontal nudity that reveals the powerful, sensually muscled legs of a gymnast or modern dancer.

Or Ruth Anne Vorhees, thinks Martin—struck suddenly by memories of the last woman he fell into stride with and eventually tried to love.

The resemblance startles him. How has he failed to notice this likeness up to now? The cocked hip and sweeping thigh, cupped tenderly in the swan's spread wing, remind him of the great round outline of Ruth Anne herself, on her side in the morning, beneath her thin satin sheets— and the thick quads rendered in the painting seem nothing less than the impressive contours of Ruth Anne Vorhees's own powerful legs, developed to the point of excess by a lifetime spent training and competing as an alpine downhill racer.

But the averted gaze, thinks Martin, stirring uncomfortably in his chair, on the face of the da Vinci Leda is a far cry from the explicit glances cast his way, during moments of both desire and disdain, by Ruth Anne Vorhees. Or so it first seems. For the longer he stares, the more he sees in the self-absorbed gaze of the da Vinci Leda a woman's propensity for guile, this look he long associated with heartfelt emotions that turns out, he's sure now, has as much to do with genuine love as the feelings behind the pale cold countenance of the man in the moon.

Swan Sucker.

How could he have missed the resemblance.

Yet these unexpected thoughts of Martin's last true flame, he's sure, arouse in him such a mix of emotions that his already troubled body feels on the verge of collapse. He struggles with his breathing. His heart hops side to side. Though two years old, the wound of his dismissal from Ruth Anne Vorhees's perilous bed seems suddenly so close beneath the surface of thin scar tissue that he feels he shouldn't risk moving. His eyes grow heavy with lethargy and self-doubt. He falls into a grip of longing that leaves him rigid with anxiety—and finally outright fear.

⁓

He wakes to the bell.

Confused, he struggles to locate himself, tumbling through a torrent of ill-formed thoughts. That's not his alarm. He's not at home. It's not morning. He's not going fishing.

And those thoughts about Ruth Anne Vorhees? They were *not* images from a nightmare, he decides, but instead actual memories boiling to the surface of his consciousness—as though fueled by a conflagration of emotions sparked by the wail of the bell ending school.

He tries to compose himself. Before him, he meets the blank stare of his dormant monitor. He reaches for the mouse, recalling how even when in the bedroom, in the shower, barefoot on the beach, when in her Tevas or in her running shoes—or even on turning to receive him from behind—Ruth Anne Vorhees, otherwise nearly always perched atop a pair of high-heeled shoes, remained on her toes, a habit of attention to her potent legs that seemed to have become the very stuff of her vigorous personality.

A nudge to the mouse brings back the da Vinci Leda to the screen. The image startles Martin. The innocent nude, the stylized Renaissance rendering, seems charged now through the lens of his still-warm memories of his striking lost love. He quickly exits the site, left with an afterimage of those faultless thighs, revealed to him in abundance the first time Ruth Anne Vorhees showed herself at his front door. They had decided to go out on a formal *date*, remembers Martin, a word they both used ironically because of their ages, as well as a long prelude of low-stakes outings during which exercise, not romance, was the aim. Or so said Ms. Vorhees from atop the balls of her feet, whether in snow, in forest, along trail or stream—at least until the moment she arrived at his door, having driven from Albion across the river to White Salmon, where they could dine with little chance of running into students from this year or years past.

Her outfit alarmed him; the April evening air remained damp and chill despite the faint scent of pollen from the distant orchards. He had seen Ruth Anne Vorhees in running shorts, bicycle leggings, the undulant stretch of her reptilian ski pants—but each glimpse of her sturdy legs offered no pretense of any activity but the athletics at hand. A dental hygienist, Ms. Vorhees seemed possessed of a body aimed at health and efficient, high-end performance—not the musky tussling her getup suggested here.

"Okay," she announced, calling up his skittish eyes to her own. She held his gaze, balancing at a dangerous pitch in the bright light cast across the threshold. Her shoes, he had noted, were as steep as lies, and her legs, stockinged black, rose and rose to a skirt made, apparently, of leather from a pint-sized pygmy goat. "I'm here to complicate your life."

Memories of this moment, and the veracity of Ruth Anne Vorhees's claim, settle on Martin as if the lassitude of despair. His hips and thighs feel numb in the chair. He forces himself to his feet; there's no way he's going to be able to grade anything this afternoon. Upright, he tugs on the mouse to check his email before heading home. He reminds himself not to forget his fish. Among messages that have collected throughout the day, he clicks on something from Ms. Hepner, the new vice-principal—probably another progress report request for a kid facing an expulsion hearing.

Martin, please see me at your earliest convenience re recent activity at your computer. No big deal—I'm sure. :)

He reads the note twice more before he's sure he understands it clearly. By then his mouth has gone dry; his tongue feels twice its size. The taste of old coffee sharpens with each breath, a cold acidic flavor as if wrung from a knot of used filters tangled about his sternum.

He reads the message again.

You gotta be kidding.

That goddamn little . . .

There's no way, he thinks, he's dealing with this kind of bullshit now. Not today. He closes his email, shuts down his computer. While the screen goes blank, all he can think of is the infantile smiley face at the end of Frau Hepner's note. What cute bit of testicide was that?

But by the time his computer falls silent, and his room grows increasingly still, everywhere Martin glances seems draped in a shadow from the da Vinci Leda and the colors of pleasure moving across Ruth Anne Vorhees's thighs.

By the time he slides into his pickup, he can't tell whether he feels more like a criminal or a pervert.

He drops the pair of bundled fish onto his waders and vest, spread out over the passenger seat to dry. The cab gives off the odor of a basement shower; the windshield seems curtained with mist until, after starting the truck, he tries the wipers and sees he's fogged up inside. He waits for the defroster to take effect while listening to the Pimsleur Level Two Spanish CD he felt moved to try again in the afterglow of the morning fishing. He could probably say a thing or two to Jack's little Latin fruitcake—if it came to that.

He recognizes he may have the chance when he arrives home and finds Jack's rig already there.

But he's too late. As soon as he steps from the garage into the kitchen, he can feel Jack's presence—and exactly what he's up to—as clearly as if a fire were already roaring in the woodstove. The . . . *dog*. He yanks open the door of the refrigerator and stuffs his fish inside, recalling instantly the terror and, later, disgust he felt as a boy on recognizing the sounds of lovemaking rising from his parents' room—the heavy, dark rhythms that rose like fear in a dream, forcing him to hold perfectly still in his bedroom next to theirs. Motionless in front of the refrigerator, the door held open in one hand, he imagines his own feelings as jumbled as the mess before him, food and foodstuffs old and new, bottles and plastic containers, packaging unopened and reused, the grime, the odors, the five kinds of salad dressing neither of them had touched since Jack arrived. His legs grow heavy, weak; he feels he needs the support of the door to remain on his feet.

The refrigerator kicks on and with it he hears the faint rumble of distant thunder, then suddenly torrents of tumbling water, the sound of rushing wind. He tries not to listen yet feels incapable of moving, and from the mess of his profound self-consciousness, he pulls up the sharp sense of feverish paranoia he so often experienced arriving at school directly from Ms. Vorhees's bed, a sensation that carried with it his own reflection in the mirror as he shaved in her spare bathroom while trying to decide whether visible the discoloring, to the point of bruising, beneath his lower lip, courtesy of shameless responses to his mouth pressed to the apex of those hearty thighs.

The house falls silent. Immediately the uproar in the back bedroom seems as faint and inconsequential as a hard-to-remember dream. Martin swings shut the refrigerator door. He closes his eyes. He inhales deeply, remembering the conversation during which his mother, three months short of dying, offered to him her *secret* about his so-called capacity as a boy to interrupt her and his father's lovemaking—how it was, she said, bedridden and frail, that from the day they brought him home until the fall he left for college, he seemed attracted or attuned to the very act that created him—or not the act itself, said his mother, correcting herself, gazing up at him from her pillow, her birdlike hand in his, but to the sex shared by her and his father, so that time and time again, throughout his growing up, he showed up at just the right time—or the wrong time, she said, smiling yet lowering her eyes, finally, not quite able to say everything, thinks Martin now, even though she had realized, she said, she had no more reason to protect him or anyone else from the truth.

What truth? he thinks, out the door before Jack—and Ms. Salazar—have a chance to discover him.

But a line of trucks parked in the turnout above the lower reach of the White Salmon cut short his idea to go fishing until his house clears. He sits idling just off the pavement, listening to Señor Pérez ask details from a secretary about an afternoon business meeting, when another pickup arrives, bouncing through puddles and slipping dangerously close past his mirror. Two guys in camo caps and camo jackets give him dirty looks. He could always go get in a fight. Instead, he calls up the moment that morning the second fish ate the fly, how it seemed a gesture more of curiosity than anything else, a sudden yet gentle pluck with the mouth as the crescent of silver rose through the dark morning surface of the river and then vanished as quickly as it had appeared. With one fish already landed, he was able to relax and enjoy this one's spirited fight, a long downstream run that ended in a pair of those end-over-end jumps that usually make him cringe with fear.

Why fear? he asks himself, reaching under his seat. What does it matter if anything goes wrong? He paws around and finally locates his flask. He pulls back out onto the county road.

Driving one-handed, he takes a shot of the cheap Scotch he keeps onboard for just this kind of occasion. Then another. Why not? What has his examined life earned him beyond heartache, fear, regret? What does it matter if he understands *why* things happen if he's unable to change the outcome, to influence in any foreseeable way the trajectory of his life? Maybe he loved Ruth Anne Vorhees. But the more he runs a comb through his tangled emotions, the more he seems to produce a kind of static electricity of feeling that does nothing but send painful sparks leaping through the levels of his consciousness.

He heads upriver, past the dam, through falling daylight filtered through the dark firs and dripping grays, recalling the long unhappy months he and Ruth Anne Vorhees spent at the end, trying to act like they still had a chance. He takes another long pull from the flask and then corks and caps it and shoves it back under the seat as he feels the tug of memories toward their failure to find something new, some hope or invitation to grow. He remembers the frightful moment, seated just as now, when he sensed that Ruth Anne Vorhees's aims to please him had taken on the aspects of procedural hygiene, with both pre- and post-operative routines that left him feeling as though he had just given blood.

Or, worse, blood had just been drawn.

He turns around at B-Z Corner, resisting the urge to stop in at the tavern and drink in the sorrow of strangers.

Besides, he still has the fresh fish at home.

—⁓—

One of them, it turns out.

The other, he discovers, lies mutilated on a serving plate in the refrigerator, a sheet of Saran Wrap pulled tight over the skeleton, chopped in two, with the whole half-fish worth of pink meat still affixed to the underside of the bones.

There's also a note.

> Marter,
> We couldn't resist.
> Feel free to finish the leftovers.
> Jack & L

He couldn't even fillet it, thinks Martin, slamming shut the refrigerator door.

By the time he reaches the river again, only two trucks remain in the turnout. Daylight has all but drained from the sky. In the dark of the woods along the steep trail into the canyon, he hears voices rising and falling above the sound of the river, until he's passed by first one pair of fishermen and then another. Near the bottom of the trail, he enters a layer of cold wet air that slowly swallows him as he breaks free of the trees.

Before him, the sweep of freestone along the final bend of the river lies empty.

He has just enough light to put up his rod and tie on a fly. He holds the leader at arm's length above his head to make sure the knot has set tight to the eye of the hook. In the front pocket of his waders, he checks if he still has his headlamp from the climb down the trail in the dark of the morning. Above him, on the road, he hears a truck pass—or the sound of the last fishermen leaving.

Even in the grip of darkness, he's able to locate the precise spot he stood in the morning and caught fish. He rolls out line, finds the back end of the belly, sends his loop far across the current. He pulls out a half-dozen more arm's lengths of line, snaps the fly back upstream to his side. Swing, D-loop, fire—the plane of the line stretches beyond view toward the blackness of the distant trees.

The fish takes at the point in the swing where both fish grabbed that morning. He pictures the boulder in the current, the patterns in the river's surface, the steelhead rising from a pack of holding fish to claim the swimming fly. The long rod bows. He lays it on its side, the tip aimed toward a point of darkness far downstream.

Later, a fish grabs again.

Later still, again.

After the third fish, at an hour he can only guess, he tells himself it's time he head home. What's the point of another steelhead hooked, fought, landed? At the same time, he feels trapped by opportunity, the sense that tonight of all nights, something impossible could unfold.

He keeps casting. Come the next fish, fighting hard in the heart of the current, he imagines him or it—one of them—*Leda*, the other one of them—he or the fish—*The Swan*.

A wild splash sounds beyond sight of his line. He holds on tight, the night deepening around him.

Beavertail

I TOOK THE CAMERA ON THE TRIPOD DOWN TO THE RIVER TO TRY TO catch the first slash of sunlight on the water. My sons were still asleep in the tent. The shots were all the same, matted and framed, as a dozen back home. Canyon walls. Dimensionless sky. The pulse of the river, at once dynamic and still, as if the needle stuck on your old rock 'n' roll phonograph. But I snapped off a dozen more, searching through the viewfinder for a glimpse of the magic all around me.

Anything could happen. That promise drew us each morning to the water. We returned despite the old pictures. *Faith is a fathomless feeling,* I thought out loud, toying with the sounds of the river. We came back each time still believing in surprise. Life will never let you down if you expect the gifts that define it.

But their father didn't think that way. I could see it clearly that morning. I knew from experience it wouldn't always be so. The best we can hope for is a memory of our convictions, not how we reached them. My sons' father failed to discover hope. Every day proved his case against the past.

In the end I couldn't help. Now I doubt I ever did. But some of us are given to wishful thinking. At any moment we create a story line that promises the happy ending. I believed Denny had a choice in the matter. I told myself over and over again that he simply needed to look at his life and be grateful. Appreciate what he had. Gaze into the river and acknowledge the joy it gave us, those handsome fish that took the fly as if moved by the very same spirit that created our own two sons.

He wouldn't hear it. *A man can't be honest and happy*, he'd say. My anger got the best of me, rising to a place I didn't want to help, to where all I could see to do was leave him to ferment in his noble suffering. The boys, at least, learned the difference between loving to fish and fishing as an excuse for not feeling loved. That's a lesson I won't let them forget.

She had a pretty stroke you don't often see in a woman. Of course it's not like it used to be. But even gals don't usually get so the rod does most the work, give into something that's not about trying to make it behave like they think it should. Few guys get there either. That's why you notice the ones who do.

They floated with me maybe half a dozen times that year. Mostly it was her and her two boys, youngsters just starting out. Far enough along though, they could handle themselves without too much attention. The old man came a couple times early and then that was it. She didn't say why. I didn't ask. I've been at this business long enough to know when I'm the problem and when I'm not.

We did the Warm Springs to Trout Creek float opening day. I think everyone got a fish on that good stretch back of the island at Mecca. I noticed right off, however, her husband seemed more interested in the next fish than the one that grabbed his fly. He didn't even want his picture took, not by his wife and not by me. Said he'd caught plenty of good trout in his life. All of the big ones he'd ever need. Whatever the hell that means.

When he stopped coming she had me pick up her and her boys where they liked to camp at Rattlesnake Canyon. It made for a long-ass drive from Madras but that's this business anyway you cut it. I'd put in at Beavertail, row hard down to their camp. Then we'd do the six or so miles to Mack's where the guys from Canyon Shuttle would drop my truck. Not a long day, really, what with her teaching her boys and not in need of twenty fish after she got a couple. And she liked to be on that hole right there at Rattlesnake at sunset, so she always had me get her back to camp pretty early, all things considered.

He owned a green and white fiberglass Hyde, not one of those dreamy all-wood Ray's like Denny owned up until three or four years ago. Not that it matters to the fish. I've always believed it's a guy thing, who has the prettiest boat. You take that a step further and you begin to see where all the trouble begins.

Denny started getting jealous from the first time we floated without him. He didn't say anything. He didn't have to. The boys and I went the first Friday after school. We missed the peak of the salmonfly hatch but the golden stones were still thick in the trees. I started with a big nymph and twice a fish hit the orange yarn I was using for a strike indicator. I didn't make the same mistake a third time. I made sure the boys had on big Stimulators, yellow or orange, it didn't really seem to matter. We hooked a bunch of good fish.

But when we got home Sunday evening, Denny wouldn't share our excitement. Or couldn't anymore. I don't know which. He asked me who we floated with and I looked at him and said, What's the matter Denny? You were with me when we booked the trip last time: *"Day after school gets out. We'll be here. Maybe the salmonflies will hang around long enough for us to spook up some fish on big dries."* You remember, Denny? I know you must.

But he acted like he didn't remember. Or maybe it wasn't an act. Maybe he had already decided something was going to go wrong. Or that it was already *going* wrong. I know I never really understood how that part of his mind worked. At least why he couldn't change it, see things a different way.

It was hardest on the boys. Tanner had caught a fish we were sure went close to twenty inches. To hear him tell it, the fish hit the fly with a splash as big as the dog chasing a tennis ball into the Willamette. Denny just looked at Tanner over the top of his wine glass like *So what?* David saw that and said, "Daddy, what's wrong?" Denny stood up, bumping the table. Wine sloshed out of his glass.

"I'm glad you guys and your mother had such a great time," he said.

I was afraid to say anything back. Whatever was going on with Denny was his business, not mine. I had tried and tried. Now I had chosen to give up trying because it had gotten me nowhere. Our boys were *thrilled* to be on the water. Denny had called me at school from work Thursday afternoon while I was cleaning up my classroom for the summer. He said we needed to cancel the float. The guy would understand. He was probably busy as hell this week. He could use the day off or find himself another client between now and Saturday morning.

I said, "Denny. That's bullshit. The boys and I are going fishing."

I don't know what came over me.

—⁓—

Come July she and her sons fished little else but wet flies. She said at this point in their learning she was more interested in teaching her boys to cast than catch big fish on a heavy stone nymph. Which makes sense when you have a stroke like hers. Both boys tended to listen to her, which says a lot about her, too. I'm tempted to call her gentle. But that wouldn't be quite right. I guess you could say she knew how to do things, so she didn't feel the need for much explaining. Maybe because of that her sons accepted what she said without a lot of question or back talk.

After her husband stopped coming she started staying back at the boat and drinking coffee or a soda while watching her boys take first licks at the best water. She'd sit there and comment on what they did right and wrong. It wasn't so much judging them but more as if she was just interested in their learning, talking to me about them as if guide to guide. She'd get going when one of them hooked a fish but not too much. She kept that part of herself screwed down pretty tight. She had said she was a teacher. But she wasn't like one I ever had.

Just into August, around the start of steelhead, she showed up with a new lens for her camera and a sack filled with nets and vials, like we were going on a science expedition, not a fishing trip. She said she was trying to figure out how the old soft hackles worked, how it was they seemed the best flies going on a big rough river like the Deschutes. I said ma'am, the way you handle a rod it probably doesn't matter much what fly you use. Those boys of yours aren't going to need to worry about flies, either, they keep listening to you. She said thank-you but I think you're wrong. This is caddis season and I know when those things change and head for the surface there's more than meets the eye that moves the trout to feed. I want to see what those bugs look like then for myself.

We horsed around in riffles throughout the day, never getting anything that looked much to her like the partridge-and-orange and partridge-and-green and other old-timey flies she and her boys used so well. She kept looking through the camera but never saw anything she wanted to shoot. You would think she wouldn't have sweat it, getting the results they did. But you could see something was bothering her, although by then I had started doubting it was all about fishing and flies.

I had a hunch when I went to drop off her and her boys at their camp and she invited me to stop for a beer. But I was wrong. I can tell you I was all wrong. We drank a couple of those good bottle beers while watching the boys fish the last light. Then she turned to me and asked real sudden why I thought her husband had stopped coming on these floats with her. I said I didn't have a clue. Not because I didn't or I'd never thought about it. But like I said before, I've been at this business long enough to know when I'm the problem and when I'm not. And one sure way to invite trouble is to offer your opinion on just about anything that matters.

"You think he's seeing someone else?" she asked.

She looked up the river toward her sons so that I couldn't see her face.

"No I don't," I said. Not that I hadn't considered it. But I'm no fool. "I really don't think it's any a my business, ma'am. Unless there's something else you're asking."

She turned and looked at me long enough I wished I hadn't said it. It was all that old guide bullshit anyway, a thing every one of us buys into now and then. Finally she shook her head and smiled. Not in a particularly friendly manner but just a smile, shrugging her shoulders like I had seen her do when she was off by herself and she failed to connect on a grab. She never did show much, one way or the other.

"All I ask, sir, is you take care of my children and me on this river. I've been paying you good money and I'm happy with your work. That's all I need from you right now."

We came home from a late-summer trip and Denny started right in on me. He said he was unhappy. I ought to know that. There was no good reason for a woman to take her sons fishing when her husband felt like this. I reminded him that he wasn't the only one who mattered in the family. We were in this together. Maybe the happiness of the boys and me mattered, too. He said what did that mean. I said figure it out. I went to bed and just closed my eyes and tried to see the river.

Denny came in late smelling of wine. He climbed into bed and put an arm around me. He said he had found something he wanted to talk about. I stiffened up, afraid. Denny said he had gone through my vest and found the card of the guide we'd floated with.

"So?" I said. I rolled over so I could look at his face.

"So what's that all about?"

The window in our bedroom faced east. When the moon rose, light fell directly onto the bed, broken up only by the shadows from the tips of tall firs left scattered between the houses in our neighborhood. It was the last place on earth I wanted to live. But to Denny it meant something, a big safe house in the suburbs, people you could be friendly to or not. At least you could count on them to keep up their end of the bargain, not let their houses go. Something like that. I never did understand. I wanted my feet in a river every chance I got. Denny seemed to want or need something else. I looked at his face in the moonlight. His eyes were in shadows. I could see nothing but I smelled my own husband, the wine on his breath rising out of the shadows. Like stench from frogwater when the river drops in early summer, just as the caddis begin to move.

"Denny," I said, "it's not about anything. He's our guide," I said. "What do you think it's about?"

He sat up in the moonlight.

"I'll tell you what I think. I think you're going over there and visiting your boyfriend the fishing guide. That's what I think."

His eyes were narrowed. His upper lip quivered like it did when he was moved by anger or fear, a pain he wielded like threats. I had seen this in Denny before. But never quite like this. I felt my heart contract.

"Denny. The boys are with me over there. What are you talking about?"

"I'm talking about you and that effing guide. That's what I'm talking about."

"What about him?" I asked.

"*What about him?*" said Denny, mimicking my voice, mocking me.

Maybe if I had been stronger, I could have faced this sort of thing. It wasn't like it was the first time. But marriage had left me feeling weak. I was tired that night. I needed sleep. It was summer and I was trying to spend time on the water with my sons before another school year started again. *I shouldn't have to play nursemaid to my husband*, I thought. Which is wrong but the truth, what I'm left with now.

"Denny," I said, turning my back to him. I closed my eyes against the moonlight. "If that's what you think, I'm sorry. But it's your problem, Denny. Not mine. You can come fishing, too, if you want."

———

She called and said she was coming over by herself. Claimed her boys had soccer. She didn't want to bore them on a steelhead float. I didn't say her boys could fish trout while she went the other way. That didn't seem the point. She could have told me her boys didn't like to get up in the black of dawn, either. Which is the only time to start if you're serious about a morning steelhead. She was that, I can tell you. Whatever else I thought, I was certain she was serious about getting her fish.

She asked me to bring a Spey rod. That surprised me. You see a pretty stroke like hers you figure they don't want to try anything else. It's bound to be clumsy for awhile. You got to be used to feeling good the way you look. I asked her about action and she stopped me. I'd seen her fish enough to know what she liked and didn't like. She said just bring what I thought was best. She was right. But you don't usually hear that. Most people think they know all about themselves and how they're going to do something new. They don't know squat.

I had her meet me at the put-in at Beavertail so we could hit that good water first thing along Cedar Island. Turns out she had camped that night at Beavertail rather than drive up from Rattlesnake. Before I helped her into the boat, I handed her the rod I'd brought. I asked if she thought it would do. I had on one of those goofy little headlamps so we could see where we were stepping and after she took the rod she looked at me squinting into the light. She didn't do anything but hand the rod back.

"It's your call," she said.

The morning was one of those you know feels so much like a fish you're afraid to really feel it for fear of jinxing it somehow. There were stars and the sharp edge of the canyon and the chill air on the water. But that wasn't it. Sometimes you just think, *This is it*. Sometimes that feeling's wrong. Or maybe it's something you do that spoils it.

I put her on the top of that long shallow bar that runs down off the bottom of the island and forms the riffle above the pool where the river comes back together. I had her work on a roll cast, just enough to make sure we could keep a fly in the water and not miss any of the low morning light. That pool there runs directly east–west, so it gets hit early when the sun pops over the rim. But we'd be long gone by then, fish or no fish.

It wasn't long before she got the hang of it. Rolling out seventy-five, eighty feet of line. Letting the rod load before turning it loose, letting it do the work. That pretty stroke didn't just come out of the blue. She understood the mechanics of the whole thing. She knew her part in the deal.

After her first time through the pool, she waded back up along the edge of the bar, said she was going to change flies. I didn't have a problem with that. It's not about flies, I said, it's about keeping it in the water, keeping it working on the end of that swinging line. She was already into her wallet, not particularly interested in my guide bs. She took out a fly. It was a little like a Spey, with those long, webby, backswept hackles. Or the Al Knudson Spider. But what it really looked like was a magnified version of the partridge and anything soft hackle she and her boys had been fishing with that summer. You could see she'd been thinking about this real hard.

"I'm going to fish this just like I've been showing my boys," she said, as if reading my thoughts. "This is still pretty much caddis water." She waved the end of the rod from side to side. "I'm going to do it all the same, just make everything bigger."

That's how smart a lady she was. How good a fly fisher. She knew things that worked, how the water moved, where fish held. She didn't try to reinvent her game. She went after it the way she knew how.

——◆——

Maybe I was testing him.

It's crazy to think he wouldn't get upset, wouldn't be beside himself with jealousy no matter how much I said it was just about the fishing, getting my August steelhead on the Deschutes. Not after the fight we'd had. But I had decided I *should* be able to go fishing alone. Even if it was with a guide, another man. I knew why I was going fishing. I knew exactly why. Maybe I *was* testing him. But if I was, it was only because I wanted to see if he could handle me doing something on my own, getting myself something all alone, without him there to help, to see it, or testify to the fact that I'd done what I set out to do.

When I got home that night, I just wanted Denny to listen to me. That's it. I just wanted to talk about fishing. Anything else we talked about then went south. There was always something beneath the surface, some wrong Denny perceived I had done to him. I knew he wasn't happy about me doing a float alone with the same guide I'd been going with. But I'll be damned if I was going to yield to those kinds of fears. Maybe the real test was whether or not we still had a marriage. Or I knew it was over and I was pushing him over the edge, trying to make it his fault, not mine.

But we never got around to fishing. I never got to say a word. I headed into the driveway instead of backing in like I usually do. It was late and I was tired. I didn't trust myself with just taillights through all those trees. Sometimes I do it. Sometimes I don't. When the headlights swung onto the steps, I saw Denny standing on the porch. My whole insides contracted. I realized suddenly I hadn't stopped to use a restroom the whole way home. I was still excited about the fish I had caught. But what was going through me wasn't just that. I looked at Denny in the headlights. I closed my eyes and prayed he would just leave me alone.

He was still there when I came up the steps. I couldn't understand what I had just been afraid of, why I hadn't wanted to see my own husband. I smiled and held out my hands the size of the biggest fish I had landed that day, just as anyone would want to share what felt like the best thing they had ever done, even if they knew it wasn't.

"Your boyfriend called," said Denny. His voice was hurt and ugly, like a dead animal in the road. His entire mouth quivered. He couldn't look me in the eye. "He said you left your rod in his truck. Said you could pick it up *'next time you went fishing.'*"

I guess he tried to mimic the voice he had heard on the phone. It was worse than a dead animal. More like something foul, decrepit, a river in a dream that turns the color and texture of house paint that smells like paper mills in the valley. I had never heard his voice like that before.

"Oh, shit," I said.

"Kind of embarrassing, isn't it."

He wouldn't listen after that. Not once. I would replay everything, every detail, how it was that morning. Learning to cast that big rod. Hooking and fighting the fish. The flies. The weather. The drift. Everything I had wanted to tell him and now I did and each time he refused to listen. Or he couldn't. I tried to remember for him precisely how the rod got left in the truck, thinking sometimes I had brought it to the boat and then left it when I decided to commit that day to steelhead and the Spey rod, don't even think about trout. But at other times I thought I might have brought it along in the boat and then left it in the truck, brought downriver by the shuttle guys, after getting back to Beavertail after the float. It shouldn't matter, I kept telling Denny. I wasn't *sure* how the rod got left behind I said again and again and again.

"You're not sure because you're *lying!*" Denny shouted, standing in the front doorway, glaring at me as if I were some kind of beast. We were inside and I thought about our sons in bed listening to this. Denny yanked a picture off the wall. It was one of mine, pretty much like all the others. I had hung it there so that the last thing I saw each time I left the house was the river, my own sort of make-believe. Denny took that picture down and threw it at me, backhand, as if snapping me with a wet towel. "If you were telling me the truth, you'd know every damn detail! You can certainly tell me everything about your fish!"

He was right. I could. I had. And he wouldn't listen.

"The problem isn't the rod, Denny," I said. I knelt down and started picking up glass. My palm hurt. Right where I hold a rod. Blood dripped from the end of my middle finger. I smeared it on the tile. "Whatever you're looking for, you're going to find it."

———

She got three fish that day. The first was the best, a heavy chromer that put a bend in that long rod to make your heart bounce. Such a clean stroke. I was proud as punch for her, pleased like nobody's business. That big fish took her a good long time. She never once trembled, never squealed, never whined like most of them do, man or woman, how they have to land this, please please don't let me lose this fish. She just took care of business the way she did.

That evening I discovered she had left her trout rod in the cab of my pickup. Not sure how it got there. Knew she would miss it so I stopped in Maupin and called her old man right away. He asked how fishing had been. I said great. Couldn't be better. His wife had got one about as good as they come. He'd be jealous when she got the pictures back. I figured I'd see them both again pretty soon. Whatever was going on between them would eventually end. Maybe even right away if he got excited about her good fish. But you never know about these things. I got another rod lying around now.

Klickitat Summer

For nearly two months the plan works perfectly. Not only is Efrén Gálvez able to take off Saturday mornings to go fishing, a break from the deadening pace of autumn picking in the Barrett orchards, but he also gets to visit Patricia Eberhard, his new girlfriend in The Dalles, a blue-eyed *gringa* who seems, as the days shorten and the heat of summer finally begins to ebb, as excited as he is to steal whatever hours they can find beyond the cool gaze of judgment cast by family and friends.

All he has to do is get a steelhead. His father, who's run the Barrett orchards since the death of Robert Barrett, known playfully as Don Bob for Efrén's entire life, loves steelhead—partly, no doubt, because of a Catholic devotion to all foods gathered fresh from the earth, but also because this had been the favored fish of his boss and friend and benefactor, the man who gave him, Rubén Gálvez, more than he could have ever imagined while scurrying like a scared rabbit through the mesquite and cholla and dusty chaparral in the mountains east of Tijuana so many years ago.

Don Bob. Along with the secure livelihood he provided for the Gálvez family, Robert Barrett had enjoyed nothing more than presenting to Efrén's father the gift of one of these treasured fish, caught sometime that day if not that very hour from the nearby Beulah or another Columbia River tributary, an occasion that often ignited the kind of feasting and drinking that seemed on the verge of erupting somewhere within the compound of Barrett pickers' shacks when the orchards grew heavy with the scent of cherries, apples, or ripening pears.

But today the nostalgic trappings of the past, and the unlikely story of his family's success, feel to Efrén like so much knee-jerk Mexican ranchero music. *Don Bob this, Don Bob that,* he can hear his father braying, damning him for failure to respect the Barrett name, were even mention of Patricia Eberhard to creep into conversation about his so-called morning of fishing. And if his father had a clue of his and his girlfriend's breakfast at Shari's, followed by an hour of heady lovemaking, barely contained, in the basement apartment beneath her mother's river-view home? Or *two* hours, thinks Efrén, checking his cell phone while studying from his pickup the final two bends of the Klickitat, the milky green surface of the river sunlit beyond the dusty shadows of the county park, a tangle of rutted wheel-tracks and primitive campsites worn into a bench of oak and ponderosa pine within a mile of the Columbia itself.

Or what they *might* have ended up doing. Efrén eases his Toyota into an open reach of shade far enough from a pair of full-sized pickups, top-heavy beneath campers, that he won't breach anyone's view when he changes into his waders. If only they'd had a little more time, he thinks, recalling the moment, lips upon her, Patricia pressed his head away, asserting it was late, he needed to go, while her breath came in quiet waves that seemed to catch in her throat before fully expelled. If only he didn't have to stoop so low as to have to lie to his own father, an act he finds all the more distasteful as he regards with increasing skepticism the river's off-color tint, a blush of glacial snowmelt from a sudden spell of Indian summer that had made it that much more difficult to argue he could take a day off to fish rather than help with the ripening fruit.

Or have to deal with these weekend warriors, thinks Efrén, his mood souring. Along the bank in full sun below the final riffle stretches an uneven line of plunkers, gear-and-bait guys hidden waist down from view by the lip of a broad sweep of freestone and glacial debris deposited by the river in high water. Nothing saps his sense of adventure more than these rank-and-file meat fishers. Yet even as he rigs up and readies his gear, Efrén keeps tabs on the plunkers, where dirty water, he's well aware, does little to diminish the workings of luck—in one form or another.

The exchange of glances between the two men at river's edge—one, rod bent, fighting a fish, the other, bent at the waist, prepared to net it—

happens so quickly that for a moment, Efrén, adrift in his own deceits, feels certain he's but imagined he's about to witness a poaching.

How could he possibly know? Yet from the cool manner the steelhead is landed and killed and quickly dispatched to an ice chest—a sequence of gestures, without trace of cheer, that reminds him of two guys changing a tire in the rain—Efrén concludes that the fish was wild, both men knew it, and the look they shared moments before the steelhead rose from the water, skewed at the bottom of the stretched and dripping mesh, was as brief and intimate as a glance passed in public between a pair of practiced adulterers.

The worst of it, thinks Efrén, slipping into the river fifty yards upstream, is that they're Mexicans—short, dark, separate, their gear the sort that fails long before it grows old. Is this why he recognized their furtive glances? The question angers him, suggesting, as it does, he shares an affinity for their petty crime—that he's privy to the private gestures of this, the lowest of acts, for no other reason than the color of his skin, the language he first learned, the culture in which he was raised. None of that should matter, thinks Efrén, feeling the first cool licks of water seeping into his waders. They're dogs no matter what their breed.

Yet even as he settles deeper into the Klickitat, adjusting his weight as the river pulls, with increasing strength, at his legs and felted boots, he feels the sharpness of his sudden anger dissipate as if dulled by the cold itself. No matter his reaction, he thinks, nothing now will undo the damage—a wild steelhead dragged from the river long before delivery of its fateful load. Worse, he discovers on reaching the deepest stretch of the wade, currents of unexpected sympathy for the two poachers, imagining the simple needs in untold scenarios that such a fish might meet—especially, now, in these lean and unsure times.

This sudden softness surprises him. Its source threatens his balance. Rod overhead, his vest bunched up around his shoulders, feeling his way across the uneven bottom, Efrén finds himself awash in waves of memories of the wild steelhead he killed a dozen years ago, a singular shame that refuses to let go of him despite every effort, on his part, to reject the humiliations of growing up brown in the Beulah valley. No matter the steelhead had been an accident—a shocking catch on the West Fork of the Beulah while first learning to trout fish with flies on gear given him by Don Bob. He had practically killed the fish, anyway, in the time it took to land it. And had somebody thought to tell him a thing about wild fish and hatchery fish? Or how, even, to tell them apart?

But the worst of it, recalls Efrén, anchoring each foot before lifting the other, the worst of it proved Don Bob's outrage, a fit of profanities shouted in response to the dead steelhead Efrén hauled proudly back to the cabin he shared with his father and mother alongside the Barrett orchards, stitched into a terraced hillside overlooking the Beulah itself. Now, he feels he understands this reaction; these fish are precious, their future long imperiled. Yet for Efrén, waist-deep in the river, there remain the dark implications of why, years later, Robert Barrett reacted with similar outrage on discovering that his daughter, Erica, had climbed into Efrén's first car, a Monte Carlo dark as *mole*, and ridden alone with him on the back roads to and from town.

Near the far bank he stumbles free of the current and rises from the river, climbing the slope of loose rock left behind by winter floods. And in the glare of the mid-morning sun, Efrén turns and gazes back at the poachers, losing himself to the sudden warmth lifting from the chalky bank, the round river stone tinted beneath a layer of summer dust and the discharge of glacial sediments carried by both heat and high water this far downstream.

The hell with them, he thinks, tugging his vest back down over the tops of his waders. *They'll learn their lesson the hard way.*

Yet this seems to Efrén an unlikely promise. He pivots and starts upstream. Look at the stunts he pulls.

It's two more crossings before he reaches the shadows still cast onto the river by the sheer walls of the mouth of the canyon, holding water that's given up fish so reliably over the past two months he's grown increasingly bold in his Saturday mornings with Patricia Eberhard.

But he finds it belittling, again, that he has to engage in this shady behavior. He's certain, anyway, his father can't possibly expect him to bring home a steelhead every time. His long tenure in the service of Don

Bob carried with it the clear message that steelheading was the most challenging of sports, that the long hours, even days, Don Bob spent fishing, while the elder Gálvez managed the day-to-day workings of the orchards, belonged to the commitment one made if he called himself a genuine steelheader.

Efrén still finds it difficult to believe his father was fooled by such nonsense. Working his fly through the top of the run, a narrow slot unlikely to produce a fish willing to rise through the swift, off-colored current, he indulges in the pleasure of casting, his loop unfolding against the dark basalt cliff, the cool air contained within the confines of the shaded canyon walls—all of this while anticipating, deeper in the run, his fly snaking through the boulders and ribbons of current where he can expect a steelhead to grab. For it's clear to him again today that this is all just that, an indulgence, an act of pleasure, not unlike the time he spends with Patricia Eberhard—and if all he were really doing was trying to bring home a fish, he'd be downriver with the plunkers—or up here wielding, instead, a conventional rod and reel, some yarn and corkies, a silver spoon, a wad of roe or tub of sand or ghost shrimp.

Delivering a fresh cast, Efrén asks himself: Is this the true meaning of class? That you can screw around playing whimsical games while the help at home tends to the fruit and fields?

An hour later he gets his fish, a hatchery hen, twenty-eight inches long measured from the top of his reel seat to the stripping guide, the scar of its clipped adipose fin smooth as a thumbnail, whereas one of its gill plates, missing a chunk the size of a coin, was probably damaged while passing through the main-stem salmon nets. It reassures him, anyway, that he's found the steelhead with little more in the way of finesse than repeated casts through the bucket of the run, a kind of artless erasure of the odds, much like the style of soccer he and his teammates had played, to such effect, throughout high school. "You have to shoot to score," Don Bob, a big fan, was fond of repeating—until, recalls Efrén, he stopped attending matches and made his daughter do the same.

He kills and bleeds the fish and wraps it in the plastic garbage sack he carries in his vest, replaced from a box in his truck each time he returns with another dead steelhead. Hungry suddenly, he imagines somewhere in the rising heat of the day, in the mix of smells gathering in the mouth of the canyon from the breeze drifting upriver off the Columbia, the faint scent of his mother's weekend posole—long a tradition in the Barrett orchards, a midday meal renowned among pickers throughout the Beulah valley, served both Saturdays and Sundays even now, years after Don Bob's death.

Yet thoughts of these meals, still dished from his mother's blackened olla, stir in Efrén fresh resentments toward the meager time he has to fish. For the arrangement with his father has been, all season, that he'll arrive by lunch, an informal agreement that grew out of the years, when he still lived at home, that Efrén was allowed to spend Saturday mornings however he pleased—even if what he did was a continuation of something started Friday night. The agreement is informal, but there's a strict code of respect still at work beneath his seemingly casual comings and goings, a code Efrén is well aware of—which bothers him, now, even more, as he recalls how often Don Bob failed to show on weekends, and how his mother faithfully withheld servings, which she carried to the Barrett house even when Don Bob arrived home closer to dinner or even well after dark.

Where was his own wife? wonders Efrén. Or Erica.

Later, as he tosses fish and gear in the cab of his pickup and quickly climbs in behind the wheel, certain he's in no real danger of getting caught but eager, nonetheless, to be off the river and safely down the road, Efrén wonders, as well, how these memories of his past, of his father's authority and his mother's posole and even her subservience to Don Bob himself, might have contributed to his own sudden impulse to approach the poachers and save them from impending trouble.

The prospects were obvious. As he started down the bank to the last crossing, he spotted, in the distance, the telltale outline of a Washington State fish-and-game patrol boat sweeping out of the basalt shadows and up through the final reach of the long arm of the Klickitat pool. At water's edge the plunkers would fail to see the boat until it was practically within casting range. These visits seemed random occurrences; you could go months and never see a game cop. They'd show up, out of the blue, inspecting for licenses and illegal fish, checking everyone—including the two poachers.

Especially them, thought Efrén.

He hurried across the river, wading with the reckless skill needed to follow the exceptional fish, the hottest wild steelhead that seemed, on occasion, of another species altogether. Without a word he fell in beside the poachers, directing them with a terse nod to notice the patrol boat just then easing its way out of the dead water backed up, far downstream, by Bonneville Dam. Before the poachers, silent as deer, responded with anything more than uneasy glances, Efrén pulled their fish from the cooler and exchanged it with the hatchery steelhead of his own.

All of it happened so quickly that as Efrén made his way up the trail to his pickup, he recalled, unwittingly, a story Don Bob used to tell, one he had heard repeated since he was a child. Given a new audience, one or a dozen listeners he hadn't told, Don Bob would carry on about a time, years back, while expanding the septic system shared by workers choosing to live, more and more, year-round in his cabins, a green INS van showed up in his driveway, its tires spitting gravel as it climbed the hill. Surprised, Don Bob turned to warn Efrén's father and three other workers of the presence of *la migra*—only to find the work site deserted, the four men having already vanished as if sparrows into the trees.

How he loved that line, thinks Efrén, now, easing his truck through the shadows, up the steep grade leaving the county park. He pictures Don Bob, gray and hard limbed, performing—maybe a little drunk, perhaps a party in honor of another dead steelhead—looking over his shoulder, first left then right, startled by the moment, alone—then finally delivering the punch line, as only a man second to no one can.

As if sparrows into the trees.

Trailing a plume of dust, Efrén spins his tires as he swings out onto the paved highway. A mile downstream the road dead-ends at a stop sign; he waits while Saturday traffic passes in both directions along the Columbia—to the east The Dalles, to the west Albion at the mouth of the Beulah valley. Sunlight through the windshield casts in harsh relief the poachers' steelhead, rigid and gray, on the seat beside him; he checks his mirrors, imagining how easy it would be, if he's not careful, to get pulled over. The traffic clears, but for a moment he remains stationary, remembering how thoughtlessly, it seemed to him, his father vanished each winter to family property still held in Guanajuato in the mountains above San Miguel de Allende, leaving him and his mother to spend the darkest, coldest, wettest months alone in their cabin, with Don Bob an uncertain presence ever since the wild steelhead Efrén killed and the way the old man could look at his mother, his father away, sending Efrén's heart racing.

A horn sounds behind Efrén. He raises a hand and waves, ignoring the rearview mirror. Then he turns left, wondering if Patricia Eberhard has ever had steelhead this fresh—or if he'll be able to notice any difference between a wild fish and all of the hatchery steelhead he's eaten since he was a boy.

Klickitat Fall

THE DARK MAKES IT TOUGH FOR GANNON OLMSTEAD TO DRIVE HIS
pickup upriver in reverse. Twisted sideways in the seat, right arm stretched
across the top of the backrest, he steers one-handed, peering through
the rear window as if backing his drift boat down to the water. He can't
see shit beyond the arc of the pickup's wimpy backup lights. Each time
he gets rolling, picking up a little speed, something throws him off—
roadside reflectors, a glance at his mirrors, the wall of night, the weird
perspective on curves so familiar he could otherwise take them with his
eyes closed—his sudden confusion sharpened as he tugs at the wheel,
disoriented by his own decision to drive, for safety's sake, on the wrong
side of the road.

At least his brakes work.

Cattywampus, he glimpses the river sliding by beneath the shimmer
of his taillights. Jockeying back on course, he grabs hold of the shift lever.
The tranny wails in protest. His breathing jumps up high in his chest—
and by the time he gets straightened out again, headed backwards up the
road, his heart, he notices, pounds like a puppy's tail inside his chest.

Okay, so he's a little pissed off.

Still a little pissed off.

At the next milepost he's startled to see the short distance he's covered from home. But he holds down his speed. Last thing he needs to
do is land his ass in the river. Creeping through a bend, the steep cut
looming outside the passenger window, he reconsiders his decision to use

the wrong lane—a strategy he immediately concludes again will cause the least alarm should he encounter someone else on the road.

Pissed off or not, thinks Gannon Olmstead, he's no fool. Four straight days with a fish, he's not about to let a little truck problem interfere with a streak of favors from the steelhead gods. Especially not on a Friday—before the wave of weekend warriors arrives.

And especially not after he's put up nearly three cord of wood in those same four days—a prettier stack of sweet-scented, hand-split oak no household has ever seen.

But for what?

A dull saw, a lame truck—and last night Elizabeth claims the steelhead fillets and fresh chanterelles and *Pinot Fu-Fu* do nothing anymore but make her tired.

And this morning?

He might as well have been sleeping *with* the woodpile.

Maybe she's just getting old, thinks Gannon.

He eyes the night, the half-lit trees, the hidden river.

He certainly wasn't about to wake her and ask for a ride—not the way she's been complaining this fall about still working.

And with those knuckleheads at the district office asking everyone to do more and more with less and less.

He's lucky he retired when he did, he thinks, trying to recognize, from this new angle, the spot he's found to tuck his truck so nobody suspects where he's fishing.

———

It was the year they closed the library, narrates Amy Fletcher.

Winding her way downriver, she enjoys the smug satisfaction she feels whenever she discovers, out of the blue, the first line of a new piece of writing.

A mile later, she's torn.

What's she got? A short story? Memoir? The self-deprecating ironies of a personal essay?

Or something as simple as a letter, subtle as verse, to the editor of the *Beulah Valley News*.

Or one to *Bryan*, her so-called boyfriend—who hasn't phoned or emailed or texted in a week.

The turd.

Watching the sweep of her headlights for roadside deer, she settles on the idea of a letter to Priscilla Iremonger, editor of the *News*—and immediately she imagines the response throughout the valley, a stir of unrest and civic shame, a great upwelling of remorse as readers, having risen in the dark of an autumn morning much like today, open their newspapers and, finding her letter, begin to pore over her words.

People say we can't eat books . . .

She composes in her head, accompanied by the low-throated hum of the pickup she's been given to patrol a stretch of river running through property recently acquired by the local land trust. Three months out of work, she jumped at the chance to get paid minimum wage for performing a service of genuine value to the community—the same impulse that inspired her to start work, four years before, as a librarian's assistant with an English degree and $78,000 of unpaid student loans.

. . . As if the intangibility of intellectual pursuit justifies votes against taxes to support a public library.

. . . As if ideas themselves, the nutrition of the spirit, are any less important than three square meals a day.

You can't eat love, either, thinks Amy. *Yet when in all of history has anyone anywhere voted against* that?

"They would if it meant raising taxes."

Upstream from the Bait House bridge, just above her turnoff to the land trust property's gated road, she imagines Bryan, dear Bryan, reading over her shoulder, the smell of him spilling over her with the flavor of unbidden lust.

As if she'll ever let *him* see her work again.

Best not even write it down, she thinks, dismissing the urge to pull to the side of the road. Her speed checked, she glances at her new Moleskine notebook, resting untouched beside her in the faint glow of the dashboard lights. With this job she'll have plenty of time to write, she tells herself—a pledge that fans an ember of guilt for all of the ideas she's entertained and failed to put down on the page.

It's a dumb line, anyway, she thinks.

Just short of the bridge, at the bend in the river beside the abandoned Bait House, she catches first sight of dawn above the rim of the valley. Only a week on the job, she's pleased by the sense that she's settled into a routine, that this glimpse of daylight at the same spot along the river foretells the predictability she's failed to create, year after year, in a daily rhythm that might include a genuine writing life. The distractions of love, she concedes, are the worst—all the more reason, she decides, to tell Bryan *They Would If It Meant* Hornsby to find someone else to absorb his cock-eyed editorial advice.

Halfway across the bridge, she spots taillights in the bend ahead—someone stopped in the middle of the road. *Deer.* She lifts her foot off the gas—and in the time it takes the pickup to stop, she sketches the opening of a story in which the deer, lying maimed in the road, has to be released from its misery, a task that requires she—

Then she remembers the William Stafford poem "Traveling Through the Dark," in which the speaker, finding a dead doe with a still-live fawn inside, chooses to push the two together into the river between the wilderness and the mountain road.

And those are *backup* lights, she sees, finally.

Not just taillights.

———

He calls it an itch, a steelhead itch.

It's really more of a vibration, internal rather than external, a hum as if his sternum were quivering like a tuning fork—a sensation he experiences in the heart of the season when it seems the river and the weather, the light in the sky and the color of the trees, align in a chorus of perfect pitch that promises a fish each time he swings the fly.

He calls it an itch because it feels a little like he's about to get laid.

If he remembers right.

Hustling in early light up the gated river road, he's sure about one thing: nobody's going to keep him off his water.

What the hell's a land trust, anyway?

Despite the new sign posted on the gate, he's not convinced he's actually trespassing. And even if he is, he figures he's got one time to plead ignorance, claim he arrived early, in the dark, and failed to spot the new rules. That's been his reasoning all week. Plus, he's been fishing this same water for ten years *before* he retired. It's like coming home and someone trying to keep you from sleeping in your own bed.

Still, he holds to the edge of the road, the preview of shadows tucked beneath the maples and spindly alders clinging to the steep drop to the river. Just in case. Warm already inside his waders, his two-hander impossible to hide, he has no intention of trying to ditch anyone—a fool's game best prevented by avoiding notice in the first place.

Yet when he reaches the deer crossing at the broad tailout above the Bait House, and he finds the pavement there still wet, releasing vapors into the rising light and chill dawn air, he glances about, sensing life in plain sight unseen by holding itself perfectly still.

Where the river pours from the mouth of the canyon, he's relieved, finally, to leave the road and drop into a stand of oaks and heavy-trunked pines. Nobody will see him now. Beneath the trees his boots fall silent atop the matted duff, spread parklike across open tracts blurred here and there by ferns and crowded seedlings. His steps stir the scent of sweat, wet hair, fresh-baked bread. He tries to remember the last time Elizabeth allowed him to kiss her thighs. He can hear the river, the sound of it washing through the moss-laced trees, altogether different than when he was on the road—and in the full light of morning, he finds it difficult, as well, to recall himself driving, just now, backwards in the dark, the images tangled, barely coherent, as if left behind by a troubling dream.

All for another fish, he thinks, his heart alive inside his chest.

—◆—

You could get used to this.

Or I could, thinks Amy, watching scraps of fog snagged by the hillside oaks, a flank of the canyon smeared the color of pumpkins.

She sits in the truck sipping coffee from the cup of her new Stanley thermos, unclear whether she's narrating or discoursing—or trying to make sense of her own life.

She raises her binoculars. Upstream the river lies all but black in a long pool shaded by a lip of the canyon mouth. Or green, she thinks, imagining a challenge from Bryan. *Screw him.* She reaches, cautiously, for her notebook—only to catch sight of something moving along the edge of the river, a sudden discord rushing downstream.

Some*one.*

Stumbling.

Chased.

Or giving chase.

She arrives in time to see an old guy in waders and a black watchman's cap reel a fish into a shallow corner of the river, leading it through a scramble of rocks with a long pole he holds low to the water. Twice the fish swirls, splashes, and scoots off between the rocks; its fins and exposed back glisten against the dark water. Edging his way across the rocks, the guy seems to keep his balance by leaning against the pull of the fish, his body flexing, this way and that, in response to the bend first tightening and then softening through the arc of the pole.

Rod, she remembers Bryan correcting her. *Poles are for flags and vaulters—or dumb jokes.*

She hangs back. Protocol requires she do nothing more than gather information; unless she received training to work armed, nobody wanted her confronting trespassing sportsmen. Screened by bankside alders, she watches the guy grab hold of the fish, clamping a broad hand around the base of its tail. He's older than she thought. He cradles the body with his other hand, lifts the entire fish briefly, and then sets it back in the shallow water parallel to his rod, aligning the tail with the butt as though measuring one against the other. On his knees he works the hook back and forth, finally twisting it out of the corner of the fish's mouth. Then he stands, slowly, bent at the waist—and he takes hold of the tail again and steers the fish headfirst between the rocks and scoots it back into the river.

It all seems lovely, even elegant—until the guy suddenly points at the river, and she realizes he's already broken out into song.

"*. . . You don't know what it's like / to love somebody / the way I love you.*"

"Nice fish," she says, coming down the bank.

His head snaps toward her as though she's caught an animal unawares.

"Nice *and* pretty," he says.

He picks up his rod and begins fiddling with the line.

She stops short of the water, just outside the range of the rod tip.

"You always let them go?"

"Wild fish. You have to."

He looks downriver and, she guesses, spots the truck.

"Of course, you probably know all the rules," he says.

"One of them, at least."

She bends down and finds a small rock and starts to toss it into the river—only to remember that's right where he's fishing. Does it matter now? She rolls the rock in her palm and then flips it backhand toward the bank.

"It's called private property," she says. "It's called no trespassing."

He steps backwards, stumbling slightly over the uneven footing. Or *feigning* the act of staggering? Mocking her? He glances over each shoulder, looks upstream and then down.

"River's not private."

"The road is."

"I've never caught a fish like that on anybody's road."

She wishes she still had rock in hand to throw—if not at him, into his fishing hole. The force of her anger catches her by surprise. She feels as though she's talking with Bryan.

She feels like shouting.

The library's full of goddamn books besides crime fiction and vampires and fucking hard-ass espionage dialogue.

Or it was.

She moves toward him until realizing both her trail shoes are covered in water.

"You have to leave," she says, pointing a finger at him as though shooing a kid off a public computer.

He looks at her, expressionless, just like the teenagers would.

Did.

"And when I don't? What? You going to shoot me?"

He turns and wades out into the river, his reel squawking as he pulls off line.

"This is posted property," she says, raising her voice.

Knee deep, he stops and looks around.

"Where?"

"At the gate at the end of the road."

"Must be a new sign."

He swings the rod side to side, animating the line.

"It was dark when I walked in."

He lies like Bryan, too.

"Bullshit," she says.

But there's nothing she can do but wait—until he finishes fishing. And then? And then she follows him to his car, gets his license plate, and files a charge. If a cell phone worked up here, she'd call the cops right now.

She watches him make a cast, the line leaping from the end of his rod.

And if she had a gun, maybe she *would* shoot him.

<hr/>

It takes him awhile to figure out she's serious, that she intends to—what? Write him up? Call the cops? *Bust* him?

Screw that.

He stays tight to the river, keeping as best he can below high water as he works his way downstream. Twice he stops to fish, wading out to cover marginal lies with a series of sharp, cack-handed casts that have no real purpose but to demonstrate who the fuck she's dealing with. If she were foolish enough to stand anywhere near him, he'd wrap the head around her neck. Instead, she follows him in her pickup—creeping along like a stalker with a hand in his pants.

Her pants.

He doesn't have to put up with this. He's sixty-three years old. He pays his taxes. His wife still has a perfectly good job. This year he bought a fishing license in five different states. *He* didn't vote to close anybody's damn library.

At the tailout above the Bait House, he decides enough is enough. He's never crossed here—but he knows from experience he's fine, if he's careful, at whatever spots the deer choose. He checks once in both directions, locating a narrow notch of dark soil in the dry grass and foliage on both banks.

It's pretty obvious.

He keeps casting and swinging the fly until he's nearly halfway across the river. There's nothing he likes more than finding an autumn fish holding in the slots and subtle depressions of a tailout—a fish that often seems more ready than any other steelhead to jump the fly, as though grown relaxed in a lie rarely pestered by gear anglers or nymphers. He loves the idea of sticking one right now. That would show her—*something*.

But when the water climbs over his knees, he reels in the line and hooks the fly to the frame of his reel. A trough of deep current sweeps through the bend along the bank, the muddy deer trail scoring the tangent. He tugs up the hem of his jacket. The footing's fine—just a bunch of freestone that'll hold as long as he's patient. He does this all of the time, he thinks, spreading his legs apart against the pull of the current, stubbing first one boot between the rocks and then the other.

He gets a little loose in the very deepest part of the slot, the current up near his belt, the rocks bigger here, harder to slide his feet around— finally shoving himself forward with the toes of his boots until he's solid again where the bottom lifts up under him.

Downstream, a wedge of slick current spears the waves of bouncing whitewater.

He holds still, making certain of his footing, peering over the top of the bank through shadows of alders and flame-bright maples. His truck's just down a ways, between the Bait House and the bridge. A rush of wind rattles the trees, scattering a shower of leaves. *Maybe Elizabeth would like to head into Albion*, he thinks, turning to check behind him. *Friday night, dinner, a movie and—*

You gotta be kidding, he thinks, spotting Ms. Posted headed his way.

She can't believe he's trying to escape. One minute he's fishing, making these pretty casts that seem a kind of poetry in geometry and physics— and the next, he's wading toward the far bank, scooting across the river like a lame dog.

She measures his progress against a quick calculation of her distance to the end of the road, the time it would take her to get out of the truck, unlock the gate, drive through, close the padlock—and then try to find him.

He could be anywhere by then.

Scrambling down the bank, she's struck by the sound of the river, a rolling pulse that rises and falls depending on which way she holds her head. She hesitates, considering the foolishness of her pursuit, the idea that it doesn't really matter if she locates him and his truck and turns him in, she's going to get paid the same whether she gives chase or not.

Which is exactly how librarians think, she can hear Bryan say—*the reason public services are a sham, why raising taxes never works.*

She's not a librarian any more than she's a cop.

She's a writer.

And writers need *something* to write about.

The water feels warm through her cold shoes. She's practically able to trot over the cobblestone-like rocks showing clearly through the shallow current. Halfway across the river, she's within shouting distance as the guy finally climbs up the far bank. She's soaked to the thighs of her Levis—but she'll be out in a minute.

Perched on top of the bank, the guy turns and watches her approach.

"The hell you think you're doing!" he hollers.

"I think I'm the one supposed to ask that!"

He holds still while she works her way toward him—then he stabs his rod tip in her direction.

"It's deeper than it looks!" he shouts, his voice coming at her like sound through a crowd. "And faster!"

"You didn't seem to have any trouble!"

She closes the distance between them, the water climbing to her pockets.

He takes several steps down the bank.

"You can't tell from there!"

She continues toward him, leaning into the current. The river sounds like waves, crashing and then receding, and she can't tell if he's really shouting or if he's just angry.

"Hey!" he says. "I'm serious!"

He comes right down to the edge of the water.

"You need to listen to me."

She stops, steadying herself, no more than a street's width away from him. She tries on the same dumb look he earlier gave her.

"*And when I don't? What?*"—raising her voice just enough so she's sure he can hear her—"*You going to shoot me?*"

The guy goes still and glares at her. Then he reaches up and pulls off his hat. He tucks his rod up under his arm and stands there, his hips cocked to one side, holding her with his eyes. His white hair against the trees looks like a crown. Or a halo. Or his head, outlined in yellow leaves, is on fire.

"Look, I mean it."

He points at her with his hat.

"If it's so important to you, I'll stay right here. You go back, get your truck, and I'll wait for you."

He pulls his hat back on.

"Serious."

Yeah, right, she thinks. *Bravo, Bryan, bravo. Another brilliant performance.* She wonders if guys take classes in this shit.

She starts toward him again—and suddenly the only thing beneath her feet is the feel of moving rocks, the rounded tops sliding free, one after another, of the toes of her shoes as she stretches her legs, searching for purchase.

The distance between them begins to grow.

She picks up speed, yellow alders sweeping past.

There's noise everywhere.

—◦—

When he sees her break loose, his first thought is, *Serves her right.*

Then he sees her eyes, the surprised look of a guy who just got hit in a fight and doesn't yet know he's hurt.

Shit, he thinks.

"Just go with it!" he hollers, trotting along the bank. He can't tell if she's trying to swim or if she's panicking. "It'll let up down a ways!"

It will, he thinks.

And then there's the goddamn bridge.

He's been in there once, three or four years ago, he can't quite recall when. He hooked a fish, he remembers, up high, first one in weeks, and immediately it got below the concrete piling, threatening to leave the pool through a mess of boulders and busted up whitewater. He thought he could follow—and he *did*, but he didn't think he was going to be dog-paddling with one arm and the rod in the other when he went down after the fish in the current.

Now everyone he knows calls it the Swimming Hole.

He hurries all the way down there, slipping through the trees and underbrush on a deer trail widened by anglers. If she can't get herself out before the bridge, he's going to have to try the same goddamn stunt.

It's going to be a lot different this time, he thinks. *She's going to be a lot harder to land.*

He thinks about pulling off his waders. But he decides it's not a good idea to get into the cold water, even if he is going to get wet. He tugs his belt tight. The good thing about waders, he thinks, is you don't have to swim to float. The bad thing is, you *can't* swim much, either.

He wades in up high in the hole, at the boulders brought in to keep the river from tearing up the road in winter at both ends of the bridge. Just like he were fishing. He thinks about trying to reach her with his rod, but he decides that's a dumb idea, he's going to want both hands free. He looks upstream, spotting her in the current. He still can't tell what's going on with her. He tries, instead, to gauge her speed and the spot in the current where she'll pass. He's sure he can get to her.

After that he'll just have to see.

———

He makes her take off her clothes.

She tries, at first, to protest—but he tells her she has to, that's the only way she's going to stop from freezing to death. He takes keys from the front of his waders, unlocks his pickup, and reaches in and starts it. He pulls a blanket from the cab.

"You're not going to warm up with those clothes on. And if you get this goddamn blanket wet—"

"Let me guess. You're going to shoot me?"

But she can't even smile, she's shivering so badly. She doesn't know how it's possible to be so cold. For a moment she's frightened to remove her top; it seems like it's just going to make the cold worse. But when she looks his way, she sees he's already climbed out off his boots and waders—and when he pulls down his wet leggings, and she sees he's got nothing on underneath, she turns away and starts removing her own clothes in earnest.

When she's down to her underwear, she checks over her shoulder.

He's shivering as badly as she is, trying to dry himself with his fleece watchman's cap.

He glances over at her.

"All of it," he says. "Every goddamn bit."

She turns her back toward him and does as she's told.

"You sure swear a lot," she says.

"Only when I'm pissed off. Or colder than goddamn shit."

She wraps the blanket around herself and climbs into the cab of the pickup.

He gets in next to her.

"I got to have some of that, too," he says.

She undoes the blanket and slides closer to him.

They sit there a long time, the engine running, the cab growing warmer and warmer, the trees all but vanishing beyond the condensation flooding the windows. When they both finally stop shivering, he tells her about the problem with his truck, that he can't drive her anywhere because it's not safe, especially in the middle of the day. She'll have to walk back to her rig, cross the bridge, head up the gated road.

Like he did this morning.

"Where the sign is?" she asks.

"What sign?" he says.

But he doesn't seem to her in any more of a hurry than she is to climb out of the warm cab. And when she starts to sense her body again, feel it naked under the blanket next to his, she suddenly starts talking about Bryan—as if Bryan explains how she's ended up here now.

"Your boyfriend?"

"He has been," she says. "I don't really know anymore."

And then all she can talk about is the problems they've been having lately, that she's been having with him.

She stops as abruptly as she started. She feels half drunk. She can't tell if it's the rising heat—or some kind of delayed response to fear. She wonders if it's even safe sitting so long in an old truck idling with the heater running.

Then she feels him shift around under the blanket. He turns and faces her.

"You want to know one of the basic facts of life?" he says.

Uh oh, she thinks. *Here we go.*

"Women like it when men are nice to them. Men like it when women are nice to them."

She sits perfectly still.

He doesn't say or do anything else.

"That's it?" she asks.

"That's it."

She looks over at him.

"You just discovered that?"

"At my age you discover lots of things all over again."

"You're not that old," she says.

"A hell of a lot older than you are."

They're both startled by a sharp knock at his door. All of the windows are fogged. He rolls down his.

"Gannon!"

She looks across into the face of a woman, at least his age, her gray hair pulled back tight, her eye shadow the same midnight blue two of the librarians she used to work with wore.

Everybody looks at each other.

"I saw your truck," says the woman.

She slumps into the seat as she watches the woman lean her head almost entirely through the window, her painted nails wrapped over the edge of the lowered glass.

"Gannon, I'm not even going to ask why these clothes out here are all wet."

Something about his mouth, the press of his lips, tells her he's disappointed that the woman—must be his wife—isn't upset.

The warmth of that disappointment—in the face of the woman's trust—just about melts her heart.

"I took the afternoon off," says the woman. "I thought maybe we could do something—if you were back from fishing."

"I can't wait," he says.

Imnaha

THEY'VE BEEN ALONE LONG ENOUGH NOW, CLOISTERED IN A CABIN AT river's edge, that the sound of the truck descending the canyon road brings them to a stop in the final mile of their evening run.

They move to the shoulder, a welt of loose gravel raised along the steep bank falling to the river. Both of them, Brewer and Perry, expect to see headlights weaving through the oaks and tall pines—although neither one of them has sensed a need, until now, for light of any kind along the pale graded road.

As the truck approaches, they follow its progress by the plume of dust boiling from the treetops, rising like smoke against the twilight sky. Yet only Perry feels moved to dwell on their immediate good fortune—the intense delight that might have easily escaped them had this stranger passed but a half-hour before, interrupting her and Brewer White's splashy streamside lovemaking.

Beside her, Brewer appears engaged in one of his protracted attempts to sound the sense of the moment, oblivious to the lingering wash of their recent, spontaneous merriment.

"Why doesn't he have his lights on?"

"Maybe his girlfriend has her head in his lap." She takes up his hand and draws close to him, locating his scent within the fragrance of sage, dust, the river—the heated grip of the close August air. "Maybe he's an ancient prospector, a Basque sheepherder or Nez Perce tribal elder, nearly blind in both eyes, who's traveled up and down this road so many times that he doesn't *need* headlights—even if he *could* see."

Brewer turns to her. He touches his lips to her brow, a gesture she recognizes as his patient dismissal of all but genuine efforts to deal with the subject at hand.

The truck—an old pickup—rattles down the last straight stretch of road on a line directly toward them.

"It could be a hunter."

"A poacher," says Perry. She wraps an arm around Brewer's waist. "If he's hunting this time of year, he's poaching."

Brewer, a head taller, glances down at her. He lifts an arm to her shoulders. The other he raises overhead and waves, signaling their presence at the edge of the road.

The truck rattles their way.

"It's dark," says Brewer.

"He can see us fine."

Right up to the last moment the truck remains aimed eye to eye at them, right until the front bumper finally begins to swing away along the line of the road, she holds herself close to Brewer. Four days alone along this remote stretch of river, four days and nights coming to know each other against the push and pull of work and desire, she leans against him, trying to feel what he feels. What kind of man is he, anyway? she wonders. Can she trust him? Can he protect her—*will* he protect her—should it come to that?

Together they watch the pickup pass. Turning away from them, the truck immediately seems as innocent to Perry as the river, no matter how swift or wild, viewed from the safety of the bank—until light through the cab window catches the passenger just so, throwing into relief a profile too much like her ex-husband's for her to possibly ignore.

Dust lifts over them. She drops her arm from Brewer's waist and pulls away.

"I think we left the cabin open."

Brewer pivots toward her.

"What do you mean?"

"It's wide open." She remembers the slap of the screen door, the wind, how the shade from the big oaks promised the very air the cabin needed so badly. She remembers her eagerness to leave work behind, find a spot upriver, step free of clothing, sweat, her clenched desire. "If they wanted to, they could walk right in."

Brewer looks at her.

He turns and takes off running, trailing the vanishing pickup toward the cabin far down the road.

~~~

Late that night, it's all a joke.

Draped naked over the downstairs bed, the curtained French doors flung open to receive the sound of the river and the cool of the windless night, they lose themselves again in laughter and yet another long digressive account of the nutty thoughts and unleashed fears that raced through each of their minds during Brewer's dizzying run.

There's also wine involved, two modest after-dinner shots apiece of Las Varitas tequila, a thimble-sized bowl of organic North Coast pot, an hour straight dancing to the reckless Brazilian carioca funk of Bonde do Rolê—plus an item of black underwear that Perry decided, mid-CD, was now as good a time as any to go slip into and, two songs later, reveal.

But come morning something has changed. She's aware while showering of a restraint in Brewer's touch, a softness to his words, a caution or tenderness or modesty. They've been someplace new, she decides— crossed a boundary, an edge, revealing aspects of themselves that leave them both more vulnerable than before.

Yet by the time they carry their poached eggs and toast and coffee to the picnic table on the patio between the lawn and shaded garden, resplendent—despite the heat—with daylilies, early dahlias, and the laughter of cosmos, she knows she's only trying to fool herself. Something happened, all right. But in the stillness of morning and the terrible clarity of the day's new light, she recognizes that their night of excess and high-pitched fun had little to do with Brewer's panicky chase—nor with their shared relief in finding the cabin untouched, their weeklong hideaway safe.

She lowers her sunglasses from her hair to the bridge of her nose. Yesterday she felt helpless, incapable of defending herself—a feeling that proves nothing she's done has freed her from the need of the protection of a man, and nowhere yet feels safe despite the distance she's tried to create between her and the ruin of her marriage.

When Brewer mentions the weather, how "it's going to blow like a mother again with this heat," she has to force herself not to react.

She gazes, instead, across the lawn, studying from behind her dark glasses the shadows cast by a single cottonwood over an eddy of the river, her mood deteriorating as the morning brightens all around them.

"So why *did* you take off running?" she asks—as if last night's renditions were as loose as they had been. She shifts her gaze, but only far enough to find Brewer beyond the splashes of color flooding the garden.

Brewer lifts his eyes to her. He sets down his pen on an open Moleskine journal where, she can see, he's been sketching the wooden gate that enchants the garden fence.

"Were you trying to prove something?" she adds.

Brewer takes off his own sunglasses and lays them alongside his sketch. She knows the routine: patient guy; will talk. He slides a napkin next to the sunglasses. He moves the sunglasses on top of the napkin.

"I told you. I heard something in your voice."

"I know you told me. But what's that supposed to mean? You *heard* something in my voice. Is this something new you're working on?"

Brewer takes the pen from his sketch and sets it on the napkin next to his sunglasses.

"You sounded afraid. It scared me."

She watches him lift his coffee cup and take a sip, his eyes returning to the gate.

"Then it hit me something bad could happen."

Perry pivots in her chair, swinging her eyes and face and every bit of her body directly at Brewer.

"So that's us? This?" She raises her hands, palms up, arms outstretched, indicating the cabin, the river, the garden, the canyon, the flowers—the two of them and the world all around. "*Un folie* fucking *à deux?*"

But she doesn't want an argument. No, she doesn't. Not now. Not right before she sits down to work.

She closes her eyes and draws a deep breath. On her face the morning feels cool as the river in the afternoon heat.

Thank God there's nothing to argue *about*, she thinks.

Thank God Brewer doesn't do *that*.

Yet as she climbs the stairs to the makeshift office she's set up in the cabin loft, she's struck by the sense of vulnerability that has suddenly invaded their working idyll. It's as if they're both afraid, she thinks—as if they both feel there's something or someone *out there* ready to do them harm.

She sets herself into the straight-backed chair in front of the card table on which sits her laptop. The familiar clutter of notepads and manila folders, open books and scribbled notes, outlines and dialogue and cryptic witticisms collected as if snippets of verse during her and Brewer's passion-laced days and nights—all of this does nothing to relieve her anxiety. She stands and goes to the window, pivots and returns to her chair. What's this *about*? she demands—disturbed, she decides, less by the odd marauding fear than by the risk she suddenly faces of losing the clarity and hope that have carried her this far through the week, a precious stint of uninterrupted work on a long-overdue biography of her hero and, of late, guiding spirit, the eminent Lester Rowntree.

Dear Lester. This close to the end of the manuscript, the name carries for her the weight of incantation. Or the sting of a curse. She sits and stares at a blank page on the screen. Then it strikes Perry that the source of her agitation lies not so much in her fear, but in the ugly irony that she feels incapable of facing fear alone—while at the same time she writes about a woman who traveled by herself through the wilds and wonders of California as if the state—and its flora—were hers for the taking.

And she did nearly all of it after divorce at age fifty-two.

Chastised, Perry returns to the window, tugs it open, kneels at the sill, and lights a cigarette. Brewer hates that she smokes. The hell with him, she thinks.

Mister *I Heard Something in Your Voice*.

Still, she recognizes her role in all of this. Look at her: the abject posture, down on her knees with the cigarette held just so, her hand aimed to nudge the smoke through the screen. Where's the goddamn wind when she needs it? But she has nothing against Brewer, she thinks. She *may* love him. Through the trees and morning heat she studies the sunlit river, a blue like a flower that isn't quite blue—or a digital blue that looks too blue to be real. What would Lester do? She doesn't need an answer. Instead she latches onto this fresh stir of outrage, the source of her thesis since she began to view the book as more than idolatry and adulation. Lester Rowntree—lonesome traveler, inveterate wildflower enthusiast, champion of native plants, renowned horticulturist, gypsy seed collector, prolific writer, and garden club celebrity—belongs shoulder to shoulder alongside the likes of Thoreau, Audubon, the craggy Californian John Muir—an icon in her own right of an American ideal wrapped up in the redemptive power of nature. Yet where was the recognition, the attention, the acclaim? How about an effing postage stamp! Who besides a smattering of Sierra Club patrons, oddball wildflower flunkies, and native plant nerds knows a lick about Lester Rowntree and her annual pilgrimages from the Sierra Nevada alpine to the Joshua Tree desert, from the Carmel foothills to the chaparral and coast ranges to the south?

Why? asks Perry, working herself up toward the fine edge of petulance and righteous indignation from which she knows she does her best writing. What was the reason for Lester Rowntree's obscurity?

Because, one, Lester Rowntree was from California—which makes her, Mr. Muir notwithstanding, no more than another hippie in the eyes of the Eastern establishment.

And, two, she was a woman.

Perry finishes her cigarette. She returns to her chair as if taking a seat behind a steering wheel.

And, most significantly, she writes, Lester Rowntree proved herself an independent woman—one who traveled and collected and camped and ventured afield alone, able to do so year after year, on the road from early spring until late fall, surviving by her wits and good sense, never in need of a partner, a man—and through it all writing and writing and writing.

"When I made the break," she said, just shy of her hundredth birthday, "life began. I had never been so happy even if I did almost starve. But I was a free woman."

Before she finishes another sentence, the screen door bangs.

She hears Brewer say something, talking to someone. She can't make out the other voice, and for a moment she considers the possibility that there isn't anyone at all, that Brewer's up and moving around, singing or whistling or even talking to himself, the way he does when working whether the work goes well or not.

That's another thing she likes about him, she thinks, her mood softening now that she's found her way back into the writing. *His* work never seems to upset him—despite the trials and uncertainty of an artist's life.

She stands at the top of the stairs, overlooking the big drawing table Brewer fashioned the day they arrived, pulling a slider off the track from in front of the washer and dryer, steering it into the main room, and laying it on top of a pair of bookcases positioned by the window. In the far corner Brewer stands slouched against the doorjamb, arms folded, legs crossed, the screen door propped open with a toe of his Crocs. She can tell he's not happy—the Cool Dude pose always gives him away—either about being disturbed while he's working, or—what?

She hesitates before starting down the stairs. She likes watching him, engaged but unaware. The tag of his T-shirt stands turned up above the collar. Through his crest of gray hair she can see a faint disc of his rosy scalp. The cant of those schoolboy hips. At the same time, what she relishes most from this vantage is the chance to inspect—even from a distance—his current work: delicate line drawings, created for her own book, of the very wildflowers pictured in Lester Rowntree's definitive text, *Hardy Californians.*

Then Brewer's arms unfold, flung forward as if yanked by ropes tied to his wrists. The screen door slams open and he plunges outside with the sound of a dog bark and a car wreck and wind tearing loose part of the cabin—and she's already halfway down the stairs and shouting his name and lost in a color of terror impossible to name.

She finds Brewer beyond the porch, kicking a man across the lawn, the blows steady, deliberate, silent beneath obscenities howled as if

Brewer himself were a madman in a movie. She runs, still shouting; she stops arm's length from him and screams his name. His feet, his legs, fall still—while down on the grass the man, bleeding from his face or head, she can't tell which, moves as if bouncing then rolls to his back and crabs frantically farther away.

"You're a idiot!" he yells, scrambling to his feet. "A fucking idiot!"

Crouched, ready to run, he continues retreating, a hand inspecting his bloodied temple.

"You'll see the fucking cops here!" he shouts.

Brewer takes a step forward. She reaches her arms to him.

At the path leading from the lawn, the man turns and takes off at an unsteady run.

She holds Brewer. His breathing settles, slows—the rhythm of recovery from their reckless acts of love.

"What happened?" she demands.

Brewer slips free of her.

"He kept asking who are we? Why are we here?"

He turns and looks at her, or toward her, his eyes twisted and wild.

"I didn't like him soon as he spoke. I didn't tell him shit."

They both hold still as they hear an engine start in the distance. Against a spike in pitch she's sure she makes out the sound of tires spinning, the splatter of gravel sprayed.

Motionless, she feels the morning heat draw the first stir of air through the canyon.

"Then he said something about us dancing last night."

She watches Brewer's eyes close. He looks as if he's going to laugh. Or start hollering obscenities at the sky.

"And pictures he took," he adds.

⌐ ~ ⌐

The wind strengthens in waves and fitful gusts throughout the morning and into the sear heat of the afternoon—no different, Perry tells herself, in front of her computer, from the rhythm of each day since they arrived on the Imnaha.

Only now the dry bite and chalky taste recall, over and over, the moment she stood listening on the lawn to Brewer explain his awful violence. She stubs out her cigarette, leaves it standing upside down in a crowd of broken butts. For a moment she watches ashes rise from the heap—how they swirl, catching the sunlight this way and that. She shakes another cigarette from her pack and lights it. The smoke rushes flat across the room.

She tries again to compose a sentence, a clear idea—then gives up and begins typing from her notes, a passage from *Hardy Californians* copied longhand onto a yellow notepad.

It took adversity to bring me the sort of life I had always longed for. Not until after my domestic happiness had gone to smash did I realize that I was free to trek up and down the long state of California, and to satisfy my insistent curiosity about plants, to find them in their homes meeting their days and seasons, to write down their tricks and manners in my notebook, to photograph their flowers, to collect their seeds, to bring home seedlings in cans just emptied of tomato juice—

Her own thoughts interrupt her.

What did he say?

"And pictures he took."

She tries to swallow, finds she can't—much as she couldn't then.

"Said he was going to put them online. A site he has."

She struggles with her breathing, imagining her mouth a dry sponge, the air cool water she's unable to drink.

"You ask me, I think it was one of those guys from yesterday," added Brewer.

She didn't tell him what she thought: his anger she understood—but to beat on someone like that? Nor that Jared, her ex-husband, had done worse. A lot worse. For a moment she relives her panic, a constriction up and down her throat as if the air itself were foul. She remembers how Brewer looked up at the trees, as though it the most natural thing in the world that moment he noticed the wind just beginning to stir the big cottonwoods. What is it he always says? "I don't care where I work. As long as I have light and space—and nobody working against me."

Then he said he was going fishing.

Just for a bit, he said. He was too riled up to work.

She felt too frightened to argue.

She pushes free of her chair and goes again to the window, holding out her arms against the sensation that she might stumble and fall. She holds her face inches from the screen, turning her head side to side, trying to align herself with the wind. She remembers her last dog, Petey, a mongrel border collie, hanging his head out the open window of her Camry.

She remembers Petey, headless, a tangle of black and white hair between their fruit trees and summer garden, after Jared took revenge with his twelve-gauge for things she never did.

She gulps at the air as if taking blows to her chest, unable to tell if these are sobs or if she's trying—and failing—to shout.

They hadn't fished since arriving. A *working* retreat they'd agreed, beforehand, to call it. But they have their gear along; they're on a river—even though they've accepted, for some time now, that she has little interest in the sport beyond what it feels like to be on the water. She can see no difference between casting a fly and casting her eyes upon flowers, birds, the weather, the seasons. Hooking and landing fish fail to capture her imagination. She's able to fabricate fabulous narratives about trips to faraway fish camps—the food, the friends, the furious pursuit of fun—yet nothing about the actual fishing, the fastidious preparations, the elaborate casts, the delicate strikes, the fine points of fighting and landing fish—none of it holds her attention the way it can screw down Brewer's focus so that it seems sometimes he views the world through a hole the size of a pinprick.

He claims this attention to detail a result of his training as an artist.

On approaching the river she felt her body contract against the possibility that Brewer could want to make love again. Violence, sex. But he put up rods and tied on flies. He wanted to fish. They waded wet, the wind now gusty, swirling the heat. They cast small Humpys on short lines. The pool was full of little trout, some of them barely big enough to get their mouths around the fly. They were bright, colorful, sharply marked. Probably steelhead smolts, he said. They were too early, this far inland, for returning summer steelhead. They were probably too far downstream, he thought, for resident trout.

They were sort of between things.

She found his calm impossible to bear. As though he hadn't just—what? Practically killed someone?

Shortly she stood on the bank and told him she'd had enough, she was going back to the cabin to work. Yet the sun held her still for a moment—until she imagined him glancing her way, inspecting the way in which her wet shorts, stroked by wind, claimed her hips and thighs.

"You going to be okay?" Brewer lifted the line off the water as if reaching up to touch his ear. "I'll be right there should anyone show up."

She *is* okay, she tells herself, blinking back tears that feel like grains of sand pitched into her eyes by the harsh canyon wind.

She's never been better in her life.

Calochortus leichtlinii.

The drawing, taped to the drafting board on Brewer's makeshift table, replicates the black-and-white photograph from a chapter of *Hardy Californians*, "Some of California's Wild Bulbs." The picture shows two flowers, side by side, each blossom different, distinct as snowflakes, yet mated as perfectly as newlyweds posed for the camera.

Which one of the two would she be? Perry wonders, downstairs to escape the heat, unable to sit still and write. *Calochortus.* Mariposa lily. Cat's ears. *Pussy* ears. She's tried so hard to acquaint herself with Pacific Coast wildflowers that she finds each genus a tangle of common and Latin names—an appropriate confusion, she finally concluded, for a story about a woman called Lester. Studying Brewer's work, she remembers her excitement on discovering a mariposa species amidst the sage and desert scrub on the Deschutes near South Junction, the delicate mauve and lavender blossoms, as solitary as poets, swaying in the wind. Brewer said they looked like some kind of hardscrabble trillium—just the sort of thing she wanted to hear to confirm her sense that the flowers were an omen, another reason she should finally agree to Brewer's offer to collaborate on her book—and all that his help implied.

It seemed a perfect solution for her failure to find a publisher while she struggled to complete the manuscript. For the real problem, she believed, was the loneliness that had begun to seep into her life two years after finally escaping her marriage to Jared Hepworth, a man she felt had come *this* close to taking her life. Worse, the years of grief and imminent danger had left her feeling unworthy of love. Try as she might, she couldn't rid herself of the sense that her disastrous marriage proved some fundamental truth about her character—or at the very least revealed such a profound lack of judgment and inability to rectify her mistakes that thoughts of coupling up again with a man seized her in such a way that she felt, through and through, as though a mispositioned limb grown numb during sleep.

Until Brewer. Yet even in his case, she recalls, leaning down to inspect the detail at the center of the flower on the left, the one she has decided represents *her*, or the female, by bringing to mind Gustave Courbet's gynecologically lush "Origin of the World"—even then she was slow to react. Mostly, she felt his botany suspect. Everything he showed her, at the start, involved fish; he'd made a name for himself, apparently, capturing the likenesses of Northwest gamefish, plus the accoutrements of the sport of fly fishing. Pretty enough, in its own right—but what did any of this work have to do with *flowers*?

He showed her. Eventually. For his early drawings, although accurate, seemed lifeless, as if the flowers themselves had been cut outdoors and carried, for inspection, inside. Of course he was often drawing from photographs. But as soon as they began to cast about for examples of local wildflowers, most of which shared lineages with species to the south, and she presented Brewer her stories about and admiration for Lester Rowntree's remarkable life, he undertook his own crash course in the language of botanical illustration, an idiom as rich in tradition, he soon discovered, as the vernacular of fly fishing. And come that day in May that they discovered along the Deschutes those mariposa lilies and, shortly thereafter, climbed out of their waders and into the back of Brewer's smartly outfitted Toyota van—well, thinks Perry, eyeing Brewer's latest work, his drawings grew nuanced, vivid, and increasingly true to life.

But is that enough? she asks herself. She recalls, incautiously, the unlikely candor of their initial lovemaking, the sense not so much of discovery but returning home. Yet when has home offered anyone an all-new season, an unknown wind—or how, at last, to walk alone out the door and find that road you never imagined?

What about when what's at stake feels bigger than even love?

From somewhere far down the river she hears a sound, something that doesn't belong to the wind, somebody headed up the road—a truck, she guesses, coming their way.

She covers Brewer's drawings. She considers, a moment, locking the front door, then stands there peering through the screen. In the distance the hum of the engine rises and falls as if riding upriver on the gusting wind—and she wonders how it is that Lester Rowntree never once described, in her writing or interviews, a time alone when she felt genuinely afraid, threatened in any profound way by someone or something *out there*.

She recalls, instead, listening to the faint thrum of the approaching engine, her hero's playful descriptions of singing to a rattlesnake, of the pestering albeit polite inquiries of park rangers, of the clamor of families in campgrounds. Strangers inevitably turned out to be helpful, wholesome, kind. There's mention of feeling momentarily vulnerable, high in the Sierra Nevada, when thunderstorms struck—or worry of getting caught away from camp after dark. Yet danger always seems remote, benign—and it never kept her home, too fearful to venture out alone.

Was the world then such a different place? Or is *she* just different, wonders Perry—so much *less capable* than the likes of Lester Rowntree, who at the age of ninety, on finally failing her driver's test, began to lie beneath the chaparral near her home, hoping to die with her independence intact.

Or did writers—especially women writers—just keep their fears—*those* kinds of fears—to themselves?

Distracted, she fails to spot Brewer until he reaches the far end of the lawn, leaving a path through the willows and trotting her way.

Or is it men who've changed?

Brewer hops up onto the porch.

"Sorry I took so long," he says.

He leans his rod in the corner where the handrail meets the cabin. The wind has knocked hers down. He picks it up and props it next to his.

"I found these."

From a vest pocket he takes out one of his Moleskine sketchbooks. He slips the elastic band from the front and lifts the ribbon inside, opening the pages as if locating a verse or prayer.

When he pulls open the screen door, she sees the drawings of spiraling columns of *Spiranthes romanzoffiana*, the elegant hooded ladies' tresses.

"There's a bunch of them where there's water seeping out of the basalt above. It's just upstream on the other side."

He stands there looking at her, the sketchbook small in his hands.

"Brewer!" she says. "There's someone coming!"

He lets his hands fall to his sides. She watches him take a deep breath. Behind him, footprints from his wading boots have already started to dry.

The wind fills with the sound of the approaching vehicle.

"That's why I'm here."

He turns and looks toward the road.

"It's not like we're going to go hide," he adds.

A cloud of dust billows their way. Suddenly the engine races—and through the trees they glimpse the pickup that Brewer ran after the evening before.

He turns back to her, rolling his shoulders inside his sleeveless vest, a gesture she's never seen before. Does he like fighting? Violence? She studies the rise and fall of his chest, a tension held there even between breaths—while in her mouth she recognizes a taste that has returned, over and over, forever.

"Come on," he says, nudging the screen door farther open with his hip. "I'll show you the flowers."

"Brewer!" she says again.

He waits—but she has nothing more to say.

Yet she doesn't move, either.

Instead, she stands there just inside the doorway, the wind funneling past the two of them. Silent, her eyes on Brewer's, she tries to convince herself that he's completely different, not at all like Jared, not in the least, that all of this is in no way close to that.

Then Brewer turns away, the screen door banging shut behind him.

He steps to the edge of the porch. He pivots and comes halfway back her way.

"The world's full of pissants," he says. "They'll suck you dry—if you let them sink their goddamn teeth into you."

She can't speak, the familiar taste in her mouth rising as if laced with bile.

"Come on," says Brewer. "Let's go look at flowers."

But she refuses.

—◆—

Later, when she and Brewer are finished having the closest thing they've ever had to a genuine argument, after Brewer has finally lost his patience, gesturing dramatically with his uncovered arms, announcing she can "suit herself" and then storming off upriver in the direction of the blooming ladies' tresses, Perry finds herself alone, still standing in the doorway, the screen door resting lightly against her shoulder. Despite the midday heat, the wind has dropped, the yard grown quiet. She can hear the river, but only as a kind of breathing, a rising and falling sound, audible inside the sudden calm. She listens for the truck, unaware how long ago it passed beyond earshot.

She steps outside.

The very worst, she remembers, was when Jared fell into fits of jealousy—founded on what, she was never sure—and tried to keep her from going anywhere on her own. She tried everything to please him— everything but that. Eventually she ran out of ways to prove she loved him. Next it was Petey. Then her garden. Then the furniture, piled in the driveway, the gasoline and flames.

She's halfway across the lawn when, somewhere upriver, she hears a truck start.

Moments later she can tell it's coming her way.

What's worse? she asks herself, as she breaks into a run—downstream, away from Brewer, toward the willows between the road and the river and her one and only chance for love.

Rattlesnake Canyon

I SIGNED A CONTRACT TO TEACH OUT OF TOWN, SEALING THE FATE OF my marriage. Patch was along, offering his own brand of moral support, patient while I visited the hospital for the drug test, a realtor who gave me the lowdown on the local market. He sipped his Italian soda and read from a posthumously published gothic novel by the late kids' genius John Bellairs, speculating on possible plot outcomes as I nursed my French roast and scanned the classifieds for apartment or condo options. One moment we were all business, preparing for our uncertain future. The next we simply looked at each other and agreed we were done for the day, enough was enough.

It was Patch's suggestion we stop at the dam and hatchery along the highway and check out the fish. Steelhead to make your heart flutter faded in and out of view, coursing through the hazy water behind the wall of glass in the viewing gallery. From the roof of the visitor center, you could see these same fish moving in the dark pool at the top of the ladder, the distance to the water doing nothing to diminish the magnitude of each startling silhouette.

At the hatchery Patch fed ponderous rainbows from a quarter's worth of cat food pellets purchased out of a gumball machine. The sturgeon were nearly incomprehensible, massive animals captured no doubt by idled logging equipment, although nothing compared to the one in the famous photo on the wall of the new kiosk, a kid on the shoulders of a man—his father, we assumed—reaching up but still unable to touch the tip of the tail of the great leviathan suspended by block and tackle alongside the two of them.

"Imagine seeing that coming up the fish ladder."

"How about chasing your fly?" offered Patch.

The Dalles. Dufur. Friend. Tygh Valley. Within an hour from our new home, we passed beneath the railroad bridge and looked directly into Shears Falls, that terrible chasm that claimed a cousin's life and no doubt countless more. A native fisherman lay squeezed into shade at the edge of his rickety Dr. Seuss platform, the long handle of his dip net standing upright like a predawn flagpole. Just before the gravel we could see the extent of the much-ballyhooed low water: skeletal bedrock and scattered freestone lay revealed as if veins of a wizened leaf.

The heat in the canyon proved startling. As soon as we assembled camp, we made for the water, deliciously cool against our bare calves, knees, and thighs. Lucy rode the current fifty yards downstream, swam up in the shade of oaks and cottonwoods, then paddled back out into the heavy water, barking at splashes raised by her thrashing paws. Drift boats and crowded rubber rafts glided by. Swarms of caddis hovered beneath the trees, a promise of things to come.

The plan that first evening was to stake out an old standby stretch of camp water and focus on Patch getting his first Deschutes redside. We showed up early, even though there were only two other campsites taken and I'd never had to contend with anyone for this low-profile spot. Fifteen minutes into the session, with Patch just beginning to follow the drift of his fly, a fellow in hip waders, sun-bleached ponytail, bare from the waist up, greeted us from a break in the willows. I apologized for the barking dog. No sweat, said our visitor—as long as she doesn't bite. At the bottom of the run, he began casting a bright lure with spinning gear. Patch stated he was ready for a break. Then our new rivermate, now carrying a fly rod, sidled up to me and asked if I minded if he fished right here, too.

I was too unnerved to argue. The fellow waded in no more than a short roll cast above me, climbed over a couple of rocks, and positioned himself directly in the narrow slot where I often found a fish on early casts. He tied an actual bobber to his line, above five feet of some kind of leadcore or dense sinking line, and then eighteen inches of leader and a big black bug—an absolutely no-bullshit, no-questions-asked, no-remorse, bottom-dredging nymphing rig—the final evolutionary step of a direction I, too, had explored now and then.

"I'm not cutting you off, am I?" he asked, glancing back at me between sudden jerks to his rod.

I made a sound as if a nurse, brandishing a syringe, just asked me to choose which butt cheek first.

"Got a good steelhead out of here last week," he added.

Then he hooked a fish. Fighting it, he crawled back over the rocks to a fanny pack he had left on the bank with his spinning rod. He unzipped the pack, dug through it, and brought out a video camera. Rod held high, he took shots of the fish languishing in the shallows. Finally, he reached down and grabbed the trout, no less impressive for its unsavory treatment, and he held it at arm's length while still filming for an audience I could only imagine.

In all of this there was something disreputable, familiar, self-aggrandizing, reflective of trajectories I could be charged with in my own career. As if none of it has meaning without the record, the witness, the story. As if, by way of this perverse logic—and it just might be true— the *memory* of the experience is as important as the experience itself.

We tried to wait the guy out, moving up a hundred yards into the broad riffles above the fertile slot. Later, when it appeared he left, we waded back down to our spot, only to meet our guest returning from camp with a fresh beer in hand. Patch was ready to give it up—head to camp, open a soda, play some Yahtzee. I checked my watch. 7:30.

"You know, Patch," I said, not quite loud enough for the guy to hear, but thinking about it, "you only get so many evenings on a river like this. I'm not going to give this one up just because some guy without manners pushes us out of our hole."

My son gave me that sweet look that said, *If I don't have a choice in the matter, let's go.*

With the river low we barely shifted gears before I spotted good water that, in the past, always seemed just a little heavy. We parked, clambered down the rocky slope, kicking up dust in the falling evening light.

Pushing through the trees, we came upon a quiet eddy tucked inside a long even run with a classic slot in the throat at the top. Two kinds of caddis swirled around our heads. The first trout I saw did one of those slow, porpoising rises that makes you think in terms of feet, not inches, although you know it couldn't have been *that* big. Patch retreated to the shadows, claiming he would rather just watch. Perhaps he saw that look in my eye, knew or at least sensed I wouldn't relax until I stuck a couple. I made one last feeble offer to stay with him, help him try to hook a fish. Maybe he needs some evidence that they're really here, I told myself, after he refused again. Maybe he knows I'm full of it—a maniac too selfish to know his own mind.

"Tomorrow night you get one," I announced, later, speaking into darkness—utterly convinced that they're here and Patch will.

From the bank he asked again if we're going now.

———

The rattlesnake lay motionless on the short path from camp to the water, Lucy already beyond it, slurping obliviously. Patch backpedaled, startled despite a history of snake encounters that had taken on near mythic dimensions in the family lore. I saw by his eyes, however, that he hadn't bought into notions of any uncanny affinities, his own powerful medicine. That's a rattlesnake right where we'd been walking, not twenty feet from camp, a wrinkle he hadn't expected in our summer idyll along the cool, blue river.

"Do they ever swim?" he asked.

I used a long dried stalk from a Queen Anne's lace blossom, poking at the snake just enough to move it on its way. It slithered off, vanishing silently into the tangled undergrowth along the path, leaving us both with the feeling—and clear understanding—that it could be *right there* and we would never know it.

"They *can* swim, but I don't think they'd like this cold water," I said.

I slipped out of my flip-flops and up to my calves into the chill moving river. Patch followed closely, glancing back at his sandals as if not yet convinced the snake had departed. I told him the story about the contest at Trestles that had to be called off after a series of El Niño storms washed rattlesnakes out of an arroyo and into the surf, where they kept trying to wriggle up onto guys' boards—a tale that sounded so spooky as we stood there in the river that I refrained from the usual details and embellishment. Straw-colored caddisflies bounced atop the surface of the water, as if tiny toys dangled from elasticized strings too slender to see. Upstream, a fish rose, one I'd seen each time we came down to the water, a dinker that nonetheless had established its territory at the end of a dead branch jutting diagonally into the water. The rises were steady, frequent, assured—a fish without fear banging away in its safe, shaded niche.

"Patch, come watch this," I said, anticipating the next rise.

"Again?" asked my patient son, willing to indulge me but only so far. "It's there again?"

The afternoon heat was fierce, debilitating, the reason relatively few people braved the canyon despite the potent fishing. It would be nicer in September, October, the chill nights and bright comfortable days—but this was August and we had time now and that was just the way it was. We spread mats directly in the dirt beneath the shade canopy, trying to nap away an hour of afternoon sun. Puddles of sweat pooled between flesh and compressed rubber. Eyes closed, I recalled Baja, the rhythm of those days, how for hours you did little but try to survive, conserve energy and fluids while waiting for the furious evening fishing. No wonder this isn't for anybody, I thought—the compressed moments of action for which all of this makes sense—but without that, none of it does, not even love can carry days like this.

I thought Patch was ready to fish two flies. With the four-weight built for his birthday that winter, he was beginning to make real casts, breaking his stroke down into two parts, straightening the line and then pitching a short loop, reducing the two parts into one. For the first time on the river, I had a clear sense of the efficacy of two flies as more than just a way to increase one's odds. For Patch the risk was what those two flies could end up looking like, the tangled mess I could make of such an arrangement myself, and the difficulty, in fading light, of rebuilding a leader and tying on new flies.

Aware of my propensity to ignore my own kind the moment the fishing turned on, we devised a new plan. Rod left behind on the bank, I would fish with Patch for approximately fifteen minutes and then, while he took a break, I would move up into the throat of the pool and get myself a fish, which often swam hard out into the river so that by the time I landed it I was back downstream where Patch waited. I know it sounds too good to be true. Who *plans* on catching fish within a schedule? But this time it worked, providing a rare sense of facility, which did nothing to diminish the deep understanding that for every time it seems sort of easy, there are a dozen times when it's clear I don't know my backside from a hot rock.

For Patch, however, it wasn't easy at all. I'm not quite sure about the sequence of events—but by the end of that second evening, he had missed several good tugs, grabbed the line on two fish and broke them off, and had another run off much of his fly line before he gained control of the reel handle, only to hold tight when the fish took off again, snapping the tippet.

I reminded him that I hadn't fought a fish off the reel until I was in my early twenties. The trout we caught in the Sierras we played with our left hand on the line, and even then it was rare to hook a fish that actually *took* line. Even his brother, I pointed out, had gained lots of experience catching little trout on the likes of the North Fork, the Malheur, and the Blitzen before landing his first Deschutes fish. This was tough stuff. I was asking him to play with the big boys.

"I thought that one trout was going to take all my line!" he reported, his mind replaying the fish while he watched his leader swing downstream, waiting for me to tell him to pick up, roll cast, cast again. "Then I looked at my reel and saw lots of line there and thought, 'Oh, he's not very far away.' Then I saw a fish jump. He looked like he was a mile away!"

"Fifty yards, at least," I suggested, not quite sure where a nine-year-old's misconceptions of distance left off and the family inclination toward hyperbole began.

Later, I failed to notice Patch had broken off *both* flies and made several casts with an empty line. This is enough to discourage anybody, especially one's faith in a father attempting to provide authentic, nurturing support. I could have kicked myself. The light was low. Fish were rising. Patch was making good casts. Any time now, I was sure, he was going to get one—only to discover a flyless leader.

There was just light enough to re-rig. Patch, however, had had enough. I reminded him that the reason he didn't have a fly on was because a fish had grabbed it. That could have been his! If anything, my enthusiasm diminished his. Clearly I needed another fish a lot worse than he needed even one.

I waded upstream and hooked one, another breathtaking trout, only to lose it when it jumped far out in the heavy current. I told myself it didn't really matter; I was pretty sure this time I was right. The young boy back in the darkness somewhere over on the bank had just got skunked again because I hadn't done my job. As that boy's father, it felt like a promise I didn't keep.

"We going now?" he asked.

—••—

We made an arrangement that night that Patch would stay in the van sleeping the next morning while I went off and tried to find a steelhead. Until then I was reluctant to leave a child behind to awaken to an empty camp, although there was another part of me just as happy to hang out drinking coffee by the river, watching guides set up with clients at the top of the run on the far side, which they would move through methodically casting, often wielding the big Spey rods that I imagined myself using one day as well. But not yet. Far from it. Steelhead remained for me as much a concept as an actual goal of my sporting career, tied to a vague sense that until I got my life in order I couldn't commit to the challenge. This is how years are wasted. And although I had encountered a small number of steelhead on the end of my fly line, to claim, at that time, that I had any real history with the sport would be like saying I appreciated fine retrievers because I happened to own one—against mounting evidence that Lucy and I existed on the same page.

This morning proved no different than most of my so-called steelhead fishing, tinged with feelings of bewilderment, hopelessness, a sense of shooting blindly into the woods. I know enough about life to understand that there are times we simply don't know what is going on, that any creative challenge requires us to accept periods of muddling unfruitfulness. No surprise that Mr. McGuane chose the title of his essay about his own protracted hunt for a first permit on a fly for his collection of fishing tales, *The Longest Silence.* The degree of difficulty marks the center of reasons why a certain breed of sportsperson is willing to trash particular aspects of his or her life. Which is no more to say than the path you choose is the one you're on and each choice eliminates others.

I returned to camp as the sun cleared the rim of the canyon, spilling heat down the steep, striated walls. Patch rested comfortably on the backseat of the van, new mosquito bites showing on his cheeks and forehead and arms. I fixed him a bowl of Lucky Charms, the ultimate in a nine-year-old's notion of breakfast cuisine. The distance between the two of us, I suddenly realized, was as great as I chose to make it. That first redside would mean as much to him as that steelhead I might have caught that morning. *We're in this together,* I thought. *None of it matters beyond that.*

His line straightened as if the fly had snagged an errant limb midcurrent. A belly formed, taut as a kite string in the evening breeze. Immediately line began peeling off Patch's reel. "Keep your tip up," I said.

He was cautious this time, finally understanding that to try to stop the fish was to lose it, break it off. He handled the reel as if it were hot to touch, or as though the fish were source of sudden jolts of electricity that shocked his fingertips. At this rate it was going to take awhile. I let him figure it out on his own.

Eventually, when the fish was close, I directed Patch to back up to the bank, an open stretch of sand deposited along the edge of the eddy. I told him it was his job to land it, put it on the beach, grab it with his own hands. This is old-school stuff but there you have it. In the end we need to know how to go it alone.

It wasn't pretty but at the start it never is. Anyway, it's not a beauty contest. Patch held up the fish with both hands, and as I took it, we both noticed the fly came free. We exchanged a look: *that* close. I got the fish back in the water, reviving it while Patch looked on, shaking his hands as if trying to dry them.

"*Now* I know why you like catching fish so much," he said, the fish suddenly gone. "My first Deschutes redside. I can't *wait* to tell my brother."

On the bank I put Patch's line back in order while he paced back and forth, still shaking his hands, saying over and over again, *Now I know, now I know.* We should not expect subtleties from our children. Unprepared for my own response, I ran my fingers over Lucy's ears.

"You want to keep fishing?"

Patch turned midstride and shook his head no.

"Then I'm going to go get one, too."

Carping Flats

Winfield is grounded until he finds a new job. For ten years he sold cookie dough for fund-raising in three different school districts, a job that's left him feeling particularly hapless now that the economy has soured. It isn't so much that he *can't* go fishing—but more along the lines that he isn't allowed to go anywhere the sport is even an option. Or so his wife figures. Keep him home long enough without wetting a line, goes the reasoning, and he'll damn well find a job—instead of heading out so he can *think* about work and his next career move.

These concerns embarrass him. Especially the part about thinking. Not that he denies himself his fair share of daydreaming while casting a fly. But the whole point of the sport has always seemed to him to be about *forgetting* the awful realities of life—and bearing down, instead, on what doesn't make a bit of difference to anyone else but him.

More vexing still is his refusal to heed his wife's requests. Not only has he given her the wrong impression about his thoughts while on the water, there's also the matter of heading to the water in the first place, a road he continues to travel despite her best efforts to cut him off cold turkey. But not exactly *real* angling water. Which is how he sidesteps the moral dilemma of whether to respect his wife's wishes—or tell her, frankly, to mind her own damn business.

They discovered the carp water as a family—Winfield, his wife, and two grade-school-aged daughters—paddling about in a secondhand Mad

River *Explorer* that grew more and more difficult to fit into from the very first day they bought it. A stiff spring wind swept in off the ocean, soon to be funneled through the Gorge at speeds the wind- and kite-boarders call *nuking*. Downriver from Portland, the wind qualified as but a gale. A shallow thumb of water spread into a reach of interconnected tidal sloughs, with whitecaps riffling all but a narrow band of smooth water in the lee of the low-gradient shorelines. Winfield had just enough experience to recognize that anywhere but these leeward edges would mean they were sailing, not just paddling. If they weren't careful, working their way back against a headwind could turn a Sunday outing into the sort of affair that lately discouraged the four of them from sharing the canoe in the first place—another kind of *nuking* the family had grown entirely too familiar with.

An elderly couple pulled their own seasoned canoe onto the grassy bank where Winfield and his family prepared to launch. He asked about the wind. The couple exchanged glances. Grandpa said he thought they would have been better off staying on the far side and then cutting across at the top of the thumb to where they stood now. Winfield took that to mean that they'd had to work pretty hard getting back in. In fact, had anybody asked him, he would have said that by the looks of them, it appeared both Grandma and Grandpa had just had their backsides whipped.

"But you've got some good helpers," offered Grandma, standing aside while Winfield and his wife settled their own canoe, stem to stern, into the edge of the wind-rippled water.

"You betcha," he agreed.

They made it across the thumb in a direct swift line, quartering downwind to the far shore and the relatively protected waters of another shallow bay. Weed grew in thick clumps over much of the inlet, as if remnants of kelp beds harvested by cutters or raked by storm. The water was opaque, a milky brown; the tips of their paddles disappeared as they dug beneath the scabby surface scraped by the wind. When they found themselves spooking fish, it took Winfield a while to identify them as fish at all—and not, perhaps, nutria, beaver, the world's biggest bullfrogs, or some other mysterious backwater creature apparently large enough to wrench the paddle out of his hands.

Things what they were at home, Winfield hadn't brought along a rod. He would have liked to argue that such circumstances merited an even more forgiving attitude toward his need for angling pleasure—but such an argument had gotten him nowhere of late. Incapable of pressing the issue, he secretly tried poking a few fish with his paddle, hoping to at least identify the species if not actually engage it in sport.

Both girls soon noticed his efforts. But rather than help with these investigations, they alerted their mother by shouting excitedly the next time they passed through the wake of a swirling fish and their father's paddle smacked the water with the sound of a pistol shot.

"Beating fish with a paddle, are we?" asked his wife, in a manner that wasn't a question at all.

"Just trying to clean some weed off," he replied.

Yet he wanted to at least *see* a fish. The muddy swirls spoke of creatures deep and broad, and even though by this time he suspected they were carp, a species for which he had always felt a certain ambivalence, he sensed it his duty to reaffirm his ascendancy as man of the house. What that had to do with catching fish, even the wily and sublime carp, remained a matter of debate. His wife, for one, found such angling efforts unconscionable. Not only did he spend inordinate amounts of time and energy pursuing fish he never brought home to eat, he also maintained the unlikely position that a husband and father who sought fish as sport provided a moral compass by which his family could maintain its bearings. Such nonsense fooled nobody, however, allowing him the impetus to go ahead and try to bonk a carp upside the head.

But debasement was never the point. He remained fairly certain of that. They followed the sweep of relatively calm water along the shore until they finally slipped around a gentle bank and turned downwind, skimming over the ruffled surface at a rapid clip. At noon they lunched and shared sodas nosed into a stand of reeds where the water opened into a broad expanse of windswept lake, none of them eager to brave the elements any farther. The paddle back gave them all an opportunity to work together, and by keeping the canoe pointed directly into the wind, they were able to make steady progress as if paddling upstream against a strong but manageable current.

In sight of the grassy bank where they had spoken with the elderly couple, his wife announced that they should begin cutting across to the far side—precisely what the old fellow had advised against.

"This thing isn't meant to go diagonally through wind," he countered. "You either go directly into it or you're headed sideways downwind."

"Says who?"

His wife turned to look at him. Both girls pulled their paddles from the water. He continued his J-stroke, trying to keep them on course. More and more his wife discounted his wish to explain how things worked. This mid-April afternoon onshore wind they were bucking, for example. Textbook, he might have argued, had not the health, well-being, and all-around cheer of his family's disposition been anywhere but foremost in his mind.

"Well?"

His wife fixed him with a well-known glare.

"Who made you the expert? The same somebody who taught you how to fish for carp with an oar?"

"A paddle, dear. These are paddles, not oars."

"Whatever."

<hr />

He doesn't return to fish in earnest for carp until May, at which point his hopes of marrying his and his daughters' fly rods to the canoe have been placed permanently on hold. He can't recall the exact reasoning. Something about the canoe being a sacred *shared* activity—that he isn't to *soil* these outings by waving his rod at the water, nor go so far as to take the girls fishing on his own. These edicts finally weary him as so much fluff. He has attempted to position himself in life as a reasonable man. But to what end?

Come the latest in a string of faultless spring afternoons, he feels numb to the usual refrain. He doesn't make enough money—even when he has a job. He's a stay-at-home dad—a reversal of roles that real men don't concede. He wants to go fishing—while there are a million things his wife has still never enjoyed in her life.

He simply isn't meeting her needs.

On the other hand, the sky today again is blue, the air still—and hours remain before the promises twilight holds. Plus, before picking up the girls from school, he tied up a wad of rabbit fur nymphs, adding them to a stillwater box he hasn't opened in nearly a year.

He loads his float tube into the back of his 4Runner. Immediately he's concerned about what his family will do for dinner. He tells his wife she can expect him home after dark. He reminds her to make sure she washes their youngest daughter's hair.

"I know how to take care of my own children," she says.

The wind is lighter than he expected when he reaches the water and begins assembling his gear. He hasn't thought about bringing anything but his five-weight, his workhouse out of the gate whether to cast size 6 weighted stone nymphs or size 20 Blue-Winged Olives—sometimes less effectively than he might like, but at least he finds himself untroubled by indecision, dealing the best he can with whatever comes his way. This attitude, he reminds himself while fashioning a new leader, is somehow tied to his problems at home, how it is his wife's needs aren't getting met. She's done *dealing with it.*

He hikes around the thumb of water they crossed on first sighting the carp, carrying the float tube on his back while sticking to the narrow band of newly sprouted annuals between the muddy shoreline and tangled greens of a Northwest's protracted spring. A garter snake slithers under his rod tip. From the channel beyond a stand of tall cottonwoods rise voices as clear as the sound of surf through fog. Ducks squawk, a pair of them beating hasty retreat through even light above the satiny surface of the dark, motionless water.

The carp are there again in the shallow bay beyond sight of the parking gravel and boat launch, showing themselves in languid swirls, tails and broad fins catching low rays of sunlight. He works his way into his fins and tube then eases into the mud, stirring up odors as he tries to get deep enough to float. Fish roll in three directions from him—thick, heavy, undisturbed. After ten minutes of labored progress, he manages to reach water a full cast from shore, only to find himself still standing, fins and boots buried in mud, unable to bring himself to cast with an oversized diaper floating uselessly around his knees.

He returns to shore and selects a new launch site. This time in he quickly begins covering fish. The action, so-called because of the numbers of big fish within immediate casting range, is nearly constant. Three hours later, twilight all but vanished, he's brought one fish to hand and broken off five others—and felt the rise and fall of his pulse rate fluctuate wildly while cast after cast creased the teeming waters of the sweetest humiliations this side of love.

Heading home, he makes a mental note to buy some heavier leader.

Getting whipped by a bunch of lowly carp seems small beans compared to his troubles at home. Then again, you have to start somewhere. On a grocery errand he secures the new spools of tippet, stouter than any he's used since casting in the surf. And, anyway, the more he thinks about it, the more he believes he broke off fish that first evening using old leader he dug out of a stuff sack he hadn't opened for years.

Shame on him.

Two weeks later his wife gives him opportunity to revisit his secret carp waters. There are accusations about a classroom visit he paid to one of his daughter's teachers, the kind of nonsense he suddenly refuses to listen to any longer. Driven by something other than his usual simple desire to go fishing, along with the five-weight he tosses into the back of the 4Runner the old ABS tube with his surf rod inside. Plus a big reel and spool with a floating shooting head. Not that he suddenly feels serious about thumping a bunch of carp—but by the time he pulls out of the driveway, he knows there's something he needs.

He has second thoughts as he leaves the city, passing through the industrial reaches, the railroad yards, the shaded slopes of Forest Park rising abruptly from the highway. Why the big rod if he is inclined to the sporting proposition? Crossing the bridge to Sauvie Island, he glimpses the effects of breeze pushing through Multnomah Channel, in no way the gale they encountered their first paddle into carp, but a lower Columbia wind nonetheless. Through the sweeping farmland, clumps of hardwoods, and sinuous hedgerows, along the narrow dike, and, finally, where the rough pavement turns to potholes and dust, he debates the merits of one rod against the other, the virtues of carp versus the number of traditional coldwater species he might be driving to cast to this very moment, and whether to trouble with the question of just what the hell he is doing going fishing in the first place while at home his wife believes he's the sort of schmuck who does things he only rarely gets around to imagining. In short, it's the kind of self-inflicted abuse out of which he senses the sport of fly fishing has evolved into its present state of rarefied airs and ritual and dogma—a final escape into poetic irrelevancies short of blowing out one's brains.

He chooses the big rod. Joined at the ferrule, it feels like an old friend, full of memories, a little heavier than he recalls. A big stick like this points to something at the heart of the matter, an admission to the inelegant itch to kick some ass. A powerful tool, it holds a simple, powerful message: *I want a fight, and I want to win.*

The fish, when he wades into the muddy shallows, are few and far between, nothing like he saw the last time. He lays out a few long casts, relishing the slow, stylized stroke needed to work the rod and heavy shooting head, scolding himself when he finally throws a tailing loop while pressing his maximum range. Shadows from trees along the shore lie all around him, but where the fish show, when they do, bright sunlight captures the disturbance on the water as if a lamp revealing the wrinkles in a dented fender. He begins shooting for individual fish. Time and again he drops the big nymph near rings and ripples and rises, where it immediately sinks as if a penny pitched into dust.

It all seems enjoyably pointless until a fish, a very large carp, appears at the precise spot the fly has last entered the muddy brown water and the new leader straightens like a leash. The rod spontaneously transforms from an instrument of delivery to one of retrieval, bent to the task like a cheap pry bar. He has a big fish on the end of his line. When was the last time he did *this*?

So big, in fact, that when it's finally swimming around his legs, forcing him to unstick his boots each time it lunges in one direction and then the next, he thinks it might somehow be dangerous, a large powerful animal fighting for its life. And ugly, too. Twice while trying to grab a hold, he raises the head entirely out of the water, where its hollow mouth and long, sinewy whiskers look as surreal as the insides of an Asiatic lily, a sea anemone, a painting by Georgia O'Keeffe. He recalls a parrot fish he once speared as a teenager that suddenly turned and latched onto the pale flesh on the inside of his forearm, leaving an exaggerated hickey that remained with him for twenty years.

He hates wounds, especially his own. He slips his entire forearm under the belly of the carp, raises it awkwardly out of the water. The fly is hooked neatly in an upper edge of its mouth, as easy to remove as a barbless Humpy from the lip of an eight-inch brook trout. He holds the fish above the water, hefting it one more time to gauge an approximate weight.

More than either daughter when they were infants, that's for sure.

He lowers the carp back into the water. Just at sunset, he's startled by a rising moon. He had no idea the time of month—nor, at that moment, he was facing east. Guess I got turned around, he thinks, heading for shore and home.

Mack's Canyon

DEEP IN THE RUN CALLED PISSANT, A TREMBLING SUGGESTION OF HOLD-ing water above Bladders, where guides give their clients one last stop in the bushes before the final mile down to Mack's, a blast of canyon wind ambushes Merit Birdwell's D-loop, crushing both it and his spirits near the end of yet another fishless day.

A second gust approaches. This one, from the opposite direction, rips water from the surface of the river as if flesh affixed to a belligerent Band-Aid—and Merit, sloshing through the tailout, fails, for the first time in weeks, to find anything even remotely funny about this latest date with futility. His hat, snatched from his head by his wind-raked cast, wallows downstream, a puddle of dark fleece slumping like a sponge. The river, all but black beneath threatening twilight skies, steadily outpaces his plunging gait, a near-perfect tempo for steelhead to hold in, notes Merit—were he not in the process of spooking every swimming creature between him and CJ Walton's drift boat tucked somewhere in the bushes downstream of the heavy water ahead.

But he'll be damned, thinks Merit, if he's going to lose his hat—a gift from Arlene Stone, whose slender and amorous arms he could be wrapped in this very moment were he not pissing away yet another day without a single tug on the end of his line. He may not be able to catch a fish, but—but what? Merit skates to a stop, staggering briefly before his boots slip into footholds between rocks, his balance stirred as if stepping from an airport conveyor—and he watches his hat slip over the lip of the tailout and immediately out of view.

At the very same instant, Merit hears the deep, familiar growl of his timeless Hardy—and as the reel gives up line, and the weight of resistance builds through the rod, he believes, for a second, even two, that he's into a fish, that somehow, miracle of miracles, the very stuff of steelhead lore, the way, throughout his angling career, his steelhead slumps have often ended, he's hooked a fish—for no other reason than that his fly was in the water.

Later, back at the boat, when he recounts this escapade to CJ, the latest in a long line of steelheading pals come and gone over the years, Merit refrains from describing the sudden calm that fell upon the river, the wind subsiding as if a wave that has just collapsed. Instead, he offers up details of a kind of parting of the skies, the great clouds tumbling over the lip of the canyon suddenly shot through with sunrays and the intimation of celestial beings. That seems more than enough; he doesn't need to overdo his case, yet another instance of the sort of profound disappointment that has him aiming, of late, for the tone of dark irony that steelheaders so often favor in the midst of a prolonged slump.

"You mean to tell me," says CJ, settling behind the oars into a molded seat fashioned out of plastic office furniture, "you thought your hat was a fish?"

CJ stubs an oar into the bank and gooses the boat over rocks and into the current. Two sharp pulls and they've spun and started downstream, the boat beginning a slow gallop. Up front, Merit turns to face his young friend, who, satisfied with his line, has already produced a cigarette and folded the oar handles in his lap, looking—at 265 pounds, give or take a twelve-pack or two—like some sort of wadered Buddha.

"I said I thought, for a moment, it *could* have been a fish," says Merit, his voice raised above the rush of the river and the wind.

But it's a line of reasoning he immediately regrets. A public defense attorney for twenty-two years, he retains the habit of quibbling over semantics, an explanation, he often suspects, for why he finds himself still dating at age fifty-four. Stirrings of failed love, coupled with the bounce of the boat, produce a sensation of hollowness high in his chest—the same feeling that preceded each and every one of his courtroom appearances. Even after purchasing a small chain of Laundromats so that he could fish, more or less, full-time, he's needed the past four years to fashion a brand of spiritual vigilance against his litigious past, a practice of mindfulness that cost him a small fortune in counseling, twice-weekly sessions he finally felt able to quit only after deepening his current relationship to a level of intimacy that has become, of late, a standing invitation into Arlene Stone's spirited bed.

The same period during which, he reminds himself, not a single steelhead has eaten his fly.

"My point," continues Merit, seated sideways to keep an eye up ahead, a stretch of tricky stickwork for which the bushes below gave Bladders its name, "was that the sudden shafts of sunlight *suggested* something great—hooking a fish, for instance—might happen."

But he still feels he's making a case—a reaction, he concludes, to his ongoing slump, a spell of futility that strikes him now as a pulse of nausea, as if the hollowness in his chest had suddenly filled with a cold, heavy gas.

Dipping the oars side to side, CJ steadies the course of the boat and eyes Merit with concern.

"It has been a long time, hasn't it!" he calls out over sound of the rapids.

Merit lowers his head, anticipating the splash at the bottom of a sharp plunge of the bow. At his temples he feels the cold damp hem of his rescued hat—and then he suddenly sees that the felt on his right boot has come unglued, the front half hanging from the sole like a limp tongue.

Is that why he couldn't overtake his hat?

"I hope she's worth it," adds CJ, his voice softening as they glide into the head of Bladders.

Feet tucked under the seat, Merit glances about the boat, looking here and there across the opaque water for signs of fish, the kind of half-hearted search he knows damn well has no connection whatsoever to actually finding and hooking a steelhead. Of course she's worth it. Why else, for six months now, has he been driving three hundred miles a pop to spend every chance he gets with Arlene Stone—she of his far-fetched dreams during a decade-long second marriage that he felt certain had the D-word forged into its steely surface the moment he met the polished couple, the twice-wed DA Charles DeWitt and his sterling, forty-going-on-who-knows-what bride-to-be.

Seasoned in angling and argument, if not all of the subtleties of love, Merit understands a thing or two about both slumps *and* hot streaks. And so when Arlene emailed the previous fall, mentioning her separation and an interest in taking him up, finally, on a casting lesson, he was, as CJ would say, all over that shit. Gazing at the water, silent now and the color of bruises bone deep, he recalls the awkward sparks that leaped between Arlene and him all those years ago when, at a party for both sides of the local legal community, he grew carried away describing the thrill of raising steelhead in low water to the teasing swing of sparsely dressed Muddlers. The DA, known courtwide as Nitwit but rarely to his face, had hosted the party to make public his impending new marriage and all it implied to defenders and prosecutors alike—and so it came as no surprise to Merit when his tales of tempting steelhead, and his offer to teach Arlene to cast for them, was finally cut short, DA DeWitt appearing suddenly at his fiancée's side to pour a long draught of sparkling Argyle down her outstretched throat, leaving Merit to study the bony articulations above Arlene's shadowy cleavage.

Steelhead, schmeelhead, thinks Merit now, not sure he really even cares about catching another steelhead for the rest of his life.

They're all the way into the tailout before Merit finally speaks up again. Two boats—the only ones they've seen that day—rattle past behind a pair of pickups on the access road. Dense clouds obscure the upper reaches of the canyon walls—and it's as if both he and CJ have silently agreed to call it a day rather than stop to fish and risk getting caught on the river after dark.

"Right when I realized the hat was hooked to the fly," says Merit, without regard for the break in conversation, "the sky looked like it was in a Winslow Homer painting. Or something by Turner." He raises a hand and gestures vacantly at the darkening clouds. "Or one of those old Chinese Zen master landscapes."

"Japan," says CJ. "Buddhists are from Japan."

"No, you're wrong." Merit pauses, his insides again stirring. He glances at the loose felt on his boot, weighs the purpose of his point.

Does he just want to be right? Or is this a valid objection, a simple clarification of fact? "People often think that. But they either forget or don't know that Chan, or Zen, was originally a Chinese thing and only really got going in Japan in the second millennium. You take Han-Shan Te-Ch'ing, for instance, not the crazy Han Shan of the Tang Dynasty, but the monk who—"

"Whatever," says CJ, pressing the boat forward with a sudden push against the oars.

Later, as they come around the final bend above the takeout at Mack's, faint as shadow in the failing light, CJ lets the boat spin backwards in the current, the wind pivoting it side to side as if jockeying an old-fashioned weather vane. CJ looks upriver, avoiding Merit's gaze—and as they float down to the concrete ramp, it seems to Merit that CJ, too, finds it remarkable that they could spend an entire day on the Deschutes in October and not touch a single fish.

Theirs is the last rig in the lot. They work in silence until CJ reels the boat up onto the trailer and straps it tight. He lights a cigarette while Merit finishes loading gear in the back of the truck.

"Well, sooner or later you're going to get over her and get a fish."

Merit swings the cooler over the side of the bed. He turns and catches but a glimpse of CJ's expression behind a glow of orange ash.

"What does that mean?"

"It means," says CJ, "that you're not catching steelhead because your mojo's gone. Or gone elsewhere. You don't need any Zen woo-woo bull-shit to see that."

Merit smiles and shakes his head. Yet at the same time he grows aware again of the feeling of emptiness in his chest, an absence of sensation that seems compressed or simply numb, he can't tell which. He turns away from CJ—and stumbles over the tongue of loose felt beneath his boot.

"I don't know what you're talking about," he says, righting himself.

CJ stands there smoking, allowing Merit time to figure it out.

"Okay, so I've been distracted." Merit lifts his hat and runs a hand through his shaggy hair. He recalls the elaborate repertoire of similar stalling gestures he practiced for approaching the bench, when everything inside him felt on the verge of melting, threatening to immobilize him. Or buckle his knees. Around him, the growing darkness seems filled with the sound of the river, the moist air stirring with misdirected hopes. *"Those who fail have ignored or taken too lightly what they deemed insignificant,"* he says, quoting Han-Shan Te-Ch'ing, his best shot of late at high ground. *"The enlightened person overlooks nothing."*

Moving through the dark, CJ looses his cigarette in an arc of tumbling ashes.

"Whatever," he says again.

—◦—

A week later, Merit Birdwell, champagne glass in hand yet still fishless since steelhead season began, stands in the fire-lit living room of Arlene Stone, inspecting her new giclée print of Tang Yin's famous *A Fisher in Autumn*, framed and hung in elegant counterpoise to another recent find, *Fish*, a sedate study of aquatic motion by the nineteenth-century artist, monk, and poet Xu Gu.

But the moment is soon lost to the artless workings of desire. Before Merit can finish summary of his ongoing slump, Arlene shushes him, initiating a smooth yet dizzying sequence of gestures that leaves him scrabbling for purchase within her emphatic embrace. Only later, draped across the davenport while Arlene tends the fire, does he note from this odd angle that the Tang Yin print appears to replicate a particular run on the Klickitat, a spot he's visited three times—without luck—since his last attempt with CJ on the Deschutes. The high rock wall of the far bank plunges into the river at a cant suggestive of the basalt flows of the upper Klickitat canyon; the immense auburn tree filling the foreground above the boated fishermen seems lifted directly from the palette of fall colors still clinging to the canyon's deciduous oaks. Viewed anew, the picture feels to Merit like a harsh affront to his streak of futility, mocking him up to the moment Arlene returns, reclaiming his attention to matters at hand.

Yet try as he might, Merit can't shake CJ's indictment, the plaintive charge that his inability to catch steelhead this season is direct evidence of passions spent elsewhere than on the water.

"Lovely, isn't it," says Arlene, intercepting Merit's gaze with a lift of eyes hovering just above his navel. She swings herself off of him, only to return, backside first, as if settling into a recliner.

"I knew you'd like it," she adds, scooching into place. "That's why I called."

Merit shifts awkwardly, repositioning his lover's tousled head. Beneath her, he feels a tremor of anxiety work its way from his stomach up high into his chest, where minutes before his desire, taut as a spring, had moved him as if waves through a humming tuning fork. He rests his arms across Arlene's silky belly—only to find himself troubled, once more, with the thought that CJ might be right.

All through dinner, Merit finds himself fashioning arguments against CJ's case. For it's not the sex, he contends, that's authored his ongoing skunk, but instead his state of mind—his failure to *embrace the moment*, as Arlene would say, cast after cast after cast. Savoring the roasted lamb, smeared with mint sauce alongside yams as sweet as pumpkin pie, he sees that he *is* distracted—that he's dealing now with a new layer of complexity in his life, in sharp contrast to the routined existence he created since leaving law so that he might focus on the few things that matter to him this late in life. Like fishing. And peace of mind. And, granted, he concedes to himself, as if carrying on his own private debate, the well-being of his heart, a concern he feels he would have soon forgotten had it not been for the goodwill and open arms of Arlene Stone.

But it's not the sex, he tells himself again.

Yet in bed that night he finds himself unable to sleep—despite a spell in Arlene's hot tub, followed by a kind of dreamy lovemaking that seemed without beginning or end. *When the mind keeps tumbling*, reads Merit, propped up by pillows as Arlene snores gently at his side, *How can vision be anything but blurred?* The book, a collection of poetry by Han-Shan Te-Ch'ing himself, known here as well as "Silly Mountain," has been on Arlene's nightstand since his first overnight stay, initiating Merit's introduction, over the past six months, to Zen and Taoist thought, subjects he knew no more about than magic or model railroading. Tonight he feels the words speak directly to him, hounding him for his failures of late to remain focused on fishing—while at the same time reminding him that just an hour before he proved incapable of holding his attention, at Arlene's request, on the long length of the upper Deschutes visible from her deck, the great river outlined by slender basalt cliffs black beneath the chill and starry autumn sky.

Instead, recalls Merit, the grip of anxiety returning to his chest, his gaze kept shifting, passing again and again over the tops of Arlene's breasts, buoyed in relief by the sudsy stir of the hot tub's steamy water.

Of course, she noticed. Yet she made nothing more of these misguided glances than to quote the same lines that Merit now, in an act of contrition, has turned to. *Stop the mind even for a moment / And all becomes transparently clear! / The moving mind is polishing mud bricks. / In stillness find the mirror!* Clearly, Arlene Stone's worth *another* ten thousand empty casts, he thinks, returning the book to the nightstand before switching off the lamp and sliding through the sheets down the length of Arlene's body.

But in the morning something goes wrong. For the first time ever, Arlene has disappeared from bed before Merit awakens. His apprehensions, he believes, had cause after all. He finds her in the kitchen; she's dressed in cycling tights, helmet, and shoes, ready to ride. He asks her what's up, where's she going, what's the hurry? Arlene tosses down the last of her coffee and says she has better things to do than lie around in bed with a guy who's too busy thinking about where he's been and where he's headed to know where he actually is.

"What's that supposed to mean?" asks Merit, thrown back to his legal past. Worse, in boxers and T-shirt, he feels at risk against the military cut of Arlene's outfit, as if he'd shown up in court in Crocs and his Capilene long johns.

"It means," says Arlene, aiming her cup at him, "you didn't say two words to me last night."

She drops the cup in the dishwasher. When the door shuts, rattling silverware in the drawer beside it, Merit decides not to point out he's sure he said more than that.

Arlene clomps about the kitchen, opening and closing drawers and cupboards, twice passing close enough that Merit slides his bare feet out of the way of her awkward shoes. When she finally finds a water bottle, in a cupboard he's sure she looked in before, he remembers to take a deep breath.

"It means," continues Arlene, struggling to remove the lid, "I'm beginning to wonder if you're going to get it—pay attention to what I'm trying to share with you—the notion of *now*, being *present*, staying in the moment."

Merit holds out a hand, offering help. But Arlene, pressing her knees together, twists the lid free. Filling the bottle, she holds it under the faucet as though trying to both strangle and drown it.

"It means," says Arlene, watching him, eyes steaming, over her shoulder, "I wonder if any of that means anything to you—or if you're just going to turn out to be another Charlie Nitwit—as selfish and self-absorbed as the next guy."

Distracted, against all reason, by the outline of Arlene's bottom, balanced as if a perfectly formed nest atop her trim and tightly wrapped legs, Merit fails to measure his reply.

"I don't get it," he says.

Arlene spins toward him, a sharp crunching noise rising from the hardwood beneath her shoes, her glare melting into a quivering lip.

"Don't, Merit." She tries twice to screw on the lid, cross-threading it each time. "That sounds just like him. As if there's a lawyer anywhere who '*doesn't get it.*'"

Arlene makes the quotation marks with raised hands, water sloshing from beneath the cocked lid. This time Merit thinks better than to offer help.

"Listen," says Arlene, reseating the lid. She inverts the bottle, checking for leaks. "I'm going to get on my bike and go for a long ride—and when I get back, I think you better be gone. Go catch your goddamn steelhead. Or figure out the difference between when you're on the river and when you're here with me."

"So last night?" asks Merit. "That was a test?"

"It's all a test," says Arlene, cinching the strap beneath her chin. She shakes the water bottle as if readying a prank with a can of beer. "Every—last—moment."

⌣

"*Great accomplishments,*" recites Merit, recalling one of Han-Shan Te-Ch'ing's maxims while he tugs on a wading boot, "*are composed of minute details.*"

Seated on the back bumper of his van, he grabs hold of the laces and, pulling, lifts his foot for CJ to see the new felt glued into place following his return from Arlene's sudden dismissal. The drive over the mountain, aflame with fresh autumn colors, did nothing to relieve his anxieties, a shot of self-doubt that rivaled his very worst spells in court. Still, this simple repair, performed as absolution, has gone a long way in helping him regain his focus.

Or is it, wonders Merit, the severity of Arlene's edict that finds him intent, for the lowest of reasons, to stick a fish and be done with this nonsense?

"*Everything in life,*" he offers CJ, stepping into his other boot, "*depends on the choices we make.*"

"Looks like you chose to do yourself kind of a half-assed job."

CJ, already in waders, rigged up and ready to go, a morning descent into the lower Beulah canyon, waggles an unlit cigarette in the direction of the second boot, which sits flat as a loafer to the pavement. Still seated, Merit spins his foot up onto its toe, revealing the boot's original felt sole, as thin as the flannel of old pajamas.

"She called before I finished. '*The universe is the hair of a horse,*' she said."

Before CJ can ask him what the hell that's supposed to mean, Merit presses his lips together and, eyebrows raised, forces a smile—a look that asks CJ, his judge and juror, *What could I do?* What he doesn't tell his friend, however, is that Arlene's call proved confusing as a smooth liar's testimony, leaving him uncertain, afterwards, whether she had hinted at an apology or prepared the ground to dump him. She quoted the literature again: "*Correct thought is no-thought.*" "*A single vacant mind has no place to go.*" "*Streams and rivers run into the ocean and yet there is no flowing.*" But where's that leave him? Them?

For try as he might, Merit can't escape the feeling that Arlene has started to build a case against him—that his failure to catch a steelhead has become evidence, in her mind, of an inability, on his part, to be present for love.

He follows CJ through a gap in the hardwoods crowding the highway above the pitch of second-growth pine and fir leading to the river below. And as they wind their way into the canyon, threading their Spey rods through shadow and tangled understory, Merit notices himself beginning to create his own case against Arlene. For the truth is, he recalls, Arlene Stone was, in her day, before marrying the DA, Charles DeWitt, a mean and pitiless public prosecutor, never above the lowest forms of witness-baiting, while equally prone to fits of pedantry that left even seasoned judges wary on her approach. What's with the Asian claptrap, anyway? Arlene Stone is no more Buddhist than a Toyota, decides Merit, a conclusion that suggests to him that his gracious lover has grown to embrace the trappings of Eastern religions in a sorry attempt to defuse her own mind—an apology, no doubt, for an inclination toward argument, allegation, and, perhaps, even coercion.

Screw her, he thinks.

And from that moment forward, claims Merit, telling CJ about it later, he just went fishing. No more worrying about if and when he'd catch another steelhead; no more fretting that catching one meant anything to anyone one way or another. A classic Zen moment, he explains to CJ. Or state of mind. Or Buddhist. Or—

"Whatever," agrees CJ, aiming a ribbon of smoke through the alders at water's edge.

Merit, still vibrating, head to toe, as if driblets of adrenaline continue to spurt through his veins, turns away from his oversized friend and stares at the blank surface of the river, searching for some sign, an indication that moments ago he was fighting a fish, a heavy, bright steelhead that seemed ready, finally, to quit—when suddenly the hook pulled free.

He can't help but tell CJ again. The air was still, the sky gray, the water chill, a glacial green. He threw a long straight line, his loop unfolding near the riprap below the train tracks on the far bank. He didn't need to mend—that's how good a cast it was. He watched his line swing, attentive to the course of the fly, the timeless arc of this strange season of empty casts—while doing nothing else but waiting.

He's hooked a half-dozen fish over the years, he tells CJ, out of this same lie. There's a deep spot right where the current bends around the tangle of debris trapped by that old snag. The fly comes around and just . . . *hangs*. The grab is always subtle. You feel something—maybe?—and the line bows, the tension builds—and finally there's life connected through the bend of the rod.

"So what happened?" asks CJ, pinching the ash off his cigarette.

Merit lets out a deep sigh, studying the river, unable to recall the moment just *before* the fly came loose, the line went slack.

"I don't know. I probably got excited—didn't wait and let it take the fly."

"You gotta let 'em turn with it."

"I probably got excited," repeats Merit, conceding the point.

CJ joins Merit at the edge of the water. The two men stand there, side by side, gazing at the river as if waiting for something to arrive.

"Happens," says CJ. "Especially when it's been a while."

In the silence that follows, Merit is surprised to find himself relatively calm. He knows it's not always your fault. Luck *does* matter. You can't control everything. In his mind's eye he sees the fish thrashing atop the water, then two terrible tumbling jumps followed, later, by a pair of angry fits of head-shaking that felt like a dog on the other end of a sock. Then the worst was over. He backed up against the current, working his way toward a patch of silty sand between the tangled roots of the riparian alders, a spot he'd used in the past to beach fish. He wondered if it was a hatchery fish or a native. Would he kill it? Take it to Arlene for a celebratory meal? Or sacramental? An offering?

Then it was gone.

"There's something so pure," says Merit, "so *unequivocal* about a lost fish." He stares at the water, trying to picture just where the steelhead was the moment it slipped free. "It's there and then it's just—"

"Gone," says CJ.

"Exactly."

"Classic."

"Poetic . . . *justice*."

CJ reaches for his cigarettes.

"Like an oil painting," adds Merit.

Merit and CJ both turn and glance at each other. Then Merit takes a broken chunk of an Arkansas stone from a pocket of his vest and begins sharpening his hook. He looks again at the river, the precise spot the steelhead grabbed the fly.

"The last person in the world he'll tell is Arlene Stone."

The Arroyo

AN ODD EXCITEMENT STIRRED ME THAT SUMMER EACH TIME I STARTED down the arroyo, a new and illusive sensation that I hadn't been able to identify beyond the typical and in this case far-fetched anticipation of what I might find feeding along the beach. So far, in a month of sporadic visits from the house I rented back in the cactus and mesquite above the south end of town, I'd found a few families and groups of friends and twice young couples swimming and picnicking and enjoying the breeze off the water, the kind of adventurous or simply resourceful people who recognize the benefits of following a dusty desert road from pavement to a low point in the dunes, carrying with them food and drinks and chairs and maybe a table and a way to make shade, people with the wherewithal to take a vehicle out onto the sand and the common sense not to get it stuck. Or how to get it unstuck if you did.

Now and then I had come upon dogs on the beach as well, all of them accompanied, most often by an adult, not a child, and naturally the dogs ate things here and there, the way dogs do, in the same manner that the seagulls and red-faced vultures on the beach gathered about garbage or dead fish or other debris that had washed up or been left on the sand.

Occasionally, I also found a few feeding pelicans, a cluster of them rising one by one with the lift of the breeze and turning to dive into bait.

Feeding pelicans and baitfish, of course, although not what I was looking for, put a keener edge on my search during several visits. But I had gotten over most of my initial bursts of hope. I hadn't seen anything besides these occasional pelicans feeding on bait, not once that fire-hose eruption that signals bigger fish on the feed, sending shiny sardines or herring into the air with the outline and texture of spray lifted by a stiff offshore wind peeling back the crest of a wave poised to break.

What I had seen, instead, were needlefish, lots of willing ladyfish that convinced me they would be fun on a smaller rod than I carried, and a few tiny jacks. And two pufferfish. Of course, for $250, give or take a few pesos, I could have hired a *pangero* and gone out and caught plenty of what I was looking for along the beach—especially dorado, probably as many dorado as I could possibly want to catch.

But this was one of those spells when I didn't have $250, give or take the pesos, to go out in a *panga* and catch as many dorado as I wanted. Instead, I had a dog named Tia. I had three kinds of dried beans and a bag of rice in the cupboard. I had plenty of work, but it was the kind that nobody would pay me for until I finished and that wasn't going to happen soon. I wanted to find a dorado—or something like it—along the beach so I could fool it and hook it and land it and kill it.

And then eat it, too.

⸺

Still, the excitement I felt each time I crossed the pavement leading into town and entered the arroyo was not the simple hope and anticipation of finding feeding fish, one of which I would have been grateful to catch and carry back to my kitchen. No matter the day, my shirt hung heavy with sweat by the time I reached the bottom of the arroyo, not the mouth down near the beach but the sandy course running the arroyo's length, a sinuous path of alluvium and runoff debris carried from thunderstorms in the mountains north of town or, far less frequently, rainfall from *chubascos* spawned at sea. The sand and silty soil ran its way through thick stands of riparian desert, the course overgrown and shady, with rarely any breeze to relieve the evening heat and humidity. Tracks crisscrossed the sand: cows, jackrabbits, rodents, coyotes or dogs, roadrunners, quail, lizards—some tracks woven around the wide furrow of a dragging tail indicating a lizard on the scale of an iguana—while here and there tracks of rattlesnakes or other, much smaller snakes rippled the way, elegant waves that never seemed to me the strokes I would expect scored into the sand when I pictured a snake moving silently through the desert night. My excitement or anticipation or whatever it was I felt when I followed the arroyo to the beach was stirred, too, by the birdlife, a parade of colorful and often noisy birds that I might have expected in a lush, tropical setting, or even Australia, but not in a harsh dry desert next to the sea. Many of the birds were long-billed predators, their beaks fashioned to snatch or dig or probe or pound or in some other way get at the multitude of insects, a few of these—moths and beetles especially—the size of the smallest birds, the hummingbirds and gnatcatchers and a vireo. I learned to recognize the songs and call of the cardinals, the orioles, the cactus wren and thrasher and flicker and Gila woodpecker. I already knew the sounds of quail and scrub jays and the mourning dove, but even these old friends I heard in a new way, leaving me all the more certain that I was going to find or discover or experience something new each time I approached the beach through the arroyo.

One morning before sunrise I passed down the arroyo and out onto the beach without a rod, without a plan but to swim at dawn, when the sea was smooth and I could walk to the beach and back to my house without feeling the heat a danger. Prior to that morning I had been reluctant to give up the best time of day to begin work. That's a benefit of having little more than beans and rice in the cupboard: stay focused. But I had just finished something, a long and difficult job, and after rising in darkness I'd had my coffee and boiled some oats and raisins and concluded that on many if not most counts I was still a free man.

The sea was slick and flat when I left the arroyo and crossed the sand to the water. Tia was with me, having decided lately that there was no good reason she should remain at home when I wasn't there. The previous day I had behaved terribly when, on finishing the big job, I borrowed a kayak, intending to drag around a fly in the bay and see if I could catch dinner that way. Though I had leashed Tia to a post on the back porch, where she was supposed to intimidate potential intruders, she had learned to turn and back away from the tension of the leash and slide her collar over her ears. When I set off in the kayak, Tia followed. A hundred yards offshore, I could see she had no intention of turning back. Instead I did.

Still seated in the kayak, nosed up onto the sand, I tried shouting and waving my arms, and then I engaged Tia in a detailed explanation why she couldn't join me. An elderly *gringa* with four dogs traipsing along the edge of the water asked in broken European-accented English if I needed help. I assured her I didn't. Finally, I climbed out of the kayak and hoisted Tia in my arms and crammed her into the front hatch. *So what's the big problem?* her brown eyes asked, an expression she offered up a number of other times when, far out in the bay, she rose to her feet and started my way while I tried with fly rod and paddle and a fresh assortment of shouts and obscenities and futile gesticulations to command her to sit or we might both be in for a slow wet journey back to the distant sand.

But today I only intended to swim. Out of habit I tightened Tia's collar and attached her to the leash tied to the porch post. She met me at the front gate. No doubt she would want to join me in the water as well, a reasonable request that I trusted wouldn't inspire the level of hysterics I had risen to the day before.

We headed away from town, following the long arc of the beach. Within a mile the curve of the shoreline left us walking almost due east, at right angles to the direction the beach ran below the homes far behind us. Summer winds blew directly onshore each afternoon along the beaches in town, winds I had learned painfully pushed jellyfish in the form of a local variety of Portuguese man-of-war toward shore. Where Tia and I walked, the afternoon wind cut sideways along the beach, and over time I'd regained my confidence and begun swimming again, albeit close to shore, in earnest.

Short of a spot I had picked out beyond probable encounters with jellyfish, we came upon a wide track crossing the sand, a shallow furrow outlined with flipper divots made by a turtle come ashore to lay eggs during the night. Was this the find I'd been anticipating each time I walked down the arroyo? The track looked as though somebody had dragged a family-sized cooler loaded with ice and drinks down to water's edge. The pattern of the divots, plus the small groove left by the tail, gave a clear picture of the turtle itself. Tia grew interested in the nest, and when she stood sniffing along the lip of the half-filled basin, I could see that if she wore a shell, she'd have been roughly the size of the animal that had dragged itself across the sand, the final leg of a journey that suddenly seemed as mysterious as the flight of dreams through sleep.

Tia set her nose and front paws in the sand covering the nest.

"Don't even think about it," I said, taking hold of her scruff and steering her back toward the water.

— ~ —

Just before arriving in the desert, I had reread Peter Mathiessen's *Far Tortuga*, his early, provocative novel that follows a group of turtle fishermen who set sail from the Caymans to net turtles commercially along reefs off the coast of Honduras. Matthiessen uses phonetic dialect for all of the fishermen's voices, setting the dialogue between wide spaces of empty page against a flat, objective, seemingly artless narrative voice. (Somewhere he mentioned that the narration contains but a single metaphor.) Like all good novels, what happens to the characters and what the novel is about differ sharply.

The novel shows primitive men doing primitive work, and it suggests that it's the nature of these men—and perhaps, at root, the nature of all men—who destroyed the very fishery that supported them. The world isn't big enough any longer, Matthiessen shows us, for turtle fishermen—much as we've come to know that it isn't big enough for whalers, for seal or otter hunters, for food and market gunners slaughtering untold numbers of ducks and egrets and the godwit and the albatross, sea- and shorebirds with value for meat or feathers or any other commodity that somebody, anybody, will buy. The list might be longer than we imagine. Salmon? Tuna? Sharks? It's a sad loss—especially if you love the sea and love the thrill of going to work in the hold of its fickle skin, its haunting depths, hunting wild animals you can turn for a profit, a way of life that offers hope, a special kind of hope, all the way to the end.

After our swim, rain began falling. We climbed out of the arroyo and crossed the pavement heading for home. Despite afternoon thunderstorms over the mountains, this was the first rain I had seen this low in the desert. It fell in heavy windswept waves from a dark sky shattered by lightning and cracks of thunder that felt as though they shook the land. I ran up to the roof of the house, a flat deck designed for a *palapa* or palm-frond awning, and grabbed the mattress I had been using to escape the heat and keep an eye out—with the help of Tia—for thieves.

They had appeared the very first night. On arrival I felt perfectly safe, undetected in a small house surrounded by desert, with only three or four other houses, all of them empty for the summer, within shouting distance. I set a camp chair on the front porch and read until dark in the breeze blowing off the water. Tired from a day of travel, I moved the chair up against the side of the house before I went inside and prepared for bed. Despite ceiling fans in all three rooms, the little house was uncomfortably warm, and I left all of the windows open, including the slider out to the back porch, with only the screens closed to keep out bugs.

Sometime the first morning I discovered the chair on the porch was gone.

I hoped somebody in the occupied houses over the rise to the north had passed by and seen the chair and carried it home. When I walked into town that morning to meet with my contact, a woman who was friends of another woman whose uncle owned the house I had rented, she agreed with my initial guess. She felt certain that either Terry or Kerry, my only two neighbors along the dusty road beyond my desert view, had grabbed the chair, assuming that it had been left accidently outside.

"Probably Terry," she said. "He's a little weird that way."

I didn't go talk to Terry or Kerry. I needed to get to work.

That evening I brought in the chair from inside the house that I had carried to the porch to read in while again enjoying the breeze. The bedroom was as hot as it had been the night before. Even with the fans on, I felt I wouldn't be able to sleep without leaving open the windows throughout the house, including the porch slider. Much later, deep in sleep after the night finally began to cool, I heard something, a noise that in my barely conscious mind sounded as if it came from the main room. In the next moment, that brief instant during which the mind is capable of stringing together an elaborate hypothesis out of the smallest piece of evidence, I became certain that the chain on the fan in the main room had somehow tangled in one of the spinning blades and now, as the noise increased, the fan was ready to break.

I jumped out of bed. The sudden loud noises convinced me that if I didn't hurry, the fan would smash to the concrete floor. The doorway into the bedroom stood two steps from the bed. Another two steps and I was in sight of the spinning fan—while tangled in the screen of the slider, a thief with a flashlight struggled to escape across the back porch.

I shouted. I reached the porch as the flashlight raced off through the night. Moments later the voice attached to the light called out to someone waiting in what sounded, when the engine started, like a small pickup, and a flurry of Spanish and movement and lights vanished through the dark.

I stood next to the screen. It lay on the porch, sliced top to bottom before the bandit got tangled in it and pulled it from its track as I made my way from my bed. Had he been all of the way inside? Clearly far enough to find the screen hooked to him as he stopped and suddenly headed the other direction. Had I lost anything? Apparently only the safety one hopes to feel wherever he or she sleeps.

Come daylight I found the deep tracks of someone running across the desert sand. Had the thief known I was there? It seemed he would have guessed had he taken the chair the evening before. Yet even an abandoned chair was no real sign that somebody was staying at the house right now. And why had the bandit cut the screen, when all he needed to do was slide it open and step inside? At a corner of the property, I found the heavy, tape-wrapped electrician dykes and a Phillips screwdriver, sharpened to a point, that the bandit had dropped while holding onto his light and hopping the barbed-wire fence. As the morning passed, I talked to a dozen different law enforcement agents from three different jurisdictions. They empathized with my bad luck—but all agreed it might have been worse.

It took me awhile to find a dog. After we got to know each other, I leashed Tia to the column on the back porch, so that she wouldn't follow her old master and she could let anybody know who was watching that she had moved into the house, too.

That same evening I hauled the mattress to the roof. Once dark settled over the desert, I locked the house, the sliders and windows included, and carried a fishing knife and a heavy rod tube to my new bed under the stars, where I slept soundly, listening to the night, the sea caressing the sand, free of the worst of the heat.

—⁓—

Come dark the evening following the rainstorm, the lights illuminating the front porch and my Roberto Bolaño novel attracted thousands of flying termites. Thousands. They covered the two bright circles cast by the spiraled bulbs set high on the front wall of the house, while at the same time growing thicker and thicker in the air, making it impossible to sit on the porch and read. Had I been near a trout stream anyplace in the world, this hatch, caused by the rain, would have caused the fish to go bonkers. But there were no trout streams in this desert, no streams of any kind in drainages this side of three separate mountain ranges, no year-round flowing water anywhere—not unless you dug deep enough into aquifers that nobody had any idea whether the rain that fell in the mountains could replenish fast enough to keep up with the growing demand from the influx of residents and visitors to the towns at the edge of this desert along the sea.

What I was witness to instead of an epic insect hatch making trout go ballistic was the start of a turtle hatch, green sea turtles coming ashore at night to deposit their eggs in nests they dug in the sand. The next morning I found two more sets of tracks. The morning after that, another. Earlier in the summer I had found a dead turtle on this same beach, its head and flippers picked at and gnawed upon by the usual scavenging visitors, and now I wondered if the dead turtle had been somehow related to the hatch, as if it had returned, as in other years, to its original birthplace, only this time to die.

Then, as the number of nests along the beach continued to grow, a few were marked. Stakes surrounded the half-filled holes. Caution tape circled the stakes. Plastic-coated chain-link fencing covered the nests. A length of white PVC pipe displayed the initials for the organization responsible for monitoring the nests. I was heartened, of course, to see that somebody, an official conservation group, had its eyes on the nests. At the same time I recognized the danger of inviting attention to protected resources.

You like turtle eggs?

No need to look any farther.

Nearly forty years ago I swallowed the contents of raw turtle eggs whole from oversized shot glasses filled with tequila. I was young, impressionable. I don't ever imagine that young people are any different than I was. I remember in Zihuatanejo seeing turtles, still alive, stacked on their backs, filling the inside of the bed of a pickup to the top of the wooden cattle slats extending higher than the cab. Depending on the part you use, I was told, turtle meat can taste like any one of five different meats—beef, pork, chicken, goat, lamb.

I passed below the turtle nests, some marked, others not, on the way to my morning swim, imagining what a few freshly laid turtle eggs might do to supplement my diet of beans and rice. I thought about the thieves who had visited my house, and how each of us deals with hunger, like pain and illness, in his or her own way.

The problems of a shrinking world are larger than most of us imagine. All of the laws, all of the rules and regulations, will only go as far as the strength of the system of enforcement put in place to uphold the laws and the rules and regulations, to punish the offenders. And we know that never works. It never works. I walked past the turtle nests day after day, resisting the temptation to dig into the sand, to look and see, while at the same time imagining just a few of the eggs, just a handful, and an omelette made with garlic and onion and tomato and three kinds of peppers, the whole of it lathered with guacamole and sharp green salsa. Tia, too, was probably tired of the chorizo I stirred into each meal with her packaged dog food.

But it was a temptation easy for me to resist. I get it—at least that much of the story: don't rob the nest if you want the tale to continue to unfold.

And this: jellyfish are the favorite food of the green sea turtle.

Then again, I'm not as hungry as other people—and nowhere have we convinced people, rich *or* poor, that a daily swim or some other exercise routine—*not* some exotic dietary supplement—is the surest path to cure what ails them.

In fifty years of travel along the coasts of the Baja peninsula, I've seen countless local fisheries exploited, decimated, and abandoned. The list doesn't depress so much as startle me: lobster here, cabrilla there, abalone, scallops, the great river of *sardinas* that once blackened the waters inside Magdalena Bay. I get this, too: if you put fishermen in bountiful waters where the life they seek is a commodity, a source of income for his needs or the needs of him and his family, he will not stop—he will not stop until the source of that income is gone, either entirely gone or grown so scarce that it's no longer worth his efforts to try to find it.

Who tried to rob me? I wondered in the days that immediately followed the attempted break-in at my rented house. Thieves? Punks? Drug users? Meth heads? Coyotes looking for nothing more than something they could pick up and carry off to sell? And who's going to protect those marked and unmarked nests on the beach, I asked myself, passing up and down the arroyo, from the same sort of person who, when faced with hunger or some other real need, considers it worth the risk to break into another man's house to see what he can find?

The problems of a shrinking world grow larger every day. I imagine it has always seemed that way. Too many people. Not enough food and resources. Where do we find water? What do we do with the poor, the uneducated, the pirates and the sleazeballs and the greedy and the insane? How do we manage to leave room for a few green sea turtles, orbiting our lives as though apparitions in the cosmos, when we have so little to show for our attempts to deal with one another?

I stumbled over many questions climbing up and down the arroyo. Perhaps, I thought, as summer drew to a close, as the worst of the heat finally began to subside, perhaps excitement wasn't what I was feeling at all. Perhaps, instead, the arroyo and wild seaside desert inspired a fresh sense of alertness, an attention to place from which questions about the path ahead must naturally arise. Where is home? What *is* home in a world grown so small? Is the very notion of home at odds with a future in which wildlife passes through our lives? Good questions. Hard questions. The kinds of questions that give our lives meaning and purpose in a way answers never can. Answers mark the end of a story. We already know what that will be.

Blue Fox Spinner

BRIGGS KEPT CALLING. HE WAS GETTING FISH NEARLY EVER DAY. AND not on a tedious o-dark-thirty march—just an hour or two mid-morning while his wife, deep in chemo, retreated from his helpless gaze.

"Big fish, too."

Chuckles, Briggs's cross-eyed pointer, filled the phone with spirited complaint.

"Ernie Delgado got a wild one on gear close to twenty pounds. 'Course all he did was bitch while he let it go."

I tried not to believe him. Like I had time to go fishing? Nine months into retirement and I was up to my eyeteeth in work, thanks to a grant from the state to build a replica nineteenth-century salmon boat, a carvel-planked double-ender complete with steam-bent frames and copper rivets throughout.

What was I thinking?

What I was thinking was that after thirty-eight years teaching high school teenagers how to build birdhouses and nightstands and jewelry boxes without cutting off their thumbs, I would finally have time to fashion something more elaborate than a plywood drift boat or cartop pram, the likes of which I spent my summers building while trying to figure out how I could possibly afford to take on a real boat.

"Then again, maybe I would've done the same."

Chuckles sounded like he had climbed into Briggs's lap.

Were they parked in his truck by the river?

"Maddie wants me to bring fish home. Says it's the only thing keeping her alive."

———

We agreed to meet in the morning. Did I feel sorry for Briggs? When my own wife died—victim, it seemed, of her fears come true—I spent the next two years trying to figure out what end of the knife to hold. When I wasn't at school I stumbled up and down the river, hooking steelhead in every imaginable lie, places I looked at now and laughed it had been so long since they'd given up fish. Alone, I felt obliged to play the fishing fool: how else make sense of this wretched gift of the gods?

At first light I pulled into the lot alongside the county museum. Out on the Columbia the lights of a tugboat pushing a barge upstream passed beyond the mouth of the Beulah as though a distant, slow-moving train. Clear skies blushed to the east. To the west a wave of black clouds spilled through the gap in the mountains as if driven upriver by the distant sea.

I put up my rod, my back to a chill breeze, the sound of the river faint beneath the thunder of trucks on the interstate. A pair of anglers crossed the footbridge leading from the hotel construction site beyond the far bank. A train whistle howled. The tugboat wailed. We were a long way from the wilderness rivers that once defined the sport—yet somehow the steelhead kept coming, their fickle numbers a reminder of how little we still knew.

By the time Briggs showed I'd watched four other anglers slip through the willows on their way into the last run of the Beulah, a rush of pretty water before it stutters and pools, finally losing itself in the breadth of the Columbia. Briggs, looking short on sleep beneath the brim of a threadbare ball cap, lit a cigarette before climbing into his waders. He assembled his gear, trimmed his knots with his teeth. As we started from the lot, we spotted Ernie Delgado, the middle-school math teacher, carrying a fish along the edge of the willows, hurrying toward a cluster of cars parked above the sluggish final reach of the Beulah.

"Sure that thing's missing a fin?" shouted Briggs.

Ernie turned our way. He held up his catch, blessing Briggs alongside it with a congenial middle finger.

Briggs served back a finger-kissed salute.

"Dude catches a lot of fish."

He stepped aside, allowing me first claim on the water.

"Sorry I'm late," he added

I didn't ask why. I didn't ask where Chuckles was, either. This deep into it, the friendship Briggs and I had managed to carve out of our very separate lives had stripped us of any need for the small talk that generally passes as polite conversation. I'd heard all of his stories; he'd heard mine. Neither of us felt inclined to talk about politics, sports, or anything to do with money—and it seemed we'd both made a vow to steer clear of our respective health issues, as though by doing so we could avoid sounding like old farts even if that's exactly what we were. When the fishing was good we checked in on one another to make sure the other guy knew—or, more accurately, so we could tell *somebody* about a good fish we caught, or one of those weird things that will happen on the water and drive you just about crazy if you don't know someone who can see it for what it was and wonder about it, too.

And it was up to Briggs if he wanted to talk about his wife.

Below the willows we found ourselves hemmed in between guys upstream and down. The breeze barked upriver with a fresh bite, but not so bad it would chase anyone off the water. Briggs said he hadn't seen it this crowded in weeks. I figured it's about what you can expect when you've been paying attention as little as I had lately.

Briggs lit another cigarette.

"The Finger didn't catch the last damn fish in this river."

He headed downstream, finally stopping just short of a gear guy who looked as if he had no intention of moving. Briggs dunked his cigarette and put the wet butt in a pocket of his jacket and waded out as close to the guy as he could get without asking for trouble. Knee deep, he pulled line off his reel and with a pretty cack-handed stroke sent a sharp loop stretching across the water.

"It's all yours!" he hollered, gesturing at a half-dozen casts worth of water between us.

I gave it my best shot—until I found myself worrying more about my supply of rivets than the shape of my loop. Neither Briggs nor the gear guy had moved a step by the time my fly nearly hung up in Briggs's boot laces; the two of them were still trying to pretend the other one didn't exist. I watched a pair of seagulls squabble on the far bank over a scrap of woven blue tarp. Have we really evolved? The question was at least as interesting as the fishing—but before I got very far with it, Briggs backed out of the river, all the excuse I needed, a couple casts later, to do the same.

I found Briggs in the parking lot talking with the fish checker, Emily something or other, the latest hired by fish and wildlife to try to keep track of what's going on with the Beulah. Like anyone has a clue. Steelhead come and steelhead go; the only guys who catch them are the ones fishing for them. The rest is theory far as I can tell. As I crossed the museum lawn, I heard Briggs say something about Ernie; Emily whatever her name smiled and shook her head.

"About the only thing they told me when I started here was to talk to Ernie Delgado. Said he could answer any questions I had, he'd been self-proclaimed watchdog on the Beulah for years."

"It's a ruse, I tell you."

Poor Emily. Probably fresh out of college and you could see in her eyes these fish were her *mission*—and here's this geezer calling her best friend on the river a two-faced poacher.

"I've looked in Ernie's freezer," Briggs said. "He has steelhead stacked in there like cordwood, half of them wild, fins intact. Doesn't even try to hide the evidence."

Briggs didn't wait for a response. He stormed off to his pickup and dropped the tailgate, letting it fall as though the lid of a dumpster. By the time I got free of Emily, apologizing for Briggs's rant, he was out of his waders and seated behind the wheel, smoking another cigarette.

"You've never seen Ernie Delgado's freezer," I said. "You don't even know where he lives."

Briggs stared straight ahead. The smoke from his cigarette, jutting like a nurse's thermometer from between his lips, curled about his ball cap and unshaved cheeks. He raised both hands to the steering wheel, squeezed it so hard I wondered if the skin at his knuckles could split.

"It just *pisses* me off. That fish he got today might've saved Maddie's life."

⌁

What happened then was textbook steelhead mojo: the harder Briggs tried, the fewer fish he caught—until he sank into a full-on skunk that lasted for weeks. No hatchery fish. No wild fish. No hookups, no grabs, nothing. I tried to tell him: just get off the river for awhile. Wait until he felt he wanted to go fishing, not like he had to catch something.

Then he *would* hook up.

But Briggs grew obsessed with the idea that steelhead he caught and cooked would keep his wife alive. It was hard to watch. You have to understand: I was at the point in my life when nothing I said or did had any desired effect on women. I had given up trying to figure out if it was them or me. All I knew was that romance felt exactly like steelheading can feel: perfect water, perfect fly, perfect cast, and . . . nothing.

Sometimes I'm *shocked* I don't move a fish.

So I couldn't really get behind the notion that steelhead Briggs caught were going to save his wife. It was a nice idea—but more and more it seemed we had little if any control over much of what mattered in our lives. Even the boat I was building seemed like it had fallen out of the blue. By all rights I was the real deal, with nearly a dozen boats to my name since the first one brought me back to earth, able to face the shadows inside an empty house. But there were scores of regional builders more qualified than I was to take on a project like this. In the end the grant I wrote was funded, I suspected, because no one on the committee knew the difference between carvel and lapstrake planking, a spritsail or a standing lug.

Still, I wasn't about to abandon Briggs, either. Deep into his skunk he showed up at the shop; he wanted to pick through my so-called sculpture, a tangle of lures and line and lead and every other kind of steelhead gear imaginable, including flies, that I had found or snagged in close to thirty years on the river. Recent winter storms had put the river out more days than not; the only fish getting caught were by gear guys. Briggs was going to join them. He'd been to Walmart but he couldn't find the right-size floats. And he'd have to drive to Portland, or go online, to find a size 2 Blue Fox Spinner, the likes of which adorned my snarl of reclaimed gear as if ripe fruit left behind by careless pickers.

Or they did before Briggs arrived.

"Isn't that Ernie Delgado's favorite lure?" I asked, watching Briggs unknit one of the bladed blue lures.

"Ernie *who*?"

Briggs twirled the spinner with a flourish—and then set out after another blue spark with a pair of flashing nail clippers.

By the time he finished, he had a pretty good start on a sculpture of his own.

"What do I owe you?" he asked.

Of course, I could have let it go; nothing in my so-called piece of art was doing anybody any good. Who needs a reminder of the mess we've made? I reached down and petted Chuckles, asleep in front of the wood-stove, a hunk of oak still between his teeth. What I did need was a hand with riveting. I had steamed and bent a bunch of the boat's oak frames, then left them clamped in place. Nailing from outside of the boat and then riveting from the inside was the one job I couldn't do alone. Why couldn't Briggs pitch in?

He tried. But after a half-dozen nails, he began having a hard time driving them, even through predrilled holes. Worse, he kept clobbering the boat, sharp whacks that resonated through the hull, doing what to the soft cedar planking I could only imagine. I tried tactfully to ask what was going on. Did he need more light? Was he having trouble getting in position to hammer? Was he *cold*? Finally, I couldn't take it anymore; I climbed out of the boat—only to discover Briggs covered in tears, snot dripping from his nose, his breath percolating in short gaspy sobs.

Alerted by my movements, Chuckles arrived, tail wagging, and began licking Briggs's face.

"She's giving up," said Briggs, an arm circled around Chuckles's neck. "Maddie's quit."

From that point on I wanted Briggs to get a fish as much as he did, maybe more so because I knew what he was in for—and he didn't—once his wife passed away. A steelhead now wasn't going to make a bit of difference to her. But for Briggs it could prove a shot at mercy as he stood before the mirror and tried to learn to live with the dead.

Three days later we were on the water at first light. The river had dropped; the fish, said Briggs, "were in." How did he know? Ernie Delgado arrived before us, but not by much; as we stepped out of the willows, we could see him downstream still fiddling with his gear, his headlamp swinging in erratic arcs as if a train engine starting to derail.

Briggs left his casting rod, rigged and ready, leaning against the willows; I figured that improved his odds tenfold. The juju in steelheading is so complex it rarely helps to adopt another angler's game. You figure now it'll be easy—and when it's not, because it's steelheading, you grow indecisive, which practically guarantees failure. You catch steelhead by persisting with what's worked in the past. Nobody experiments when he thinks he really has a chance to hang one.

I imagine a wave of fish passing out of the Columbia that morning and heading up the Beulah. But maybe there were only two. Briggs had insisted I lead the way through the run; was he still thinking in terms of luck, cause and effect, the rewards of gracious behavior? Halfway down the run I spotted Ernie tight to a fish. I turned upstream to say something about it to Briggs—and he was into one as well, a fish I saw once as it rushed downstream and cleared the water nearly directly in front of me, its reckless flight captured by the rising light behind me.

A wild fish? Something about its outline or attitude. Or was it my concern for Briggs that tweaked my perceptions? It was impossible to tell one way or the other. The verdict, I hoped, would arrive soon enough.

But then the unimaginable happened: while Briggs's steelhead was racing downstream, Ernie Delgado's fish was headed in the opposite direction. In moments the two fish met, lines crossed, and the next anyone knew, Briggs and Ernie were hooked together and whether either one still had a fish on his line was anybody's guess.

They both *acted* like they did. Which meant neither of them was willing to let up and give the other one a chance to land one or maybe even both fish.

A sadder spectacle you'll never see—both men pulling and reeling and, in moments, shouting up and down the river, each one letting the other know he was a this and a that and if he would only—

I couldn't take it. Since leaving the high school, I can't handle conflict and confrontation. I don't know why. I ran up the bank and grabbed Briggs's casting rod and came back down to the water and cast the Blue Fox Spinner over both lines, where I figured a fish might still be. Both Briggs and Ernie were so shocked by what I had done that I had the whole mess snagged and practically to my feet before either of them could react.

Then they came running, Briggs with his Spey rod, Ernie his casting rod, the two of them red in the face although Briggs, by the time he got close, looked like he might blow a gasket. Meanwhile the fish, both of them, came in sideways, nose to nose; at first they didn't look much different from all of the other junk I'd been pulling out of the river and hanging up in the shop. Just more of it. But I could see what mattered most: a wild fish and a hatchery fish—and before either Briggs or Ernie got a look, I had them both unhooked and held by the tails, their noses in the water.

"The hatchery one's mine," said Ernie. "I know it. I saw when it jumped."

"You're full of shit," said Briggs, huffing and puffing as if he had just run a four-minute mile. "Mine jumped, too. Missing its fin. Seen it clear as day."

"Get that fish back in the water!"

Emily bounced to a stop, her dark ringlets settling around her face.

"Get that wild fish in the water. All the way."

I slid the wild steelhead, a pretty hen that had to go close to ten pounds, forward a couple of feet. I looked at Ernie, Briggs, Emily. Suddenly I was back at the high school, dealing with kids again.

"Nice fish, Ernie," I said, letting the wild hen go. She lay there a moment, quiet as a cloud, then moved off with a slow flex of her broad tail. "I gotta say—you really are one hell of an angler."

Ernie started to say something—but I didn't give him a chance. "Briggs, you gonna keep this?"

I held up the fish—eight, maybe nine pounds—just a regular old hatchery buck that was placed on this good earth to make an angler's day.

Briggs stepped forward and slid a hand into the fish's gills.

"Don't mind if I do," he said, raising the fish for all of us to see.

"That's two—one wild, one hatchery," said Emily, tallying the information on her tablet or phone or whatever it was. "Any others today?"

We all shook our heads. I turned to Ernie and asked him what his fish ate. By the time he got done telling me, Briggs was gone. I drove home and mixed up a batch of fairing compound, and I went to work on the dings he had left scattered on the hull of the new boat.